Logistics of a Distribution System

To the memory of
Guy Chantrill RASC
Distribution Logistics pioneer

Logistics of a Distribution System

Peter and Nigel Attwood

Gower

Published by
Gower Publishing Company Limited
Gower House
Croft Road
Aldershot
Hants GU11 3HR
England

Gower Publishing Company Limited.
Distributed in the United States by
Ashgate Publishing Company
Old Post Road
Brookfield
Vermont 05036
USA

CIP catalogue records for this book are available from the British Library and the US Library of Congress

ISBN 0 566 09098 8

Typeset by Poole Typesetting (Wessex) Limited, Bournemouth and printed in Great Britain by Billing and Sons Limited, Worcester.

Contents

List of figures

List of tables

1   Logistics and distribution

Distributing goods from places of manufacture or storage to places of consumption requires good management, starting with planning followed by organizing and controlling the operations. That is a simple statement which is easier to say than to do, as many a manager has discovered. A better understanding of logistics, however, will go a long way towards improving distribution efficiency.

The term *logistics* is familiar to those readers with a military background because, originally, it was used to describe the movement of men and materials for the purpose of winning battles in times of war. Although it still applies to movements today, these are movements that have commercial or industrial objectives, though the principles are the same regardless of what has to be moved or distributed.

In the context of distribution, logistics involves tactics or day-to-day operations in order to achieve distribution objectives. Therefore, logistics is central to decision-making at the operational level, and it can apply to every branch of an organization at some time or another. An understanding of logistics is essential for planning and operating a distribution system successfully.

Depending upon its origins, logistics is often seen as being synonymous with distribution activities, either the physical distribution of products, supply chain management, pipeline management, or supply and transport. Whichever description is used, the basic definition of logistics is the same; namely, getting the right goods to the correct place at the time and in the condition required by the customers. The National Council for Physical Distribution Management has defined logistics as:

> 'the integration of two or more activities for the purpose of planning, implementing and controlling the efficient flow of materials and products from the point of origin to the point of consumption.'

Logistics, simply speaking, means making available the resources that are needed for achieving an objective, but this requires more information before it can be put into practice. Logistics can only handle simple facts; when it comes to distribution, the basic facts or data are usually quantities and costs. Processing such data is complex and time consuming, and this is where a computer comes into its own. Like distribution systems, computers come in all shapes and sizes and there is one to suit every system.

DISTRIBUTION LOGISTICS

Logistics is the means to achieve an end and not the end itself. It is therefore only a tool of distribution, and cannot take over the decision-making function of the manager. In fact, it is just a collection of mathematical systems designed to help managers put their decisions into action with the aid of a processing tool – the computer.

Distribution logistics is the organization of a system for supplying products to customers in a satisfactory manner – that is, supplying the *RIGHT PRODUCTS* to the *RIGHT PLACES* at the *RIGHT TIMES* for the *LEAST COST*. Since distribution is a service, it costs money without directly producing an income, although indirectly it makes an essential contribution. Thus the primary aim of a distribution manager is to reduce the cost of supplying goods to customers while maintaining or improving the level of service provided. In its broadest sense, logistics refers to the flow of both materials and products, and includes procurement as well as physical distribution. The total system is illustrated in Figure 1.1.

This book is concerned with the logistics of moving products from the production warehouse to the customers via depots and sales outlets; in other words, it refers only to physical distribution in Figure 1.1. Distribution is a dynamic function because it is continually changing with time. Quite often these changes are outside the control of distribution managers, yet logistics, like plans, must take them into account. Strategic planning is necessary for this purpose.

Strategic plans for distribution are based upon the general objectives of the system as a whole, because they are concerned with policies and procedures. Logistics, however, is important for specific planning, and applies more to operations which are really sub-divisions or functions of the strategies.

The fundamental strategy of a distribution system is to match production outputs to the market demand by holding goods until they are required before delivering them to customers. It follows that the two basic functions of distribution are warehousing and transporting products.

THE FUNCTIONAL DISTRIBUTION SYSTEM

Production and marketing functions are linked together in Figure 1.2 into a distribution chain which shows the relationships between components. Essentially, distribution is a service that must be an overhead cost on both production and marketing; therefore, reducing distribution costs will increase company profits. It is easiest to reduce costs when their sources have been recognized, and this is the advantage of preparing a logical sequence of distribution operations with the aid of a distribution chain for the company.

Value of distribution

The company must measure distribution value in terms of the service offered to customers and its cost. Value can be increased by providing a better service or by reducing the costs. When every person in the functional distribution system knows

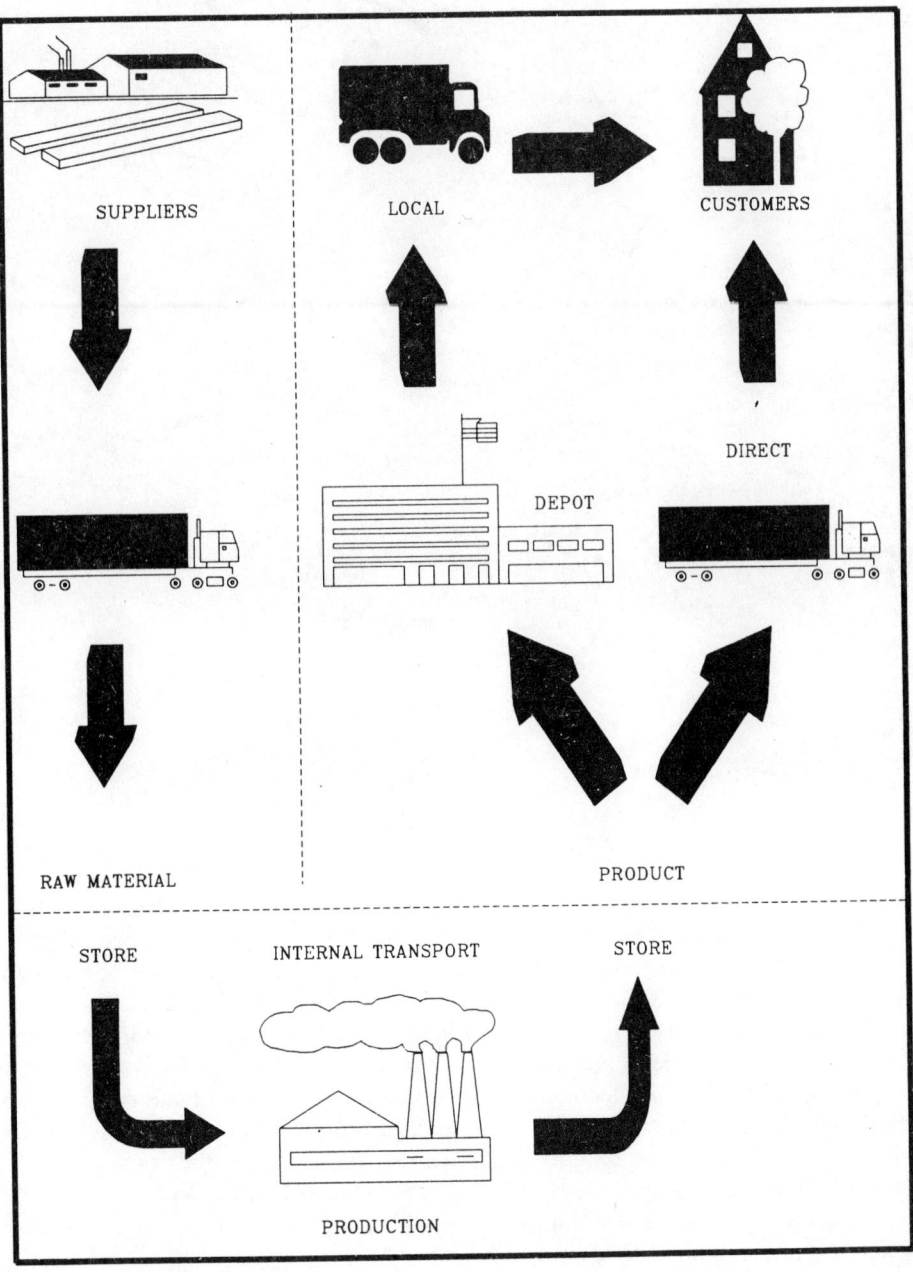

Figure 1.1   Total logistics system

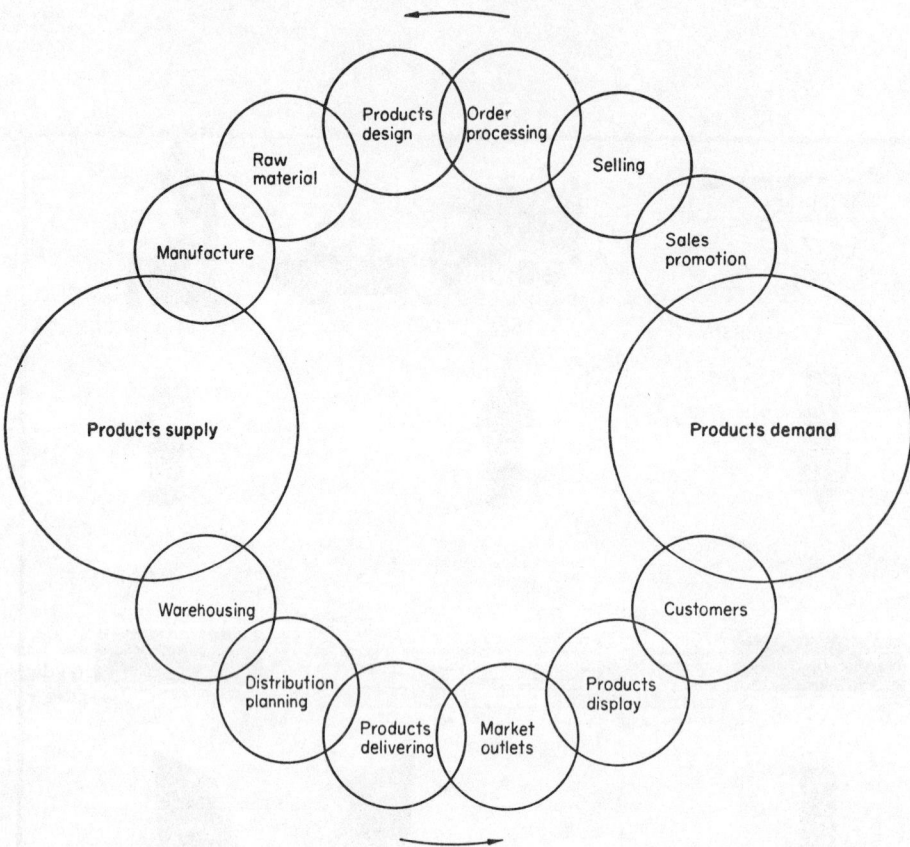

Figure 1.2   Distribution chain

the lines of authority and responsibility in its management structure, then they will realize that there is a communication bond between each job and the managing director. The functional relationships in an ideal distribution management structure are shown in Figure 1.3 by the lines of communication that join the functions.

In general terms, the company must have an official communications network so that information flows smoothly through the whole structure, because facts are the life blood of a logistics system. The *real* facts are communicated accurately when people in an organization know *why* the information is wanted and they trust that it will be used effectively. Such communication must be well planned and organized so that it encourages its development as the recognized procedure for obeying orders and instructions. It must be quite clear who is the issuing authority and who is responsible for executing the orders. If the line between them is recorded officially and included in a carefully indexed manual, it will be possible to compile an operating code for all to follow.

It is important to stress that a logistics system is best prepared when those people responsible for operating it think in an organized way. The greatest benefit from organized thinking is that communications are more effective, because everyone in the company is aware of its structure as a whole and not as a collection of bits and

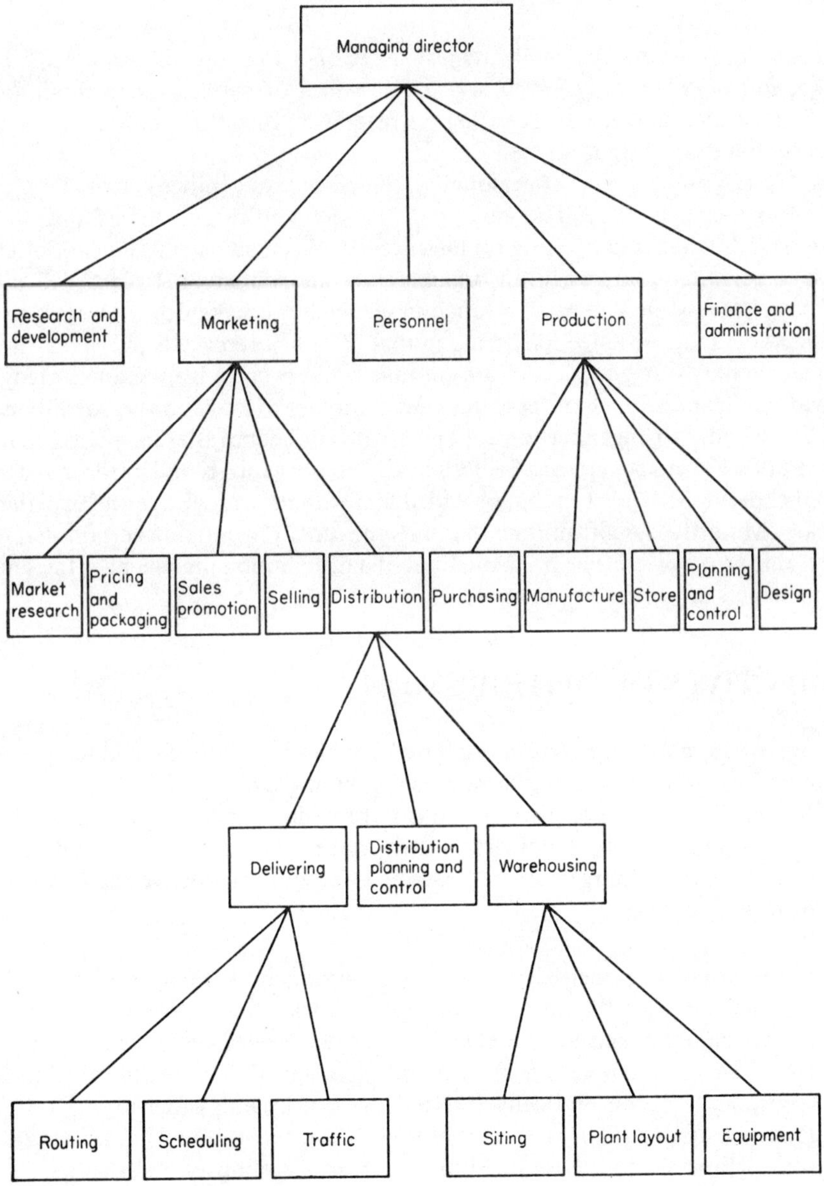

Figure 1.3   Functional management structure for distribution

pieces. At any level, people will function more logically when the full implications of their own jobs are properly understood, and good communications help to do this.

Leadership

The oldest, most natural and greatest asset of a manager is leadership. It is a projection of personality which is a combination of persuasion, compulsion and example setting that encourages others to react in a respectful way. Organization is a science, but leadership is an art.

Art is the manifestation of personality; therefore leadership is personal, regardless of an organization's size. The 'boss' must be seen and recognized as a person who understands what is happening on lower levels. Electronic communications cannot replace personal contacts in an organization, and impersonal plans will only be partially successful. The human touch in leadership breaks down barriers to communication and resistance to change so that trust will replace fear.

The qualities of a good leader are courage, willpower, judgement, knowledge and broad-mindedness. Each of these qualities combines to make the personality necessary for a leader to engender respect and create confidence that his plans are for the benefit of all. A manager must be both leader and organizer, and a true manager is a product of the environment that provided him with the knowledge and experience of his job. Maturity is a gift of time that must be repaid by making certain that others are trained to succeed. The basic qualities of a distribution manager are the same for all managers anywhere in the world.

OBJECTIVES OF DISTRIBUTION

The distribution manager has to organize his staff into a coordinated team, because teamwork is vital for working towards a common goal.

The overall objective of distribution is to provide a service to the marketing and production functions by holding and delivering products efficiently and economically. Secondary objectives can be related to warehousing, delivering and planning the distribution system:

1 *Warehousing* is principally a service to production, being designed to hold products of manufacture, to transform stocks from production units into marketing units, and to assemble loads for delivery to customers.
2 *Delivering* is a marketing service, being designed for transporting products according to orders and delivering them into the hands of customers.
3 *Planning the distribution system* must be designed to coordinate warehousing with delivering, to advise on siting factories warehouses and depots, to route delivery vehicles, to schedule deliveries, and to control operations in accordance with requirements.

The costs of distribution are related to these three objectives, but they will vary according to the number, sizes and types of warehouse and vehicle as well as the personnel employed:

1   *Number of warehouses*: transport costs and delivery delays will decrease as the number of warehouses increases, but stockholding and operating costs will rise.
2   *Sizes of warehouses*: the unit cost of distributing goods will decrease as the size of a warehouse increases, but capital and land costs will also increase.
3   *Location of warehouses*: transport costs depend upon the location of a warehouse in relation to the source of the greatest volume of products to be distributed.
4   *Vehicles*: the number of vehicles required will increase with the number of warehouses; as vehicle size increases the product unit operating cost will reduce, while different vehicle types will be required for different products or routes.

TOTAL COST OF DISTRIBUTION

The total cost approach can be defined as the minimization of the combined expenses of supplying goods to customers efficiently; that is, supplying the *right* goods to the *right* places at the *right* times for the *right* costs. Distribution expenses are a liability on a company, and that costs money . . . in other words, it loses money when the planning is *wrong*! Planning must consider the system as a whole, otherwise the advantages of combining various costs will be lost.

Always included in the range of total distribution costs are transportation, warehousing and inventory carrying expenses associated with finished goods; other costs that need to be added are order processing, customer servicing and data processing related to distribution. The real disadvantage of treating these costs separately is that significant trade-offs may exist between them. For example, as the number of warehouses increases, the delivery costs will reduce, because the distances between warehouses and customers decreases, however, capital, warehousing and inventory carrying costs will increase. Since the system has to be seen as a whole, the concept of total cost is important when making strategic distribution decisions.

Although total cost is important, it does not go far enough. Distribution operations depend to a great extent on what happens in other areas. Often, manufacturing and marketing decisions will have a greater impact on distribution effectiveness than the decisions of the distribution manager. Not only should the needs of physical distribution be known in those other functional areas, but the information from related management functions also needs to be integrated into the distribution logistics information system. The total cost approach requires farsightedness and an ability to see beyond the boundaries of a particular function.

The computer is an ideal tool for farsighted managers with imagination, because they can help to visualize different strategies for achieving their objectives but are unable to decide how the strategies will perform in practice because of the lack of evidence of the possible results. Nowadays, models and programs of managers' ideas can be devised so that the probable results can be simulated with a computer in order to compare alternatives and make better decisions. The manager must be able to communicate his ideas to subordinates so they can collect every piece of information that will make the simulations as real as possible. This is one of the differences between an out of date and an up to date manager . . . today's good manager is capable of motivating subordinates to provide factual information for computers to process quickly and accurately in order to give credence to new strategies that could give the edge over competitors.

Accurate information is vital – every individual operation must be carefully defined and costed – so that the calculations will be reliable indicators of what can happen when the strategies are implemented. The managers have to learn to trust their staff, and the employees have to learn that the future of their employment rests upon the reliability of their work.

The most important facts in any business relate to income and expenditure, because the difference between them represents a profit or loss. Often, it is easier to reduce costs than to increase prices or sales; therefore, every little cost has to be analysed correctly in order to see how it affects the overall picture. For this reason, the total cost concept is a valuable attribute for developing dynamic management thinking. In the past, the manager had to look at individual costs in isolation and speculate on their overall influence, but today the costs can be manipulated dynamically with simulation models in order to come up with answers that can prevent potential disasters. Like each link in a chain, the weakest piece of information represents the total strength of a management decision based on logistics.

A TOTAL COST MODEL

Development of a total cost model for distribution involves strategies for all its functions over a broad geographical area which, after 1992 in Europe, will include crossing national boundaries – the single European market will probably have to follow the USA's pattern. In the US, integration has gingerly developed over the years into the so-called *total cost model* in which distribution costs are considered in unison. Here, it is illustrated with an actual study, in order.

The purpose of this industrial study from the US is to illustrate the importance of integrating logistical cost information into the process of decision-making. The need for integration is greatest with strategies for holding costs down or keeping standards of customer service up. It concerns the distribution of wire netting in rolls from two factories in the steel belt of the eastern USA to widely dispersed markets throughout the country. Distribution was just one of the components of the total cost, but it represented roughly ten percent of total sales, which was too much.

Each factory produced a particular range of wire netting rolls, and they were freighted to eight depots at strategic sites closer to the markets (see Figure 1.4). It was uncertain whether the number of depots or their locations were optimal, so the study started with an examination of the costs incurred and the services provided, using Cleveland Consulting Associates' LOCATE computer program. The following data files were generated for computations:

1 Potential depot sites.
2 Total quantities of wire netting rolls consumed in each of the markets.
3 Freight rates for each class of delivery between depots and markets.

The total cost approach to distribution logistics considers every activity in the system as a whole, and computes the total cost of each alternative strategy. The activities that were integrated in this study were:

1 Despatching the wire netting rolls from two factories.
2 Freighting the goods to regional depots – varying in number from five to eleven.

Figure 1.4 Distribution of wire netting rolls in the US

3 Inventory control – holding stocks at the depots.
4 Materials handling at the depots themselves.
5 Local distribution to retail outlets.

Of course, each activity had a total cost for all its operations, so the amount of information collected was considerable. This information was collated in order to obtain costs for operating different numbers of depots (namely, five, six, seven, eight, nine, ten and eleven). Each time it was assumed that the same quantities of wire netting rolls were handled, based on sales forecasts for the period ahead.

The total cost for each activity was computed for each of the seven alternatives, and they were incorporated into Figure 1.5 which was used to make the overall decision. The graphs for the different activities show how their costs would vary with the number of depots, and the situation was very confused until the total cost was computed for each alternative. Delivery costs would be least with five depots; while in contrast, freighting costs would be least with eleven depots. However, the total cost graph showed that the least total cost would be incurred with six depots, and that was the alternative strategy finally chosen.

Just as each distribution activity can affect the total cost of distribution, so distribution can affect the total cost of running a business. A lack of information from other functional areas such as production and marketing can influence distribution operations. The following are examples of the need for information: transportation operations will be more economical when information on production schedules is available so that vehicle loads from factories to depots can be better

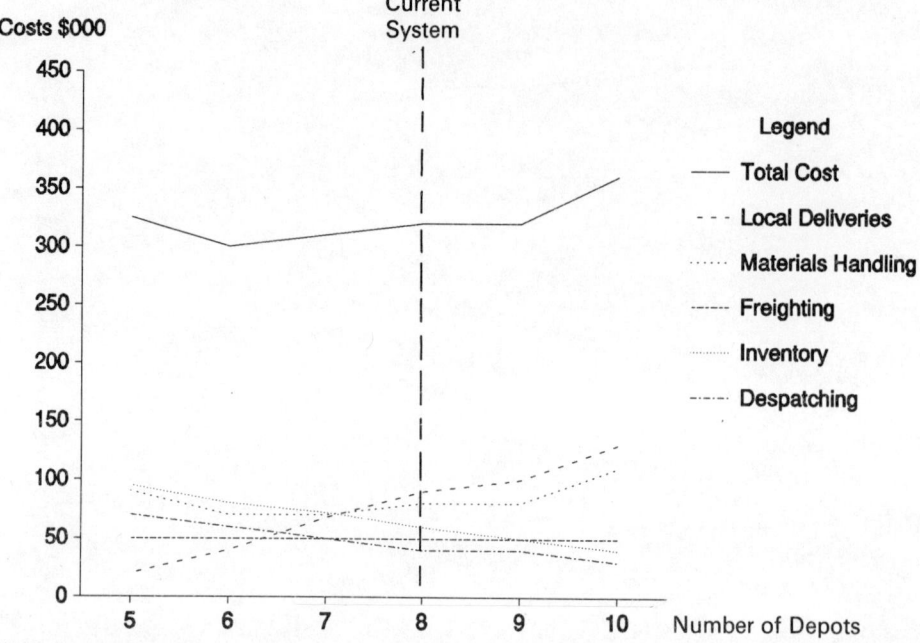

Figure 1.5   Total cost graph

planned; sales information helps to plan the inventory needed at depots, the design of materials handling equipment, the size of local distribution networks, and the personnel to be recruited; likewise, distribution plans provide information that will help the production function to organize its throughputs and the marketing function to promote its sales campaigns.

A logistics information system that includes cost minimization programs is particularly appropriate when the basic strategy is to use the lowest cost supplier without detracting from service to customers. If the aim is to provide superior service, then a good logistics system can provide timely and reliable information for improving decision-making that will be a significant aid to achieving strategic objectives.

In summarizing, the total cost concept enables distribution managers to arrive at an optimal balance between delivering, warehousing and stocking goods which will support their efforts to integrate all logistics activities from a strategic viewpoint, because they will know what is involved logistically and how to acquire and integrate the right information. The need for integration is especially strong when low cost or superior customer service strategies are required to compete in markets.

THE LOGISTICS SYSTEM

A logistics system comprises all the movements necessary for achieving an objective. Nowadays, it usually refers to industrial objectives in general and distribution objectives in particular; therefore, this section describes only the distribution logistics system and its management. The objective of managing a distribution logistics system is to maximize the economic value of the products moved from places of production to places of consumption by reducing the costs involved.

Logistics activities

The activities of a logistics system for distributing products include warehousing, transportation, communications and control; each represents a variety of choices before the final system design becomes specific. Some of the more important variables are:

1 *Number and location of warehouses*
   Warehouses may be established at each production plant or located strategically near the markets; their size will depend upon the demands for specific items, and this will determine the number required. For consumer products, local retail outlets are usually the end of the distribution line; however, most local retailers are primarily display and selling locations which are by-passed by distributors. Changing the number and location of warehouses will change the number of customers who are close to them – that is, product availability – and this will change the total costs of warehousing and carrying inventory.

2 *Modes of transportation*
   Transportation modes vary considerably; from plane or ship to train or truck; each has different costs, times, handling and packing characteristics, as well as, reliability and needs for a different data processing method. The choice of transportation mode will also influence other activities of the logistics system.

3 *Communications and control*
   The activities of a system are linked by a communications network which controls the movement of products. Again the choice is wide and interactive; from PTT services (mail, telegraph and telephone) to private services (messengers, radio and computer data links).

4 *Information processing*
   When designing a logistics system, the choice of information processing is between centralized or decentralized systems, depending upon the inputs and outputs. Usually, the alternatives are on-line, semi-automatic, manual, or a mix of all three.

5 *Product availability*
   Limits must be set for the percentage of customers whose orders will be delivered within specified times, times which will vary considerably according to product types and selling prices.

6 *Service reliability*
   The reliability of satisfying demands is another variable; it depends upon the products being where expected when they are needed. Other things being equal, service reliability can be improved by increasing stocks; however, stock levels are affected by the type of product, inventory control, transportation mode and information flow. Together with product availability, reliability determines the quality of service provided to customers.

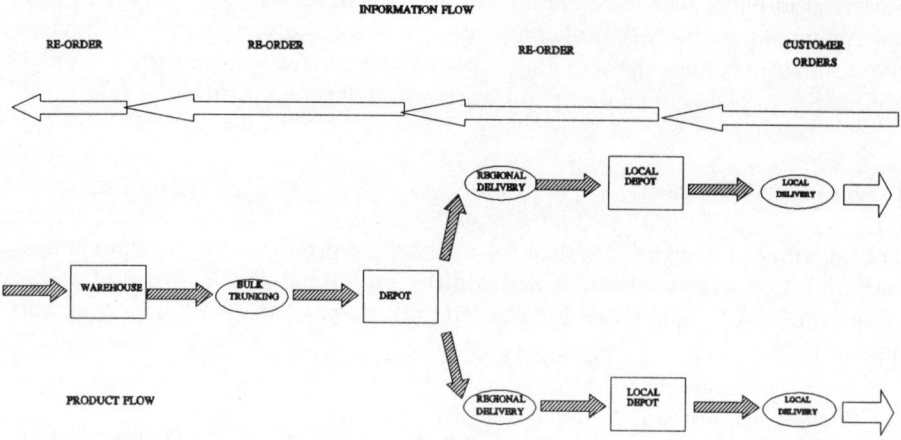

Figure 1.6   Flow lines in a distribution logistics system

7   *Types of products*

Product design affects plant location, manufacturing methods, warehousing, materials handling, packing designs, transportation modes and service reliability; consequently, the types of products to be distributed will have the greatest effect of all on a logistics system.

Logistics system structure

The simplest form of a logistics system can be described simply by the stocks and movements of products through the system, as shown in Figure 1.6. Like each manufacturing operation, each distribution movement changes the product; the former changes its design utility, while the latter changes its location utility. The stock points in a logistics system separate each movement in order to make it easier to schedule and control the movements. Figure 1.6 shows that the flow of products and the flow of information are interdependent.

Time is critical in logistics management because it is needed both for the movement of products and for dealing with the information received. Naturally, more time is needed to move products than to convey information, so a backlog of orders is commonplace in most distribution systems. This is where efficiency is vital, because delays increase costs and make dissatisfied customers. Rapid communications and transportation can reduce the range and size of stocks that have to be held, while at the same time both product availability and service will be improved.

Both the speed of communication and transportation have increased considerably in recent years, although the flow of products will never be as fast as the flow of information. Electronic transmissions of information exceed the speed of vocal sounds, yet they can be controlled far more accurately thanks to the development of computers. Without the aid of a computer, analysing large volumes of data would be so laborious and time-consuming that it would never be attempted; nor would distribution have been able to move with the times.

COMPUTERS AND DISTRIBUTION LOGISTICS

It is not intended to go into the details of computing techniques and languages in a book on distribution; however, a brief description of computers will help to understand their relationships with distribution planning. There are two distinct families of computer – *analogue* and *digital*. An analogue computer produces values, for example, the speedometer of a car is analogue because it indicates relative speeds; on the other hand, a tachometer is digital because it operates numerically. Digital computers are valuable management tools that can store and manipulate numbers or letters in order to perform logical operations according to a preset program. Analogue computers have not yet been applied to distribution management due to the complex nature of the models for simulating networks, deliveries and inventories; therefore only digital computers are described here.

The *central processing unit* (CPU) of a computer performs mathematical calculations following instructions from a *program* – part of the software – using data supplied by the peripheral equipment, which also records the results. Since electronic devices perform operations so quickly – in millionths of a second – the slower input and output equipment for transforming physical movements into electronic signals is responsible for controlling the rate of working. This is one of the main reasons why magnetic disks have replaced punched cards for transferring information to and from the CPU before displaying it on paper print-outs or a video screen. The reading of data from a magnetic disk approaches 100 000 characters per second, far too fast for human keyboard operators or electrical typewriters, so now computers are being taught to program themselves.

Programming

The instructions to a computer must be coded in a form that it can understand, namely, a program of binary numbers that either complete or break an electronic circuit – fundamentally, the computer only knows 'yes' or 'no' – but it will respond so quickly that it can be programmed to perform complicated logistic calculations.

When managers are able to cope with 'simple' electronic logic they will be in a far better position to give effective instructions to the 'human computers' that control the behaviour of people!

The electronic computer operates by continuously alternating between analysing an instruction ('yes' or 'no') and obeying it, but the instructions have to be 'written' in a language that produces the desired results. A number of standard languages are available that can be stored in a computer memory so that its operator is able to use program packages in the correct language in order to perform certain manipulations. To use a standard program it is necessary to provide an input of data to the CPU. The detail and format of that input varies with the type of computer system used, but the reliability of the results will depend upon the accuracy of the data supplied to the computer.

Originally, computers were very large and clumsy – so-called *mainframe* computers – however, the development of microchips has reduced the size of a memory store from the size of a house to that of a matchbox, and this has reduced the cost of owning a computer to suit the pockets of most people. In fact, the microcomputer is popularly known as the *personal computer*, or simply a PC. For most companies, buying a microcomputer is now more of a routine expense than a major investment decision. Consequently, software programs are available that enable unskilled operators to perform functions that were the prerogative of experts only a few years ago.

SUMMARY OF LOGISTICS AND DISTRIBUTION

Whereas distribution concerns the movements of products from the site of manufacture via storage to the places of consumption, logistics relates to the planning and control of these movements.

Logistics stems from the Greek word *logistikon* or 'the science of computing', and the French word *logis* which refers to the movement and billeting of troops. Obviously, the modern concept of logistics, which is the computer-controlled movement of products, owes something to both sources. Actually, logistics is an inexact science, because the control information can vary between the precise and the problematical. Problems arise from uncertainty; however, experience can minimize uncertainty, although it will never eliminate the need for commonsense, imagination, anticipation and innovation – the everyday manifestations of logic.

The planning and control of movements with the aid of logistics requires intelligent preparation and systematic management of the resources for the objectives. The objectives of a distribution system are to provide customers with the best service for the least cost.

All appropriate logistics systems can improve the service to customers, but at a price. The degree of automatic control provided by a system must be balanced against the cost of its implementation and, like most good things in life, the best distribution logistics system is a compromise.

Unless a computer-based system receives accurate information, it cannot provide the right results; however, with factual data it will operate quickly, reliably, conveniently and economically. With respect to distribution, the facts come from the activities to be controlled, namely, ordering, warehousing and delivering. Added to these main activities are:

- receiving, identifying and sorting goods;
- processing, assembling and despatching orders;
- operating, controlling and maintaining handling equipment and vehicles;
- accounting, budgeting and evaluating costs;
- collecting, analysing and communicating information.

Simply speaking, all these activities follow the cycle of planning and control, presented diagrammatically in Figure 1.7. Regardless of the activity we are considering, the same questions apply. The 'we' in Figure 1.7 may be personnel, transport vehicles, forklift trucks, pallets, cartons or packets of tea; the questions will always be relevant.

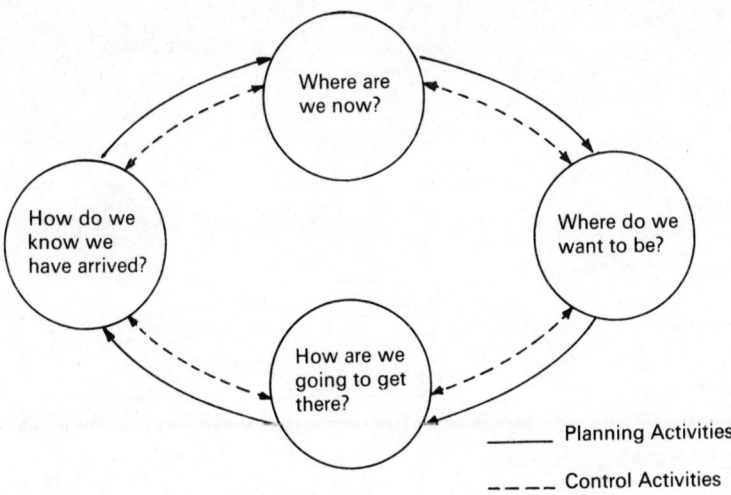

Figure 1.7   Distribution logistics cycle

2   Distribution planning

The first stage of planning a distribution system is to define the system in broad outline so that strategies for the overall plan can be developed. This outline must consider both the present conditions and the expected future trends. Future trends will be approximate until confirmed, but incorporating them will suggest the best general strategies to be employed.

A strategic plan must be flexible so that it can allow for a considerable variation in operating characteristics from the original specification. It is in this area of operations that scientific planning can be of great value for deciding the most suitable strategy.

STRATEGIC PLANNING

Strategic planning always precedes functional planning at all levels of an organization, because it means preparing plans for achieving objectives – the broader the objectives, the broader the strategic plans must be. The normal procedure starts with an assessment of your current strengths and weaknesses, of your company and its competitors, followed by the assessment of the market potentials. Then the objectives have to be reviewed in the light of how well your capabilities and those of the competitor match up with the potentials in order to prepare plans that can meet the objective requirements. The outcome of the planning process will be a selection of products for markets and methods for distributing them economically according to the level and importance of their objectives.

Corporate strategy

At the top, corporate strategic planning concerns the way that a company is structured to meet the Board's directives, but the production, marketing, distribution and finance functions must have equal status. Consequently, conflicts will be reduced or amicably resolved, while the functions are unified in purpose. At lower levels, functional strategic planning involves preparing plans for the ways that each function can contribute effectively to the corporate objectives. So, planning is interrelated at all levels of an organization, and distribution logistics is a link between corporate planning and operational plans for both the production and the marketing functions.

Distribution strategy

The basic question for the distribution strategy is how can products be moved to obtain a market advantage? Consider the following two examples:

1   Superior customer service gave an equipment manufacturer the edge over his competitors, because he was able to supply replacement equipment from stocks when any item sold to a customer needed repairs. Formerly, the company had sent a service mechanic to the customer's premises whenever a breakdown occurred, but the distances and times involved often caused delays. Under the new scheme, stocks of replacement items were strategically placed around the country from where they could be delivered to customers quickly on loan while faulty items were being repaired. The company soon had a competitive advantage in the market.
2   Keeping up with fashion was an important marketing strategy for a knitwear manufacturer, but a long development time for each new line was affecting its competitiveness. This was reduced with computer-aided designing linked to a network of computer terminals in the purchasing offices of customers. Ordering information was then immediately available whenever market trends changed and a shorter lead time between manufacturing and selling ensured that the company's new fashions were reaching customers sooner than its competitors.

When the distribution manager participates in corporate strategic planning, the plans can be developed iteratively so that they respond more quickly to market changes or production requirements. Since each plan is logistically evaluated in terms of the best customer service and the least operating costs so that the most competitive prices will result. Likewise, the corporate plans will take into account the best inventory carrying levels, as well as materials handling and delivery methods.

LOGISTICS OF PLANNING

The art of controlling movements is the essence of distribution management, since the aim is to achieve a correct balance between the service offered to customers and the lowest operating costs. Costs are easier to measure than customer service, which includes timely deliveries, correctly processed orders and effectively dealing with complaints and emergencies. The cost of supplying service is largely that of inventory control associated with forecasting customer requirements, setting correct inventory levels at depots, scheduling production runs, despatching goods from warehouses on time, allocating items in short supply and planning deliveries. In view of the number of activities involved in distributing goods, it is better to treat the system as a whole rather than trying to optimize each activity separately. That will keep inventory levels at an overall economic position and replenishments will be controlled from the centre instead of each warehouse having to call on the others when stock-outs occur.

Satisfying the customers

Planning replenishment orders in advance is easier when product shortfalls can be predicted for an integrated system; particularly if the requirements of the distribution system are balanced with the production capacity or supplies availability. Accurate forecasts of demand will help to phase replenishments, but good forecasts require information on demands rather than sales or deliveries in order to distinguish regular orders from one-off orders, such as when restocking a warehouse. A good forecast based on a statistical model can include external factors and changes in the patterns of orders. Often, it is preferable to make forecasts for a product range rather than for individual items; the quantities forecast can then be pro-rated down to the items in a range. Such a total forecast is used to establish production runs more effectively than cumulating the requirements of each depot. However, planners must be prepared for abnormal demands such as faster sales promotions.

The level of customer service depends upon the inventory levels at local depots and the ability to draw on other depots; therefore, integrating service with demand is vital. A distribution plan, for example, may aim to provide a 90% service level on standard items from local depots and to supply less regular items from central stocks within a 24-hour period. Conversely, another plan may be designed to give a 95% service level for all items at every depot. The choice depends upon many things, but they all affect the investment needed for inventory control.

An integrated distribution plan can provide the information for setting levels of service, and it will be able to forecast stock levels needed at each depot for each service level and product demand.

Replenishing inventories

The main benefit of integrated distribution planning is the timely replenishment of stocks, because it is performed in phases for each product at each distribution centre, based on costs and service levels. The aim should be to replenish stocks whenever the expected level falls below the safety level, and planning in advance will prevent stock-outs. Replenishments can be set in a number of different ways:

- with economic order quantities (EOQ);
- by ordering minimum quantities or values based on experience;
- by forecasting for varying periods;
- by adding together the requirements over a period of time.

Whichever method is chosen, time-phased planning should review stocks at regular intervals so that each product at each depot can be replenished as soon as it falls below a predicted level. The forecasting of future demand requires a knowledge of statistical methods and setting long-term inventory levels for the whole distribution system; therefore, good central planning is advisable. As a result, changes may have to be introduced in some cases, or computer programs modified to combine inventory control with demand forecasts based on customer service levels. It is suggested that integrated distribution planning can be implemented in three phases.

Inventory planning – Phase 1

Introducing a single integrated inventory control system will show details of the current stocks and the predicted demand at each depot in the distribution network. If it is accompanied with basic forecasting, the system will be able to predict the demand for each product at each depot, as well as across several depots or across the entire network. Combining these forecasts with safety stock levels enables re-order points to be calculated for each depot, so that replenishment orders can be placed when the current stocks fall below the re-order points. Such information can be readily seen on a video display screen if it is stored in a computer's memory; the planner responsible for inventory control and customer service levels will then be able to see the product stocks currently being held at each location.

In the first phase it is essential to keep the forecasting and safety stock calculations as simple as possible, yet to provide accurate and reliable forecasts. The following methods for forecasting are suitable:

- moving averages;
- single exponential smoothing;
- manual adjustments.

It is wise to take other factors into account such as seasonal fluctuations, sales promotions and political changes; however, the marketing function will be in the best position to quantify such forecasts. Similarly, people in the marketing field should be able to keep track of movements in demand, either at one location or for all areas. From such records it will be easy to see trends and to incorporate them into future forecasts.

A safety stock level at each depot will ensure maximum customer satisfaction when ordering, and there are three simple methods for calculating it:

- determine a fixed quantity;
- find the mean demand over a number of periods;
- match statistically the desired customer satisfaction percentage with its necessary stock level.

Tables should be prepared for the range of products supplied from each depot according to sales volume or value, and depending upon their nature; an item will then have its own safety stock level (for example, an expensive luxury product has a slow-moving demand compared with a fast-moving, popular product).

Re-order times occur when the inventory level reaches the safety stock level plus the replenishment lead time required for each item. When a single inventory planner controls the inventory for all depots in a distribution system, bulk replenishments can be adjusted easily according to the overall requirements. Consequently, production runs will be longer and more economic.

Inventory planning – Phase 2

Whereas the replenishment calculations in Phase 1 are simple, in Phase 2 the forecasting is more sophisticated. There are plenty of statistical techniques for calculating stock forecasts, and all attempt to analyse demand trends over certain periods of time. Some complex algorithms are available that are very successful for particular products when used carefully. One approach to forecasting that has become popular in recent years is *focus forecasting*, because it has proved to be useful in practice. Using a number of different forecasting techniques, a computer program compares the results for each product over the previous three months with the forecast results in order to select the appropriate technique for each situation and product.

The second phase of implementing integrated distribution planning introduces automatic stock re-ordering to take over routine checks once the basic forecasting calculations have been carried out. Obviously, there will be many peaks and troughs in the product demand graphs; therefore, smoothing rules should be applied so that production runs can also be better planned. One rule involves the use of *sensitivity thresholds* for the most economic re-order quantities, preferably across the whole distribution system.

A program will be needed for tracking replenishment orders, because in Phase 1 a replenishment could be regarded as a purchase order on the production plant from a depot, but now orders will be placed automatically. So it is a good idea to create a replenishment order which is both a *purchase* and a *sales invoice*, and which can also be used to track items *in transit*. Such a feature simplifies ordering, order processing, despatching and receiving activities, thereby reducing the amount of clerical work required.

When the production control people are using the same computer hardware, it is possible to integrate depot replenishing with production schedules. This becomes more significant during the third phase when the time factor is introduced. Phase 2 is when to compare the distribution system with production so that integration problems can be resolved prior to introducing the more complex time-phase planned orders.

Inventory planning – Phase 3

The essential task of planning order times is to extend forecasting and safety stocks over longer periods, and to compare past requirements with current stocks and future forecasts. Doing this month by month helps to plan replenishments in order to meet the customer service requirements and inventory investment objectives. The planned quantities can then be transferred to the production schedule, which is used for production control and the procurement of raw materials.

It is usual to plan replenishments for each depot separately; they can be regarded as the demand quantities on a central warehouse. In this way the logistical requirements can be planned for parts or the whole of the distribution system over longer periods. There is one disadvantage of overall planning, in that short-term imbalances can occur between local depots.

Against that disadvantage can be set the benefit of having more information available in time for planning deliveries. When the forecasts are made in terms of the weight, volume and nature of goods to be moved to the different locations, the number of vehicles and personnel can then be estimated in advance for maximum performance efficiency. This will be useful for making contingency plans. In the longer term, demand forecasts will be useful for deciding such things as warehouse locations, fleet sizes, materials handling and stock control, right back to the production departments.

Conclusion

Integrated inventory control is an excellent way of reducing the money tied up in stocks and work-in-progress. It is wise to implement it in phases so that any changes needed can be better incorporated into the whole set-up. Using standard computer hardware throughout the organization enables the different departments to use the same software, while the development of operating programs will be more economical. Finally, it fosters better teamwork because everyone is aiming at the same goals.

INTRODUCING THE COMPUTER

The computer is invaluable for saving time and effort where large amounts of data have to be analysed and processed in figures or words; therefore, it is an important tool for routine distribution work. Mathematical methods can be used better for planning operations than planning strategies, although even then, continually changing circumstances make them difficult to implement without modifications. When a situation is fairly stable, however, or when orders are regular, a computer can perform repetitive operations more effectively, particularly for such laborious tasks as invoicing or stock-taking.

Computers for planning

Transportation planning readily lends itself to computerization, and developments in this field date back to the 1950s when the Chicago Area Transportation Study produced a complete package of computer programs for distribution models and assignment data analyses. Later, increased computer size and capacity led to the development of programming languages like Cobol and Fortran that allow managers to write their own programs for specific jobs. Faster and larger computers made programming easier for complex distribution systems in the 1980s, while in the 1990s the microcomputer revolution has had an impact on smaller companies and logistics activities within the distribution system itself.

It is not the intention of this book to describe computing languages and techniques in detail, but to help distribution planning managers to understand the relationships between computing and distribution planning and control. Even so, an outline of the basic elements of computing will be useful. There are two types of computer – analogue and digital; the former deal with the manipulation of values and are not yet applied to planning strategies; however, the second group can handle data in the form of characters like numbers or letters, so digital computers have plenty of applications for the logistics of distribution.

For managers who are less knowledgeable with computers, the speedometer of a car is analogue because the position of a pointer represents the speed of travel, just like the slider of a slide rule; on the other hand, a Chinese abacus for counting beads, or the game of Scrabble that uses letters, are both digital. Numerical manipulations are very important for planning distribution operations, and something needs to be said about digital computers in order to understand how computers – macro or micro – can be used to reduce the tedium of many distribution operations.

Description of computers

The basic elements of a digital computer system are the CPU that performs the individual manipulations, and the peripherals which supply the data to the CPU and display the results from it. The input to the larger mainframe computers may be punched cards, paper tape or magnetic tapes and disks; whilst the input to a microcomputer is its keyboard. The output of a computer is usually some form of typewriter that produces the results in a printed form, or it may be a video display. The speed of the input and output peripherals controls the speed of obtaining results with a computer. A typical reader for an input of punched cards can cope with 1 000 characters per second (bytes), but an output reader can manage only half this rate, so it is slow compared with the other equipment. A magnetic input or output reader can handle more than 100 000 characters per second; unfortunately, it can only be read by a CPU, and is unintelligible to a human being. The fastest practical output is a line printer. Normally, a line printer makes a horizontal line of characters on stationery which is fed continuously through the machine. Characters are made up from a large number of dots and any letter, figure or graphic can be printed to suit all requirements. The average line printer can print out more than 1 000 lines a minute, which is much too fast for the human eye; however, outputs are displayed on a video screen at the same time.

Microcomputers are fast enough for systems that are controlled manually by people, because their keyboards and printers are designed for speeds that can be handled by the fastest hands and eyes. A good keyboard operator is capable of typing around 400 letters or eight lines per minute.

Recent developments in computing

The development of computers has proceeded so quickly in recent years that their size is being reduced all the time; a modern portable computer can perform as many operations as a 1950s computer that had a memory occupying a large room and weighing many tons! Microcomputers are ideal for adapting to the requirements of most distribution systems, but they can also be connected to a larger mainframe computer as an input terminal. Alternatively, they may be connected by telephone links to multi-user computers in order to allow individuals to have access to the whole system, and to put 'computer power where the people and the problems are', according to one expert.

So much for computer hardware; now a few words about the software that comprises the instructions which tell the hardware what to do. A set of instructions or commands is called a *program*; each program is made in the language that a computer can understand. Nowadays, most computers speak the same language, but formerly each computer manufacturer had its own specific language. Since IBM became the great name in the computing field, it is not surprising that today most popular computers are known as *IBM compatible*, because they can function with IBM programs.

Software programs are either pre-packaged and available at a price, or they can be self-made for specific applications. Obviously, the CPU of a microcomputer is limited in the range of operations due to its compactness; therefore, it is essential to get sound advice before choosing a computer for particular distribution applications, not to mention the software. Some programs are specific for applications such as accounting, customer records or delivery routing; however, others can generate different applications like graphics, spreadsheets or word processing. A third type of software which can evolve its own environment is still in its infancy, but it has the potential for integrating different types of program. A user will then be free to move around the alternatives for different modes of analysis or presentation, as required, which will enhance creative problem-solving.

Another key aspect of computer operation is *user-friendliness*. That term is rather misleading because all computer systems should be *friendly* to the user rather than hostile! Actually, *user-friendly* means that a system improves the creativity of the user, but there is more to it than that; a system must also encourage and support team participation with the sharing of processes and data.

Evolution of microcomputers

There have been three stages in the evolution of professional applications for the microcomputer. Firstly, individual manual tasks were transferred to computers in order to increase the capacities of people and to reduce costs. Secondly, programs were developed to undertake tasks that required innovative skills in order to bring together different elements of a single activity normally performed by a group of people. Thirdly, computers became tools of change, so that the latest hardware and software are the means to achieve much higher aims, such as improving the efficiency and effectiveness of organizations.

The acquisition of a microcomputer depends upon the distribution system in question; the Canadian National Railway adopted a coordinated approach with a central information group that approved all the hardware and software for it. Hundreds of personal computers were acquired, and the complete system was standardized so that the large number of inputs and outputs could be interchanged. This reduced the costs of operating a widespread national network, but it would have been less suitable for an organization where experimentation was an advantage. In such a case, different software packages would allow users to innovate and develop new ideas which would be too expensive for a central information processor to handle. One of the advantages of microcomputers for distribution is the adaptability of their software and the freedom to use data and procedures without centralized approval.

Other factors have to be taken into account when introducing computers – the cost aspect is most important. Whereas microcomputers are more flexible and personal, large computers are more cost effective, and they ensure greater accuracy, integrity and security of information (databases). These aspects would be undermined by the proliferation of independent databases on microcomputers for different purposes and analysis in different ways. Whatever the merits of the different choices, the influence of senior managers will have an effect on the evolution of microcomputers in the future of distribution systems.

Implications for management

The introduction of computers into a distribution system, microcomputers in particular, will improve the coordination and control of daily operations. It will be possible to use more powerful techniques for order picking, despatching, scheduling deliveries, for monitoring transport vehicles and their fuel consumptions, as well as for automating inspections and maintenance procedures. In addition, microcomputers are suitable for financial analyses, word processing and other administrative chores. They can be linked together for electronic communications during ordering and similar marketing operations, for preparing mailing lists, and for passing on instructions to the field staff.

What will happen when managers have more time on their hands? According to Parkinson's Law, they will find other work to fill the time available – probably things that they have overlooked previously, such as improving the control of customer service, coordinating delivery operations, or learning how to make better use of the computer! On the other hand, automating the control of operations could reduce the need for so many supervisors, and their expertise would be available for other work. In any case, those managers who are able to take advantage of the new computer capabilities will be the ones who survive and advance.

LINEAR PROGRAMMING FOR DISTRIBUTION PLANNING

Linear programming is an operations research (OR) technique that has been applied to distribution strategies, particularly, for the purpose of using limited resources to the best advantage. Solutions to strategic problems previously had to be found by repeated trial and error without any guarantee that the best solutions would result; however, OR techniques have overcome that.

There are different basic forms of linear programming that can be used with or without a computer. The *Distribution Method* of linear programming can be used manually, but the *Simplex Method* better lends itself to computerized calculations; both use matrix algebra which is suitable for finding optimal solutions as opposed to exact solutions.

Planning deliveries with linear programming

Here is an example of the distribution method for delivering standard vehicle loads to customers – a computer program is not necessary, although software packages are available for more complicated distribution planning problems.

A supplier of automotive electrical equipment had three depots located at different places in order to deliver to a number of automobile assembly plants; the objective in this case was to find the most economical distribution network for delivering to five plants from three depots.

The data required for solving this kind of problem includes the cost of each delivery, the demands at each location and the stocks available at each depot. In the distribution method of linear programming, the available stocks have to equal or exceed the demand requirements, and the matrix algebra for solving such problems proceeds in steps (iteration). The first step is preparing a table of the number of loads required and available; this is known as a *distribution matrix*. The next step is to decide the allocations from depots to plants that are feasible for meeting the overall objective. Their respective costs can then be compared in order to find the best combinations.

More than one solution can be optimal; in other words, they have the same minimal costs. Therefore, the final choice will depend on circumstances and preferences. Often, the best solutions are found by comparing the cost of each new solution with the current system; otherwise, an initial solution is found with the so-called *north-west corner convention*. In this convention, the sequence of steps starts at the upper left hand corner of the distribution matrix, and stocks are allocated successively to the least expensive routes until all the demands are satisfied.

This example has been kept simple in order to explain the method for allocating supplies economically. The supplies are represented by standard vehicle loads to be delivered, and the relative costs of each delivery are expressed in monetary units, from a depot to a plant. You can insert your own cost figures and values when adapting this method to your own distribution system.

USING ITERATION

As mentioned earlier, matrix algebra aims at developing solutions to allocation problems iteratively, by a succession of logical steps. It starts with an initial feasible matrix in which all the demands are satisfied from the available stocks; alternative solutions are then compared with it in order to find the best.

Iteration example

In the case of the automotive electrical equipment supplier, the actual vehicle loads are shown in Figure 2.1 as stocks available at the three depots, or as demands required at the five plants. In total, 26 loads are required and they are available.

Next, the cost of delivering one load from each depot to each plant (in cost units) is inserted into the top right hand corner of each empty square of the matrix (see Figure 2.2). The costs will vary, therefore the objective is to optimize them.

Initial feasible solution

The initial feasible solution can now be obtained with the *north-west corner convention*, starting at the upper left hand corner of the matrix (namely, square XJ in Figure 2.2). All eight loads of stock at depot X can be delivered to plant J which requires nine loads; the other load required can be delivered from depot Y. This leaves eight loads in stock at depot Y, so six of them can be delivered to satisfy the whole demand at plant K, while the other two loads are available for plant L; however, plant L requires three loads, and the third load will have to come from

PLANT DEPOT	J	K	L	M	N	STOCK
X						8
Y						9
Z						9
DEMAND	9	6	3	4	4	26

Figure 2.1 Distribution matrix

PLANT DEPOT	J	K	L	M	N	STOCK
X	2	5	3	2	5	8
Y	5	3	6	7	8	9
Z	2	8	5	5	4	9
DEMAND	9	6	3	4	4	26

Figure 2.2 Distribution costs

depot Z. The other eight loads left at depot Z can then be shared equally between plants M and N in order to satisfy their requirements. This solution is feasible because all the available loads have been allocated from stock. In feasible solution, all the allocation squares are adjacent to each other so that there is a continuous path through the matrix, as can be seen in Figure 2.3.

PLANT DEPOT	J	K	L	M	N	STOCK
X	8 ^2	^5	^3	^2	^5	8
Y	1 ^5	6 ^3	2 ^6	^7	^8	9
Z	^2	^8	1 ^5	4 ^5	4 ^4	9
DEMAND	9	6	3	4	4	26

Figure 2.3   Initial feasible solution

Distribution costs

After completing the initial feasible solution, the next thing is to see if its total distribution cost can be reduced. The total cost is the sum of the individual distribution costs, and the cost of each distribution is the number of loads delivered multiplied by the cost units per load. For the initial feasible solution the total distribution cost is 92 units.

Changing the initial distributions may improve the solution by reducing the total cost. This is done by calculating the opportunity cost for each square of the distribution matrix. An opportunity cost will be positive if it can improve the solution, if not it will be negative. Obviously, the opportunity cost of an allocation in the initial solution will be zero, as shown in the bottom left hand corner of squares in Figure 2.4.

Opportunity costs

It has to be assumed that the distribution costs are contributed partly by the demand at a plant and partly by the stock at a depot; the positive or negative opportunity costs can then be found by iteration:

$$\text{distribution cost} = \text{demand cost} + \text{stock cost}$$

Step 1:   Starting with the first feasible distribution square XJ in the matrix of Figure 2.5, the distribution cost per load is two units. Therefore, if that cost is contributed entirely by plant J, the demand cost at J is two units and its stock cost at X is zero. These values are added to the matrix.

Step 2:   Move to the next feasible allocation square YJ, where the distribution

PLANT / DEPOT	J	K	L	M	N	STOCK
X	2 / 8 / 0	5	3	2	5	8
Y	5 / 1 / 0	3 / 6 / 0	6 / 2 / 0	7	8	9
Z	2	8	5 / 1 / 0	5 / 4 / 0	4 / 4 / 0	9
DEMAND	9	6	3	4	4	26

Figure 2.4   Initial solution opportunity costs

STOCK COSTS	PLANT / DEPOT	DEMAND COSTS					
		2	0	3	3	2	
		J	K	L	M	N	STOCK
0	X	2 / 8 / 0	5	3	2	5	8
3	Y	5 / 1 / 0	3 / 6 / 0	6 / 2 / 0	7	8	9
2	Z	2	8	5 / 1 / 0	5 / 4 / 0	4 / 4 / 0	9
	DEMAND	9	6	3	4	4	26

Figure 2.5   Demand and stock costs

cost is five units. The demand cost at plant J is known, therefore, the stock cost at depot Y must be $5 - 2 = 3$ units.

Step 3:   The next square is YK; since its distribution cost is three units and the stock cost is also three units, the demand cost at plant K must be zero.

Step 4:   The distribution cost of square YL is six units, and the stock cost is again three units; therefore the demand cost at plant L is three units.

Step 5:   Continuing to square ZL shows that its distribution cost of five units is divided between plant L and depot Z. Since the demand cost at L is three units, the stock cost at Z is $5 - 3 = 2$ units.

Step 6:   Using the stock cost of two units for square ZM, where the distribution cost is five units, the demand cost at M must be $5 - 2 = 3$ units.

Step 7:   Depot Z can also deliver to plant N which has a distribution cost of four units, and this means that the demand cost at N is two units.

Now the opportunity costs of the other squares can be calculated in a similar manner in order to complete the demand and stock costs of other squares:

$$\text{opportunity cost} = \text{demand cost} + \text{stock cost} - \text{distribution cost}$$

Step 8:   In square XK, both the stock cost and the demand cost are zero, while the distribution cost is five units; therefore, the opportunity cost is negative. No improvement can be made by delivering loads from depot X to plant K.

Step 9:   Repeat the calculation for square XL and the opportunity cost is zero; again, no improvement can be made.

Step 10:   For square XM, the opportunity cost is $0 + 3 - 2 = +1$, which means that using this combination of plant and depot can reduce the total distribution cost by one unit.

Step 11:   The opportunity cost for square XN is $0 + 2 - 5 = -3$, and this allocation offers no benefit.

Step 12:   From depot Y, where the stock cost is three units, the opportunity cost for square YM is $3 + 3 - 7 = -1$, and no advantage will result from using this allocation.

Step 13:   In square YN, the opportunity cost is $3 + 2 - 8 = -3$, and no advantage results.

Step 14:   From depot Z to plant J, square ZJ, an advantage will result because the opportunity cost is $2 + 2 - 2 = +2$.

Step 15:   In square ZK, the negative opportunity cost of $2 + 0 - 8 = -6$ shows that there will be no improvement here.

Revising the initial solution

The opportunity costs can now be inserted into the distribution matrix along with the distribution costs (shown in Figure 2.6). Improvements can be made only when the opportunity cost is positive, and the matrix is revised starting with the biggest opportunity. In this case it is square ZJ.

The demand at plant J is for nine loads, and nine are available at depot Z; therefore, this allocation should be considered first, and it is put into the revised

STOCK COSTS	PLANT DEPOT	DEMAND COSTS 2 — J	0 — K	3 — L	3 — M	2 — N	STOCK
0	X	2 / 8 / 0	5 / −5	3 / 0	2 / +1	5 / −3	8
3	Y	5 / 1 / 0	3 / 6 / 0	6 / 2 / 0	7 / −1	8 / −3	9
2	Z	2 / +2	8 / −6	5 / 1 / 0	5 / 4 / 0	4 / 4 / 0	9
	DEMAND	9	6	3	4	4	26

Figure 2.6 Opportunity costs

PLANT DEPOT	J	K	L	M	N	STOCK
X	2 / 0	5 / −5	3 / 3 / 0	2 / 4 / +1	5 / 1 / −3	8
Y	5 / 0	3 / 6 / 0	6 / 0	7 / −1	8 / 3 / −3	9
Z	2 / 9 / +2	8 / −6	5 / 0	5 / 0	4 / 0	9
DEMAND	9	6	3	4	4	26

Figure 2.7 Revised solution

feasibility solution of Figure 2.7. The next best alternative allocation is from depot X to plant M, where four loads are required. When this alternative has been done, only four loads will remain at depot X and they should be allocated to the next best squares. The opportunity costs of XJ and XL are both zero, but the demand at J has already been satisfied; therefore, three loads will have to go to plant L, and the remaining load to plant N.

The rest of the demand required at N, namely three loads, should be delivered from depot Z, because the opportunity cost of square ZN is zero; but no stock is left at depot Z, and the allocation to plant N will have to come from depot Y.

There are only six loads in stock at depot Y now, and six are required by plant K; that, then, is the final allocation. The revised distribution matrix is shown in Figure 2.7.

Conclusion

Delivering goods from depots to plants can be improved logistically with linear programming, as can be seen in this example. The total cost of the revised solution is 82 units, as opposed to 92 units in the initial solution; this is an improvement of nearly 12%. When considering an existing distribution system, that system is taken as the initial feasible solution, and iteration will show if its total cost can be reduced by the presence of positive opportunity costs.

That was an example of a stable system, but when the demands are variable, the simplex method should be used, preferably with a computer software package.

Simplex method

The objective of the simplex method for solving a problem is to convert the inequalities into independent linear equations by inserting conventional terms to represent them. For example, non-negative *slack variables* can represent any restrictions before making the equations into a matrix which can be manipulated routinely with iteration after finding a feasible solution. The steps continue until an optimal solution is obtained.

PLANNING A DISTRIBUTION SYSTEM

Two logistics methods are suitable for planning a distribution system: optimization and simulation. The former uses linear programming for a range of operations, and the latter uses spreadsheets for comparing the merits of a few alternatives. The usual objective of plans is to minimize operating costs subject to certain constraints, such as the variable demands of customers for goods, the stocks available at warehouses (including capacities and handling methods), and types of transport vehicles used for deliveries. A spreadsheet can best show the flow lines and volumes between locations, but optimization is able to show how resources can be used for the best opportunities.

When considering plans for improving an existing system, simulation is often advisable, because the system is likely to have evolved gradually, making it difficult to obtain the *optimal* configuration. With a simulation spreadsheet it is easier to incorporate random variables, uncertain constraints and general costs. This has a practical appeal to distribution managers, but the manipulation of figures, although more satisfying to computer operators, needs specific programs.

Heuristics

In reality, many distribution decisions are heuristic, or more colloquially *rules of thumb*, because they rely upon past experience using regression analysis. Heuristics proceeds by:

1 Developing a concept of what is expected.
2 Using that concept to assist searching, selecting and assigning meaning to facts.
3 Improving the concept continually as more information and interpretations become available.

Heuristic programming combines mathematical optimization with creative simulation. When a large number of facts have to be examined, the time and effort can be reduced by doing so in such a way that the ones most likely to produce a solution are considered first. This is certainly faster than random hunting or starting from first principles – regression analysis means working backwards from the final goal.

Planning creatively

Planning a distribution system is a complete function that includes deciding the number, locations and capacities of warehouses, the routes, number and sizes of transport vehicles, as well as providing customer services that include timely deliveries according to orders for the least cost. The values of these parameters change with time, which means that plans must be dynamic. Unfortunately, this means considering every eventuality, and that is well nigh impossible without a computer and the appropriate programs; however, modern techniques of logistics and operations research make it easier realistically to analyse the information collected.

Creative thinking starts with defining objectives, then developing strategies and making plans to achieve the objectives. Finally, the activities have to be controlled and the results measured. After evaluating how well the objectives have been met, the findings should be used to revise future plans.

3   Analysing demand

A great advantage of analysing demand from the distribution point is to discover the levels of service required by customers, and to determine the costs of distributing goods to them. Demand analysis aims at searching out and measuring market throughputs so that management can forecast both the volume of sales and the distribution needs. Once this is done, the demand can be manipulated according to the resources available.

Forecasting demand

In any company, the forecast or estimated demand will be the pivot for all planning operations. Successful estimates must be dynamic because they will be tools for guiding decision makers by showing them the probable results from different strategies.

Market research

The basic principles of scientific research are collecting information, analysing it in order to develop strategies, and testing these strategies by experimentation. Market research must apply these principles with reference to market demand. A major task of analysing market demand is to find out what the public wants, and to determine the value of past service levels in relation to future requirements.

MARKET DEMAND

The concept of market demand varies with the objectives for analysing it, but here it is being analysed for the purpose of planning a distribution system. The most common marketing factors that determine the demand for a product are its price, its sales promotion and its utility. These factors affect the value of the product and the distribution method. Analysis will improve the value, because it is a systematic examination of everything related to a particular objective.

Elasticity of demand

In general, the sensitivity of a market to changes in products or distribution methods is the elasticity of demand. More precisely, it is the percentage increase or decrease in product demand that results from a marketing change. Conceivably, there may be an expectation flexibility value for each factor that affects the demand for products.

Demand analysis

Demand is a variable factor that is sensitive to the customers, products, costs, times and levels of service in a system. This sensitivity can be measured statistically by correlating the numerical demand for a product with each of these sensitivity factors. The results must be expressed mathematically in order to compare distribution strategies meaningfully.

Correlation analysis. After collecting data concerning the factors that are believed to affect a certain demand, figures for the product sales have to be analysed carefully before and after a particular operational change. The ratio of these figures will be a coefficient of the change in demand that results; it will be greater than unity if sales increase after the change, or less than unity if they decrease.

Example of changing demand. A bakery changed the day for delivering pre-packed cakes to a seaside resort from Wednesday to Friday, and this was believed to be the reason for an increased demand. Due to this change, the mean customer order size increased from 120 trays to 150 trays. The coefficient of demand can be expressed as

$$\frac{150}{120} = 1.25$$

or an increase of 25% in sales due to changing the delivery day.

Similarly, demand coefficients can be calculated for different days of the week or other changes that affect sales, such as the type of packing, the design of a vehicle, or the time of year. Each of these factors will have a coefficient of demand that influences the distribution quantity. An equation can be prepared for any situation to include all the factors that affect the demand in order to plan for the expected sales. The sales expected will be obtained from the original (or normal) quantity multiplied by the demand coefficient for each factor involved successively.

In the bakery example, the normal procedure for distributing to the seaside resort was delivering on Wednesday (coefficient $= d$), packing the cakes on trays (coefficient $= p$), using a small general van (coefficient $= v$) and delivering during the holiday season (coefficient $= h$). The results from testing alternative procedures are presented in Table 3.1, and they were used to forecast the expected sales quantity with the aid of correlation analysis.

The bakery wanted to know the throughput that could be expected during an off-season period if the delivery day was on a Friday, if the cakes were packed in cardboard boxes, and if a purpose-built baker's van was used. The expected

Table 3.1   *Demand coefficients for distributing cakes*

Distribution factors that can change	Mean order size (dozens)		Coefficient of demand
	Pre-change	Post-change	
Delivering on Friday	120	150	$d = 1.25$
Packing in boxes	150	165	$p = 1.10$
Purpose-built van	165	165	$v = 1.00$
Off-season period	165	75	$h = 0.45$

throughput (T_E) could be calculated from the correlation equation that included the normal throughput ($_N$) and the coefficients (d, p, v and h).

$$
\begin{aligned}
T_E &= T_N (d \times p \times v \times h) \\
&= 120 (1.25 \times 1.10 \times 1.00 \times 0.45) \\
&= 120 \times 0.62 \\
&= 75 \text{ trays}
\end{aligned}
$$

The throughput to be sold with the new delivery procedure would be 62% of that for the normal procedure; it was expected to be 75 trays of cakes per customer, on average.

Obviously, correlation analysis can be used whenever future trends have to be decided; the expected results from distribution changes will be estimated instead of tested, and reliability may suffer slightly as a consequence.

Criteria for good forecasting. There are many ways of guessing future demands, but good forecasts will be the most appropriate and effective for given circumstances. An effective forecast must comply with the accuracy desired; it must be feasible so that its achievement can be expected with known certainty; it must be flexible in order to cope with changing conditions; and it must be appropriate to the situation under review.

The value of a good forecast depends upon the data available and the method used for analysing it. Value will be improved by comparing the actual results with the expected results, and there must be a reasonable degree of correlation between them.

Normal demand

The normal demand for a product is the demand that can be expected for most of the time. Any difference between the actual and expected results will be a measure of the circumstances. The data used for normal demand calculations must include all known circumstances such as different competitions, changed populations, economic crisis or wartime conditions. Normal demand is the most frequent demand that will occur in a market sample, while average demand is the mean for the sample. A little thought will indicate that 'normal' is more appropriate than 'average', which may be an impractical fraction.

Patterns of demand

The dynamic nature of distribution is reflected by the patterns of demand for products. Patterns refer to the changes in demand with time. Some patterns of demand that can be expected to affect a distribution system are given in Figure 3.2. The slope of a graph will be its coefficient of change; in the trend pattern graph, the mean slope is:

$$\frac{800 \ \text{tons}}{5 \ \text{years}}$$

This equals 160 tons per year rate of increase, which means that the throughput can be expected to increase annually by 160 tons if this trend continues. Graphs can be used to show cost patterns as well as demand patterns.

SYSTEMS ANALYSIS

The decisions made by managers are part of a system. Simply speaking, every system, however large or small, has an objective that can be achieved in a number of ways. Choosing the best of these alternatives is fundamental to decision-making. When making decisions for solving problems, it always helps to analyse a problem in order to find out why it exists, and to develop alternative ways of solving it. This is the essence of systems analysis.

Analysing a distribution system means examining all components of its logistics network to determine how well each (and ultimately, the whole) system is functioning. Analysis can be a simple procedure like a *time and motion* study of a driver unloading goods from his vehicle; or it can be worldwide when it involves air freight deliveries. Observations provide the data that will be analysed statistically or incorporated into programmed models of the logistics network. A model simulates a *real* system so that it can be manipulated mathematically to obtain solutions without the danger of making expensive mistakes.

Logistics systems analysis must begin with a focal point – the objective – and every component of the system is examined in terms of what it should do and what it costs. The value of anything in the distribution system depends upon two conflicting terms: the quality of service, and the cost of providing it:

$$\text{Value ratio} = \frac{\text{Quality}}{\text{Cost}}$$

Value can be increased by improving the quality of service, or by reducing the cost of providing it. It is impossible to quantify quality, therefore it has to be standardized so that the value of a system can be evaluated. For obvious reasons, every little saving that can be made will contribute to improving the value of the system. It is not necessary to analyse the system as a whole, but a saving means a change and that means making a decision. With a change in the distribution system both production and marketing will be affected, but an advantage to one could be a disadvantage to the other; this is why an evaluation of the whole system is important. Partial analysis is useful for aspects of the system, but analysis is not really effective until the performance of the entire system is examined.

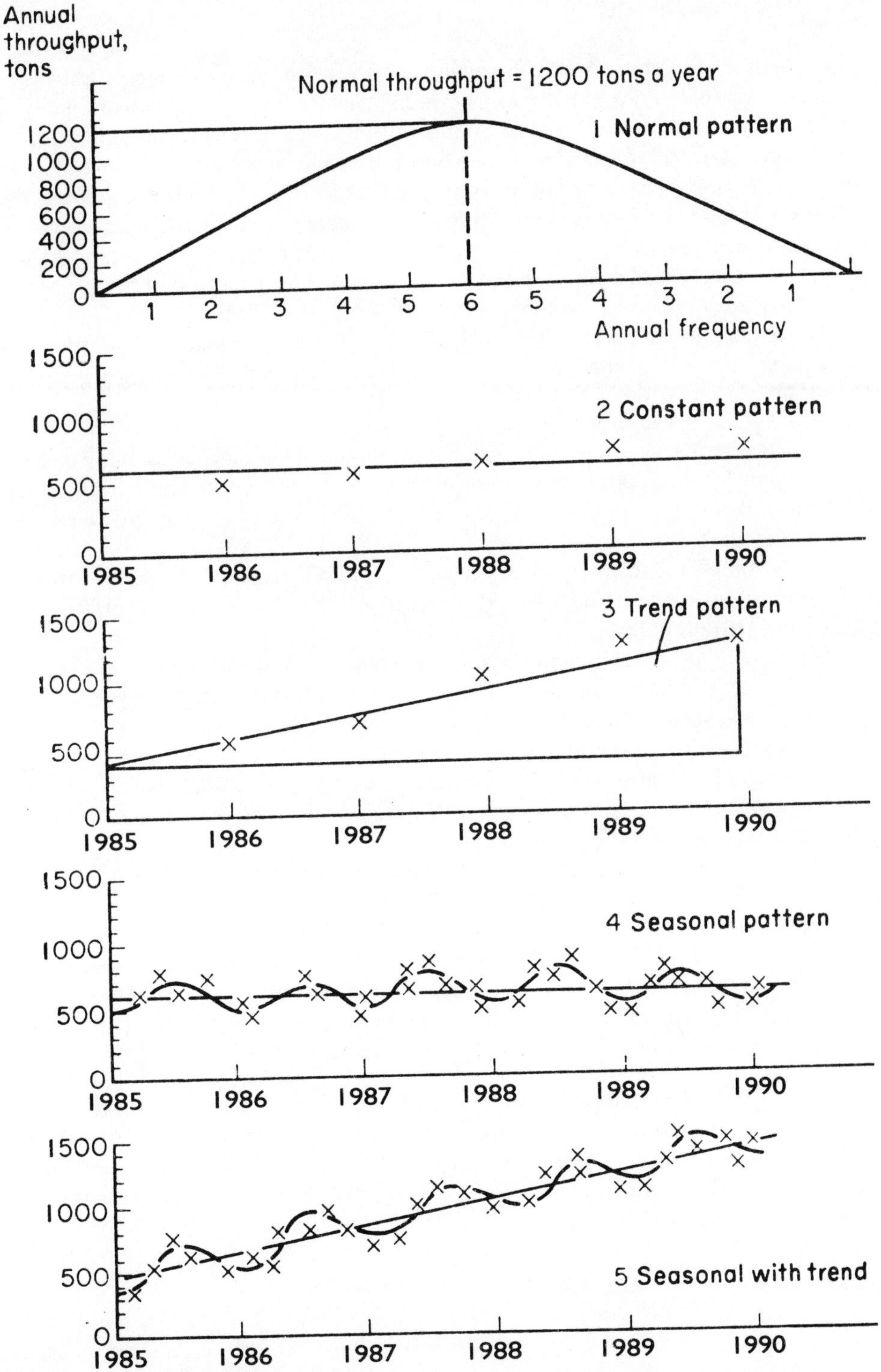

Figure 3.2   **Patterns of demand**

Logistics systems design

Since logistics encompasses a wide range of activities, the design of a logistics system is a complex undertaking that requires special techniques, such as network analysis or simulation, but only after quantifiable objectives have been identified. Before a design can start, there must be agreement on the objectives, and any constraints to the system must be specified. Constraints are factors that will affect achieving the objectives, and usually they cannot be changed under any circumstances; for example, personnel regulations that are legal, existing machines or buildings that are too expensive to change, delivery rates that are part of a contract, physical restrictions to the use of a certain route, or the schedules of a public carrier.

The data collected and analysed will affect the design of a logistics system which can be no better than the basic data utilized. The following checklists include the types of information required for the database:

Logistics system design checklists: the information required for designing a logistics system for managing distribution comprises a thorough examination of the products themselves, the facilities required, the sales procedure, the customers and the competition.

Product data: (1) throughput; (2) packaging; (3) stock level; (4) seasonality; (5) transportation; (6) manufacture; (7) marketing; (8) order quantities; (9) regional demands; (10) profitability.

Facilities data: (1) production capacities and handling equipment; (2) central warehousing; (3) depots capacities and equipment; (4) order processing; (5) transportation; (6) vehicles loading and unloading; (7) retail outlets; (8) data collection; (9) data processing; (10) administrative controls.

Sales data: (1) locations of sales offices; (2) sales areas and staff; (3) order sizes; (4) order processing; (5) market research; (6) pricing; (7) sales promotions; (8) complaints; (9) invoicing; (10) financial controls.

Customer data: (1) location and population area; (2) premises; (3) orders; (4) deliveries; (5) special requirements; (6) order frequency; (7) sales volumes; (8) profit margins; (9) method of payment; (10) credit allowances.

Competition data: (1) competitive products; (2) competitive order processing; (3) competitive delivering; (4) competitive efficiency; (5) competitive facilities; (6) competitive service and prices; (7) market promotions; (8) sales lost to competition; (9) competitive advertising; (10) competitive data processing.

The purpose of collecting all this information is to analyse it and find the present composition and costs of the distribution network so as to compare it with the competition and proposals for new designs. As recorded earlier, two methods of analysis are suitable for systems design, and they are illustrated with reference to the distribution system.

Network analysis and the distribution system

The design of a distribution system proceeds in stages; therefore, network analysis which links components of the system is very useful for deciding the best sequence of operations, and for discovering which are the most critical in terms of time and costs. Network analysis helps managers to recognize that the sequence of events will depend upon the activities that lead up to those events. Some cannot start before others, and some cannot finish before others. Whereas some can proceed at the same time. Each activity has a duration and each event has a time.

The resources available and used will affect whether activities can be performed in parallel or in succession, and preparing a network shows their relationships. In the example that follows, numbers have been assigned to the events in sequence, and the connections show whether the activities preceding them have to be in parallel or in succession.

ANALYSIS OF EXPORTING WINES

A wine cooperative in the east of Spain exported wines to countries in Western Europe, and it was facing strong competition in these foreign markets. It decided to analyse the distribution system because it was responsible for half the selling price in one instance; namely, the exportation of red Rioja wine to the UK.

Distribution procedure

After an order was received from the importers in London, the regulations for exporting wine to the UK had to be checked and an application made for an export permit. Then the stocks were checked to see if the wine required was available, along with a check on the appropriate packaging materials for bottles, so that arrangements could be made for delivering the order. Other things that had to be arranged were insurance of the wine in transit, an import licence into the UK, the routes and transport reservations, and the associated paperwork. All these events were listed along with the events that initiated and completed them (see Table 3.3).

This procedure is valuable for recognizing the inter-relationships between events in order to prepare a network in which they are connected by the various activities. In this case, the sequence starts with the receipt of an order, the wine stocks and export regulations can then be checked; if the stocks are available, packaging can be decided, an export permit applied for, the order picked and transportation arranged. After that, insurance can be taken out, an invoice sent to the customer and the order made ready for dispatch; finally, the customer will receive the goods and pay for them.

In a network of events, some activities are more critical than others, either in terms of time or cost; they therefore have to be controlled carefully, otherwise the delivery date and price will be exceeded. It is advisable to prepare contingency plans for the critical activities in order to implement an alternative when necessary. This procedure is known as *critical path analysis*. The critical path for this wine exporting example can be seen in Figure 3.4.

The earliest time to reach an event is the shortest network path to that event in terms of combined activity durations; for instance, there are two paths to reach event (6), either via (1), (2) and (4), or via (1) and (3). However, both require two days because the link (4) to (6) is a dummy one that involves no time; therefore, the earliest time to reach event (6) is two days. The earliest time for completing the

Table 3.3   Exporting activities

No.	Starting event	Description of connecting activity	Duration (days)	Added cost (%)	Ending event	No.
1	Order received	Checking wine stocks	1	0	Stock available	2
1	− − − − − − − − − − −	Checking export regulations	1	0	Export regulations known	3
2	Stock available	Preparing packages required	1	9	Packing available	4
3	Export regulations known	Applying for export permit	3	4	Export permit ready	5
3	− − − − − − − − − − −	Choosing transportation route	1	1	Transport decided	6
4	Packaging available	Dummy	–	–	− − − − − − − − −	6
4	− − − − − − − − − − −	Order picking and packing	2	8	Order ready for despatch	9
5	Export permit ready	Dummy	–	–	− − − − − − − − −	9
6	Transport decided	Reserving transport space	3	1	Transport available	7
7	Transport available	Dummy	–	–	Order ready for despatch	9
7	− − − − − − − − − − −	Preparing Bill of lading	1	1	Bill of lading ready	8
8	Bill of lading ready	Dummy	–	–	Order ready for despatch	9
9	Order for despatch	Arranging transport insurance	½	4	Insurance available	10
9	− − − − − − − − − − −	Preparing customer's invoice	½	0	Invoide sent to customer	12
9	− − − − − − − − − − −	Loading order for despatch	1	2	Order despatched	11
10	Insurance available	Dummy	–	–	− − − − − − − − −	11
11	Order despatched	Transportation to UK	10	50	Order arrived in UK	13
12	Invoice posted	Mailing invoice	4	0	Invoice received by customer	14
13	Order in UK	Transportation to customer	2	0	Order received by customer	14
			30 days			

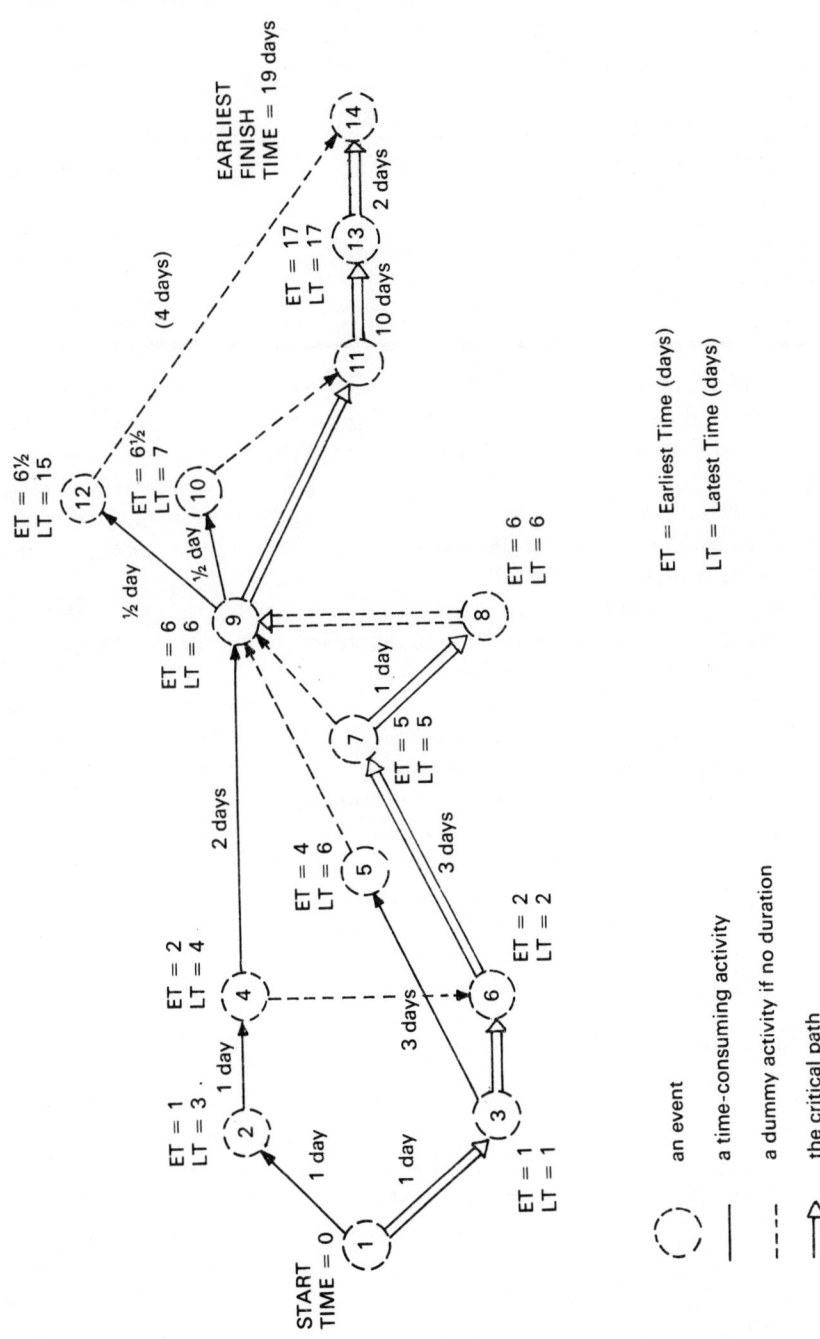

Figure 3.4 Network analysis for exporting wine

Table 3.5   Added costs for exporting wine

Activity	Added costs (%)
Packaging the wine in bottles	9
Getting export permission	4
Preparing transportation	2
Order picking and packing	8
Administration	5
Loading for despatch	2
Transportation	50
Total added costs	80

delivery of a consignment of wine from the Spanish cellar to the UK customer is the least number of days needed to have all the events completed, namely 19 days.

The planned time before the customer receives this wine consignment is 19 days, and the network activities that require this time are said to be on a *critical path*, for it is vital that the events along it are completed on time. In other words, they have no time in hand (called *slack time*). Some events do have slack time available, indicating that their completion is not critical.

The slack time available for an event is found by subtracting the earliest completion date from the latest completion date. Obviously, this is zero for event (14), where the planned date for receiving a consignment is the same as the earliest expected date for completion. Thus, the latest time for completing an event is the final date less the time from that event to the final date. In the case of event (11), it is 19 days – (2 days + 10 days) = 7 days. Event (11) is on the critical path because there is no slack time between the latest time and the earliest time.

The critical path is along the links connecting all the events with zero slack time. Here it is (1)–(3)–(6)–(7)–(8)–(9)–(11)–(13)–(14) and any delays along this path will increase the time to reach the final delivery date. Any time saved when performing the activities along this path will advance the final delivery date, or will be available to cancel out any delays.

Delivery costs

In the same way that there are critical times for events leading up to the final delivery of a consignment, the costs of completing these events are also critical, so any savings will improve the margin between the price and the total costs. In the example described here, the costs have been expressed as percentages, and each activity adds to the total cost of the wine at the cellar in Spain (shown in Table 3.5). The selling price was taken as double the cost of the wine stock in the cellar, which includes all distribution costs plus the profit margin:

$$\text{Selling price} = \text{stock cost} + \text{distribution costs} + \text{profit margin}$$
$$= 100 \qquad\qquad + 80 \qquad\qquad + 20$$
$$= 200\%$$

Critical costs must be examined first, should the selling price need to be reduced. Presently, the wine is exported in bottles, but this requires a lot of space so that the cheapest form of transport (by sea) also requires the longest time. When wine is transported in casks, the space required in the hold of a ship is reduced from $5m^3$ per 1 000 litres of wine to 1.5^3. A custom-built bulk container for that volume of wine would require only $1m^3$, and air freight might be worth considering; however, the cost of bottling the wine after receipt would increase the total cost.

Although the paperwork related to exporting wine does not add much cost, speed is a more important consideration for reducing the distribution time. In this case, telephonic and fax communications are quicker than postal mail. Compromises between costs and time could also produce improvements; for example, road or rail transport modes.

It is hoped that this example has shown the reader how network analysis can help to improve the design of a distribution system through a careful examination of every part of that system. It involves logical thinking in which the association of ideas is essential for the generation of new procedures. When delivery times are *not* critical, delivery costs may be!

COMPUTER SIMULATION

Simulation is the most widely used computer technique for logistics planning, and it involves the manipulation of mathematical models according to operational variations. Reliability is improved by making computer models as realistic as possible, and taking into account such factors as the availability of different transport modes, transportation costs, locations of customers and depots, service requirements, inventory holding and warehouse operations. The great benefit of simulation is being able to determine the likely results in alternative situations. In fact, it can turn hindsight into foresight.

Computer simulations permit distribution managers to test the outcomes of their decisions before implementing them, rather like the way that aircraft designers use wind tunnels to pre-test their new designs. The basic purpose of simulation is to imitate the operation of a system during a period of time without the traumas of real life. This makes it possible to test new strategies or procedures, and to get prior notice of how they will interact in practice.

When the model of a system or sub-system has been designed and programmed, its accuracy must be tested to see how well it complies with real life. One way is to use real data as the input and to compare the simulated results with the results that were actually obtained. In a case of inventory simulation, the input could be past customer orders and the outputs could be the total value of stocks, the number of back orders, the replenishments, and the re-ordering frequency. Once the accuracy of a simulation model has been determined, the behaviour of various elements in the system can be predicted through experimentation.

For example, by increasing the reserves of certain goods in a warehouse inventory to cover an extra week, the effects could be seen by analysing the simulated results of such a change on the number of back orders and the value of the stocks. Other elements of an inventory system could be changed in order to get prior knowledge of their probable effects on the real distribution system. Simulation can provide answers to questions like:

- How many warehouses are needed?
- Which customers can be supplied from each warehouse?
- What volume can be supplied from each warehouse?
- When are rail deliveries preferred to road deliveries?
- Which routes are the most effective and why?
- Would sales improve if the customers reduced their order cycle times?
- What would happen if the minimum order size increased?
- Is it better to own or lease vehicles?
- What is the optimal number of staff for operating a depot?
- What is the break-even point between customer service and distribution costs by product?

Testing a proposed plan of campaign with a simulation model requires a computer, because of the large number of calculations involved. In a particular case in the US, there were three alternative methods for distributing consumer goods: first, directly from the factory to shops; second, a number of depots that could handle specialized lines; and third, general depots that could be allocated to different regions. The first alternative was viable for large order quantities, the second for customers selling a narrow range of goods, and the third for a wider range. Programs were made and the computer was told to try different numbers, sizes and locations of the depots for each alternative. The annual sales for the previous year provided the data, and the costs and service levels were determined for each of the alternatives – each set required 75 million individual calculations and would have been impossible without a computer. The optimum number of depots was determined for the second and third alternatives, along with the minimum consignment size necessary to make the first one viable. The expected costs and service levels were then found.

Systems analysis is an activity that ideally lends itself to computerization because it involves considerable numbers of repetitive steps, and this is particularly important in the areas of planning and scheduling. In systems analysis it is not a case of computers just being substitutes for regular ordinary equipment when handling conventional planning and scheduling procedures; but it refers to the appropriate techniques for making vector diagrams. These techniques include PERT (project evaluation and review technique), which estimates operational times and analyses operations to find critical paths in order to present a dynamic picture of changing priorities; CPM (critical path method), which is suitable for scheduling complex deliveries, comparing costs and allocating resources; and SS (systems simulation), which can simulate the effect of changing the elements in a system in order to determine probable outcomes.

Systems simulation

A simulation model is a description of a system that can be manipulated in order to measure the effect of changing its variables. The description may be a written statement of the operations that compose the system, and includes how they vary or relate to one another. To be able to manipulate the model, the written statement has to be converted into a flow diagram to show the logical sequences and relationships before translating it into mathematical equations. When the common denominator of these equations relates to the overall objective of the system they can be varied simultaneously. In a distribution system, the costs of operations for a given customer service level represent the common factors.

To discover the effect of changing the variables in a system, the simulation requires an input of data which has to be processed so that the output data is then ready for analysis and evaluation. Processing the input data with a computer requires a program written in a language that the computer can understand. The speed of a computer enables changes to be simulated in a very short time, and allows the manager to keep one step ahead of market fluctuations.

Simulation is a means of obtaining experience with ideas and concepts before they are put into practice. It is a technique for accumulating experience, learning from it and developing a better system, or for comparing alternative systems. Consequently, simulation is a substitute for real-life experience without the risks, high costs or loss of time.

There is no single method for developing a systems simulation model, but the following list of steps can be used as a general guide:

1 Describe the system and relate its variable factors.
2 Express the variables in quantitative terms.
3 Eliminate the unimportant factors.
4 Prepare a flow diagram of the inter-relationships.
5 Convert the relationships into computer programs.
6 Collect input data.
7 Test the model with past information.
8 Change the variables and re-process the information.
9 Analyse the output data.
10 Implement the revised system.

An example of using system simulations to analyse a problem involving the supply of fuel to Scottish fishing ports is given below.

ANALYSING DEMANDS FOR FUEL SUPPLIES

Fuel supplies for fishing boats based at small ports in the Western Isles of Scotland were shipped from an oil storage depot on the mainland at Oban (01) to five Hebridean Islands: Colonsay (02), Coll (03), Mull (04), Barra (05) and South Uist (06). The simulation model developed by the shipping company required information about the varying demands for fuel oil at the five island fishing ports, and about the capacities of two supply tanker vessels. This model allowed the company operations manager to schedule deliveries after specifying an initial set of parameters for the performance of his ships and the demand conditions at the ports. Simulation allowed a number of alternatives to be tested and analysed so as to evaluate the replacement of ships, the expansion of storage facilities at the ports and to route the sailings efficiently.

In the first steps of designing a systems simulation model, specifications of the demands and a description of the supply requirements are required. These specifications are then coded into a computer program which has to be verified and tested. The final steps involve implementing the system within the operational framework.

1   *Description of the system*: the shipping company had an Apple II microcomputer for simulating the movement schedules for two ships that supplied the demands for fuel oil at five small ports. The daily consumption at each port was based upon past records; the company leased the storage facilities at these ports, and it was possible to expand the capacities at some of them. The objective was to develop an operational model for satisfying variable demands.
2   *Preparation of a flow chart*: the initial design of the simulation model is shown in Figure 3.6
3   *Development of computer program*: the simulation program was written in BASIC for a microcomputer so that the operator could select a supply ship, a number of ports and a period of time. Fuel oil storage levels were updated daily, and the daily demand at each port was treated as a random variable. As the time to re-order supplies approached, a supply ship was assigned to that port. At each decision point in the network, the manager received details of fuel oil levels in the storage tanks at all the ports and the whereabouts of each ship with the stocks it carried. This information let the manager know what stocks were available and the distances between the ships and the ports. The simulation output was expressed as delivery costs per litre, distances travelled, number of calls to the ports, average storage levels, and minimum levels permitted at each port.
4   *Collection of information*: the objective of this simulation was to allow the manager to assess the chances of a single ship satisfying the demand requirements at a set of five ports. The model was designed to be interactive so that operational decisions could be made during each simulation run by replicating the outcomes of daily decisions. Oban was the supply port, and the fuel records were stored in a computer file along with the requirements at all five delivery ports. A ship was then selected and the costs of delivering the requirements were calculated over the simulation period.
5   *Changing the variables*: since fuel consumption varied randomly at the ports, the amounts they required each day for the simulation model were taken from a normal probability distribution graph based upon past daily stock levels. Random variations are best analysed with Monte Carlo simulation, which is performed by picking events (stock levels) at random, such as would be the case with a roulette wheel.

Plotting the daily stock levels at each port over a representative period of time produced a curve like that in Figure 3.7. The vertical axis is the cumulative probability of the percentage volume consumptions which are shown along the horizontal axis. Thus, 25% of the time, the daily consumption was nearly 10% of the storage volume at a port, 50% of the consumption was 21% of the storage volume, and 75% of the time it was 34% of the volume.

Monte Carlo simulation used random weekly fuel consumptions from a table of random numbers (see Table 3.8). The table was generated by computer completely at random from hundreds of figures. The first number in the upper left hand corner of the table – 05 – means a probable week's fuel oil consump-

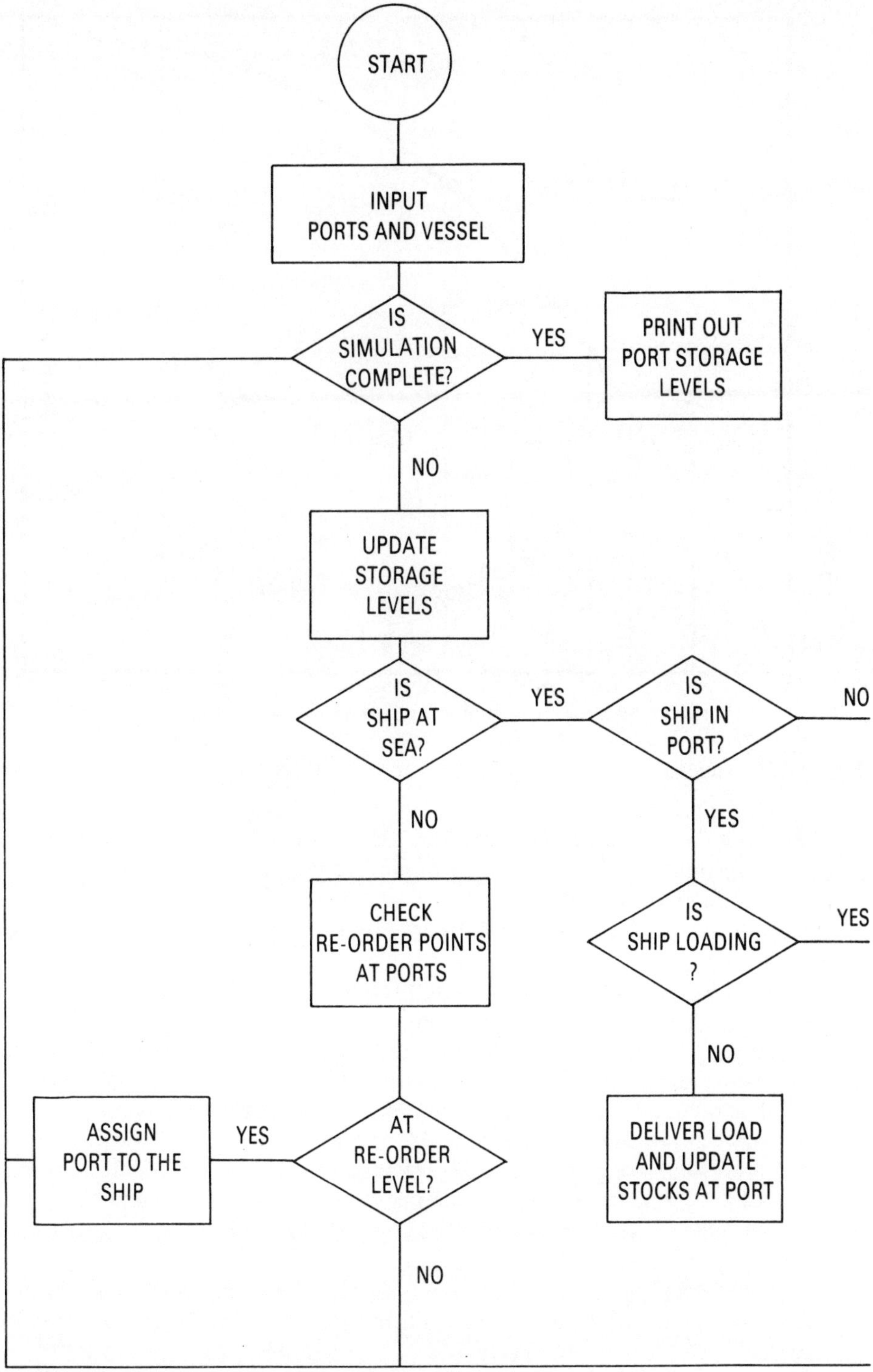

Figure 3.6   Flow chart for simulation analysis

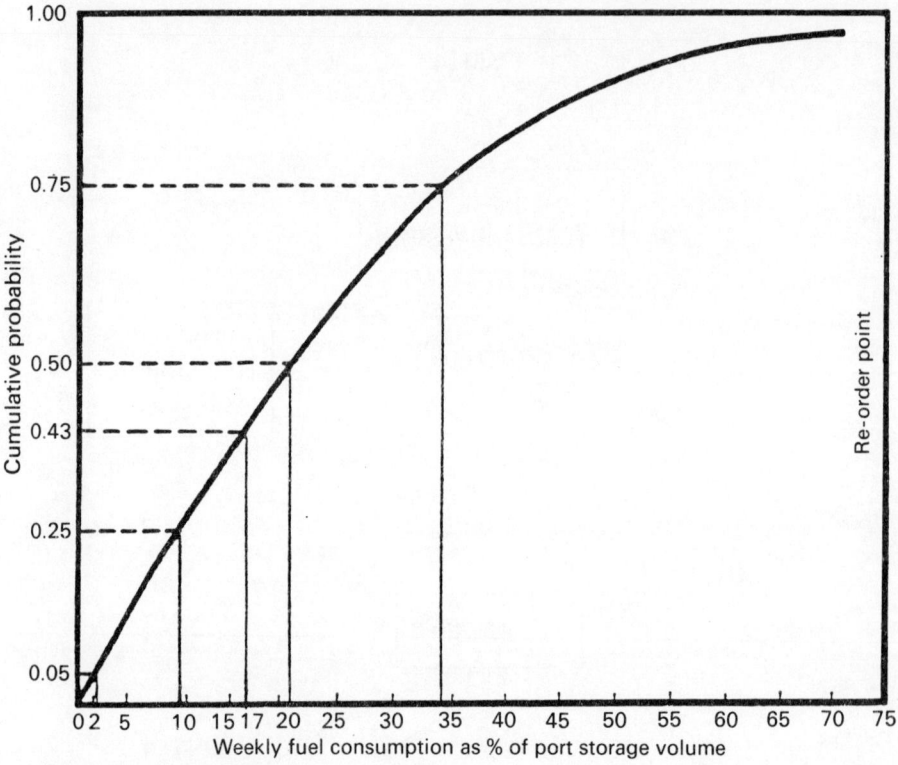

Figure 3.7   Fuel stock levels

tion of 0.05 or 5%, which from the curve in Figure 3.7 is approximately 2% of the storage volume at the port in question. The consumption for the next week would be determined by the second number in the table of random numbers (43), which means 0.43 on the normal curve, equivalent to 17% of the storage volume.

Table 3.9 represents the consumption for 20 weeks. The port superintendent would have to re-order fuel oil for weeks 6, 8, 9, 11, 12, 14 and 15 when the storage level fell to below 25% of storage capacity. Each day, the fuel oil available at each port was recorded, and when a port reached its re-order point (based upon the mean daily consumption) and a desirable safety margin, a summary was printed of the fuel available at each of the ports and the position of the nearest supply ship. The manager was then able to decide how to route a ship so that the expected arrival times could be computed. If a port did not reach its re-order point for several weeks, it could be excluded from the route. Otherwise, topping up its storage tank might be an economical thing to do after checking with a costing program based on operating costs for a ship per litre-kilometre. When the volume on board a ship fell below 5%, it had to return to Oban for supplies.

The simulation continued for all the weeks in the period under consideration; a summary was then printed out, including the average cost per litre of fuel oil

Table 3.8   Random numbers

05	04	31	17	21
43	06	61	47	78
31	85	99	63	92
10	47	39	30	36
39	80	05	45	53
94	20	87	97	04
63	43	14	33	07
99	50	51	80	11
65	29	51	29	85
80	83	09	53	45
87	16	71	77	59
77	58	82	37	85
24	40	43	03	94
99	07	39	40	71
05	17	36	22	20
08	04	63	25	15
63	71	78	62	46
05	67	76	50	85
07	55	97	43	99
49	17	34	63	62
39	56	01	25	83
91	19	08	99	68
22	61	19	61	08
03	67	69	29	02
51	91	76	33	80

delivered, the total distance sailed by the ship, the total volume of fuel oil delivered and the number of deliveries by the ship. A sample printout is shown in Figure 3.10.

6   *Implementation*: the simulation model was used to evaluate the ability of a ship to service the fuel oil requirements of the five ports. The impact of different demands and storage tank capacities at the ports could be assessed on the basis of the costs per litre delivered. Similarly, the use of different ships could also be evaluated, should a new ship have to be considered.

Conclusion

The development of microcomputer models for simulating distribution systems can improve the accuracy of forecasting results, and they can reduce the time needed to obtain cost estimates. Decisions are more reliable when past records are analysed, but it must be stressed that the results will depend largely on the suitability of the programs developed. Participation in the process of developing a simulation model gives a valuable insight into future requirements. Finally, it has to be said that

Table 3.9   Fuel consumption

		Fuel consumption at port	
Week numbers	Random numbers	Weekly	Cumulative
1	05	2	2
2	43	17	19
3	31	13	32
4	31	13	45
5	39	16	61 re-order
6	94	60	60
7	63	28	88 re-order
8	99	75	75 re-order
9	65	30	30
10	80	42	72 re-order
11	87	50	50
12	77	15	65
13	24	10	75 re-order
14	99	75	75 re-order
15	05	2	2
16	08	4	6
17	63	28	34
18	05	2	36
19	07	4	40
20	49	20	60

```
WEEKS SIMULATED      20
SHIP NAME            LOCH AWE
CAPACITY             55,000 LITRES
SPEED                12.5 KNOTS (22 KM/HR)
OPERATING COST       £2412.50 PER WEEK
TOTAL DISTANCE       125,403 KM
TOTAL DELIVERIES     3,580,110 LITRES
```

DELIVERY PORT	DELIVERIES	OPERATING COSTS
01	762,554	£20588.90
02	388,173	£10480.70
03	415,822	£11227.20
04	1,038,301	£28034.10
05	975,451	£26337.20

COST PER LITRE DELIVERED = £0.027

Figure 3.10   Simulation summary printout

analysing a system should be a team effort for investigating where improvements can be made. Effective systems design involves six basic steps:

1 Describing the objectives and constraints.
2 Organizing the activities into a network.
3 Developing a simulation model.
4 Collecting data and recording it.
5 Analysing the data in order to evaluate the introduction of changes.
6 Implementing the simulation results in order to test them in practice.

4 Deciding supply sites

The sources of supplies for a distribution system are usually warehouses situated somewhere between the manufacturing plants and the markets. The actual sites for the supply warehouses will depend upon locations and throughputs of the customers, as well as the cost of delivering the goods. Deciding where to site warehouses will have to be a compromise between least cost and greatest service to customers.

Since supply points are the heart of a distribution system, deciding the number and sites of warehouses is crucial. The cost of warehousing must be balanced against the savings that will accrue from mass production, or the increased sales expected from such an investment. There is no scientific method for making these decisions, but commonsense plays a major role in siting warehouses economically and effectively. Variations in distribution activities make it vital to study each system on its own merits, but a logical approach will always produce a rational system that has a good chance of success.

LOCATING SUPPLIES FOR DISTRIBUTION

Supplies are the flow medium for a distribution system, being common to all its functions and operations. The location of these supplies must optimize the objectives for planning the distribution system. These overall objectives must compromise the requirements of production and marketing, so that the objectives for warehousing and delivering are compatible.

The best location for the source of supplies differs with each system under consideration, but some factors for investigation are general:

1   Type of distribution system.
2   Production requirements.
3   Market demand.
4   Operating costs.
5   Ordering requirements.

6   Centre of demand.
7   Availability of land or premises.
8   Design of warehouses.

Industrial specialization makes it necessary to distribute goods from sources of supply to locations of demand, and there are many combinations of sources and locations. The combination finally chosen will determine the functions of a distribution system and the resource requirements.

Functions of distribution

Basically, the functions of distribution are warehousing and delivering. Warehousing is the function of storing the products of manufacture until they are required by a market. Storage is necessary in order to smoothe out fluctuations in manufacture and market demand. Delivering is the function of transporting products from the sources of supply to the locations of demand. When these places are some distance apart, transportation is essential. The method of delivery depends upon the nature of the products, the available transport and the distribution throughputs.

The warehousing function begins with the receipt of products from a factory; they are then stored safely before being transferred to the delivery function as demanded. The delivery function begins by assembling the products for transportation to the customers (customers, however, may be intermediary distributors, and not the ultimate consumers).

The basic functions of a distribution system are illustrated schematically in Figure 4.1. The system is assumed to start with production and end with customers. First, planning must look at the market demand, and analyse it to determine the supply resources needed. Later, planning reverses this sequence by considering the siting and design of supply points before returning to customers. Planning is made more flexible for distribution purposes when a two way approach is adopted.

Supply sites

The supply sites for a distribution system have to be situated strategically in relation to the sources of raw material for production and the locations of market demand. An optimal supply site involves minimal distribution costs.

Costs are reduced when the sources of supply are sited at points where distribution costs are large; for example, costs are large when bulky materials have to be transported to or from remote areas. It is usual to site a source of supply at the location of raw materials for production when they are bulky, as in the case of minerals, timber or oil. On the other hand, it is more economic to site the supply point of manufactured goods in the area of greatest market demand.

The rough location of a supply site can be determined with an educated guess based upon past experience and knowledge of distribution methods. It is best to consider distributing to the whole market from one site first, and then to consider more than one supply point. Economically, the number of supply sites can be found by comparing costs for the same level of service. Experience shows that one central

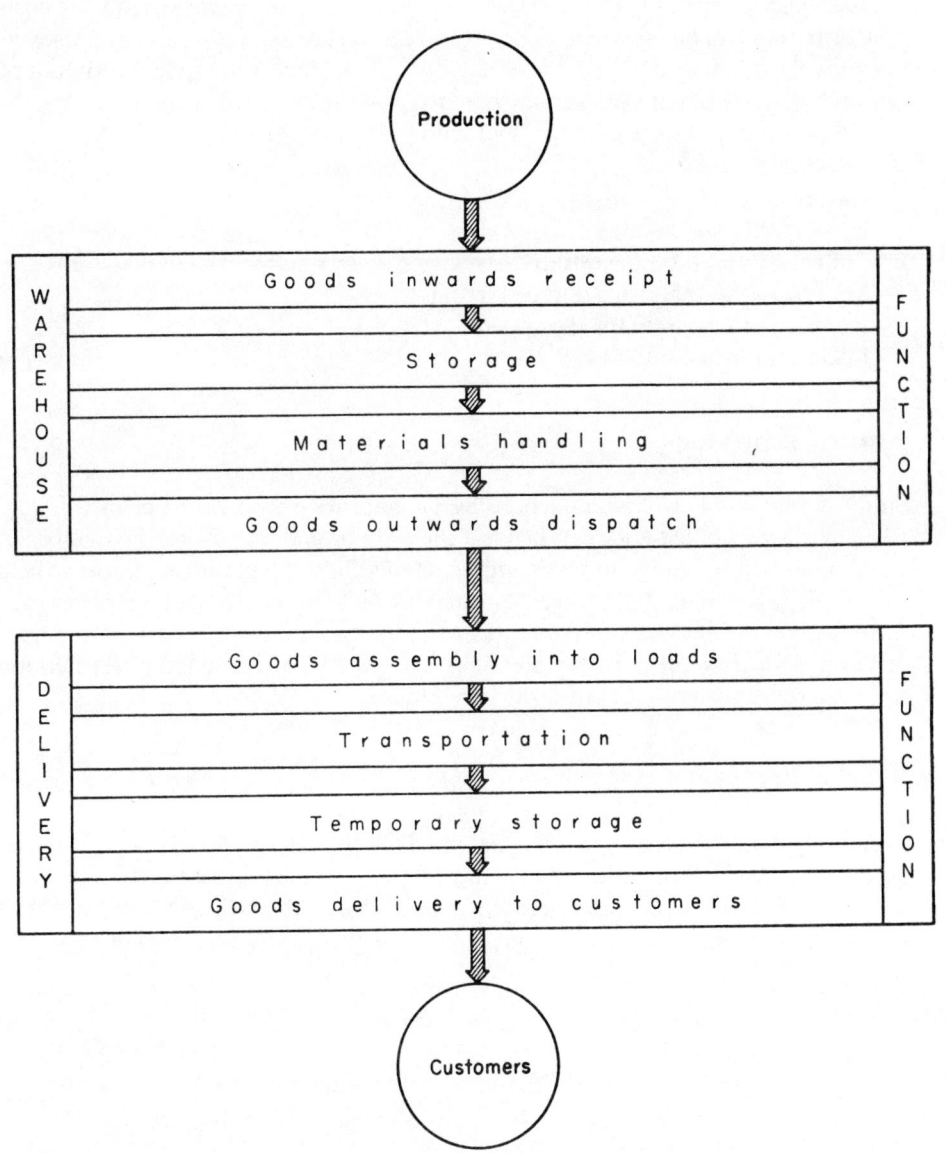

Figure 4.1   Distribution system

warehouse must carry supplies of all product items, and so must two warehouses; three, though, need carry only half the range each.

Since a distribution system is dynamic, it must be reviewed at regular intervals and plans modified in the light of changes. In this way, costs will be kept as low as possible, and the service provided will be as effective as is necessary.

The supply points are usually warehouses, and the focal point for reducing costs of distribution will be their sites. Siting warehouses requires a careful comparison of costs involved before it is possible to decide if the warehousing function should be centralized or regional. All supply site decisions must result from studying the overall policies, and they will be influenced by the following factors:

1   Nature of goods to be distributed.
2   Level of service required by customers.
3   Individual and total operating costs.
4   Methods of warehousing and delivering.
5   Planning of resources for the system.
6   Effectiveness of controls.

Nature of products

Siting supply points will be influenced by the nature of products to be distributed, particularly perishable goods. When the shelf-life of goods is short, the number of warehouses will be many; however, improved methods of handling and storage help to provide wider market coverage. Seasonal production necessitates complete stock turns within the season, and some distributors find that it is easier to organize inventory control when a single warehouse is operated. Once again, the best solution will require compromise between the variables.

Level of service

In many instances, speedy delivery is essential for providing a level of service that is acceptable. The level of service is most important to the marketing function, because it affects sales. When customers require speedy or variable deliveries, decentralization of warehouses is preferable, but control of the service level is more effective from a single supply site.

Operating costs

Optimal sites for sources of supply are affected by production costs, marketing costs, labour costs, stockholding costs and delivery costs. One central warehouse requires less capital investment than several regional warehouses, but the cost of delivering goods will be higher. Decentralized warehousing has the advantages of reducing delivery costs, improving customer service and decreasing warehouse capacities. However, these advantages must be balanced against the disadvantages of greater investment in buildings, equipment and labour.

A regional warehouse can be made the central supply point for a market region or a local production plant. This configuration can influence operating costs, but it will provide better control and improve customer service.

Method of warehousing

The size of a warehouse affects the area of a site needed, which may determine its suitability at a particular location. The area for a warehouse site must take into account, in addition to accessibility of receiving and dispatching goods, parking vehicles and constructing roadways. When capital investment in the land and buildings at a supply site is high, one central warehouse will be favoured; however, investment charges can be reduced by selecting a 'green field' site away from a town. Regional warehouses are less costly for bulk manufactured goods or for simple constructions.

Method of delivering

The geographical location of supply points has a direct bearing upon transport costs, and it is essential to include a study of the delivery methods when investigating a supply site. The delivery method selected will also influence the ancillary requirements; for instance, sea transportation requires access to harbours, while air, rail or road transport have their own particular requirements that affect optimal sites.

Planning of resources

The fewer the supply points in a distribution system, the fewer the resources required and the easier it will be to plan the system. The planning objectives are criteria for siting supply points. First, supply points must be located where they ensure the best service level, and second, this service has to be provided for the least transportation, stockholding and controlling costs.

Effectiveness of control

The control network in a system depends upon good communications for effectiveness. Control effectiveness is proportional to the suitability of a communications medium and the number of links in the network; by and large, speed is essential, and the fewer the links the better. Centralized control is most direct, but it is least flexible. Normally, a few supply sites are best for the effective control of a distribution system.

Siting considerations

From the production viewpoint, the number of supply sites must maximize production efficiencies and minimize production costs. These conflicting requirements make it necessary to compromise in order to select an optimal site.

Preparing models of a distribution system allows its variables to be manipulated to achieve the best compromise without risking capital. The first model to be considered should be a centralized system, and then the number of stages can be increased when the customer service required justifies it.

The central site can be found roughly with coordinates of the demand locations. More precise supply sites requires an analysis of the market demand and distribution costs.

When one or more optimal sites have been determined for a system, a network can be developed which includes delivery routes and schedules. The final stage of planning will be testing the sites proposed experimentally to discover the level of service that can be provided and the operating costs.

METHODS OF SITING

The objectives for siting supply points must ensure a satisfactory level of service and keep costs down. An optimal site will comply with both requirements, but it will be found only after a systematic search and appraisal of alternative sites.

Exhaustive search method

This method for siting supply points is infallible, because every possible site is considered and compared with the objectives for the system. Delivering costs are the most important variable when controlling a system, and the supply site has a great effect on them in the form of delivery distances.

Usually, delivery costs are proportional to distances between the supply site and customer locations, and an exhaustive search investigates all distances involved for different combinations. All possible costs will be collected and examined. Examinations are enhanced by drawing maps that pinpoint delivery costs. Maps that show 'iso-cost' contour lines assist planning by defining cost areas. Iso-cost contours are lines drawn through points of similar cost, and these are illustrated in Figure 4.2 for delivering goods to four countries.

Iso-cost contour maps

The distribution costs related to a particular system can be plotted on a map as an aid to planning in order to improve their value. Contour lines can be drawn through all points with the same cost concentrically around the optimal site. The optimal site will be found with cost coordinates. Locating the supply site elsewhere increases the distribution costs, but this may be unavoidable in some instances.

In order to keep unavoidable costs to a minimum, iso-cost contours will define the least cost limits when searching for alternative sites. The optimal supply site in Figure 4.2 is at Antwerp, and iso-cost contours encircle it at 10% cost increase intervals.

The centre of least delivery cost is found by cost coordinates at right angles to each other, and the search for a supply site must be made in this vicinity first. When no site is available, the cost of supply from neighbouring areas will have to be considered. In the map for the Low Countries, the supply site can be moved 100 kilometres north of Antwerp, to Rotterdam, before the total cost of distribution

Figure 4.2   Iso-cost contour map

increases by 10%; however, it can move only 50 kilometres west, to Ghent, for the same increase.

Systematic search methods

The great volume of calculation and investigation involved with the exhaustive search method can be reduced by omitting unusual situations, like very low or high demands. A less complicated method consists of estimating the demand through-puts for market areas and assuming that the best site will be found in the area of greatest demand. A rough search can be performed by dividing the whole region into areas and examining them systematically. These areas may be arbitrarily based upon 10 kilometre grid squares, and Ordnance Survey maps are useful for this purpose.

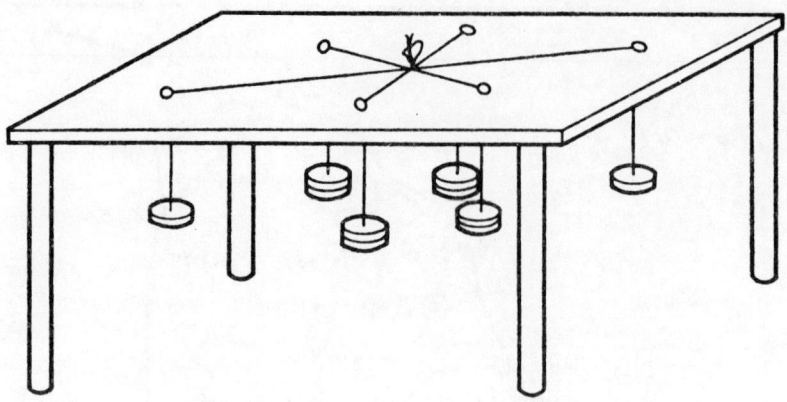

Figure 4.3   Analogue siting simulator

Analogue siting methods

Siting problems can be solved mechanically with animated diagrams or models. One simple working model comprises a map pasted on a wooden board or table with holes drilled at each demand location. A thin string is then passed through each hole and their ends knotted together above the table. The throughput at each demand location is represented by an equivalent weight attached to the end of its string below the table, as shown in Figure 4.3. When the appropriate number of weights has been added, the different string tensions will pull on the knot above the table, but the knot will be free to move and it will settle when the tensions are in equilibrium. The optimal supply site is found from the map as the place where the knot settles.

Natural obstacles like rivers and mountains can be circumnavigated by sticking pins into the map at places of strategic passages that avoid them. Other analogue siting methods make use of electric current and variable resistances, but they are more complex to construct.

SITING ACCORDING TO DEMAND

Supply points for a distribution system can be sited quite precisely with reference to the demand locations and delivery routes leading to them. Combining warehousing and delivering costs allows optimal supply sites to be determined. Warehousing costs can be considered as being fixed, but delivery costs increase with the distance from the warehouse source of supply. Since the smallest costs will be found close to the supply site, overall costs are least when that site is in the vicinity of the greatest demand. This condition applies regardless of the number of supply sites required.

It follows that the size of demand is initially more important than delivery distances. The demand locations can be joined together as a demand network to find the area of greatest demand. Distance will become important only when there is more than one area with the greatest demand.

Line theorem

Distribution costs basically depend upon the throughput of goods and the delivery distances. Throughput affects total costs more than distance, because it is directly related to the market demand. Consequently, it is advisable to consider demand before distance.

The line theorem states that the supply site with the greatest throughput depends upon the magnitude of individual demands in a system. It assumes that all demands are effective at locations that can be connected together into a line network. The network will be simplified by combining minor branches with major ones until a single main line results. There are a number of procedures for establishing the main line of the system and determining the location of the greatest demand.

The location of the greatest demand along the main line is found by summing the individual demands, starting at one end. The optimal supply point will be the location of greatest demand. When the sum of individual demands equals or just exceeds half the total demand for the system, this location will be a supply point. This point is confirmed by summing the demands from the opposite end of the line. However, if a different location is reached that is equal to half the total demand there will be two equal supply points for the system. They can be reduced to one point only when the respective delivery distances are calculated.

First, the procedures for finding centres of greatest demand will be considered before studying actual cases where distance is involved.

Two demand locations system: the simplest distribution system comprises just two locations of market demand, and the optimal supply point will be at the location with the greater demand. In this case, the least volume of goods will have to be transported to the other location. When each location has the same demand, all points on the line connecting them will be equally optimal. A two demand locations system is shown in Figure 4.4(a).

Three demand locations system: when there are three locations of market demand they must be considered on the same supply line, but its length is unimportant. The optimal supply site will be at the location with a larger demand than the other two combined together. When each demand is less than the other two, the central location will be the optimal supply site. The different configurations of a three locations system are shown in Figure 4.4(b).

Branch line system: a system with a number of branch lines can be reduced to a single main line by eliminating branches with the smallest demands. The system shown in Figure 4.4(c) has two branches, and the branch containing the greater demand will be the main line. The demand in a branch line is considered to affect the main line demand at the junction.

Considering the demand in a system, a line with branches is an extension of a two locations system. Delivering to locations of a branch line, the distance up the branch has to be covered regardless of the supply site, and demand is effective at the junction and not at some distance from it.

Loop line system: sometimes, two or more branch lines are combined into a loop, as shown in Figure 4.4(d). The loop can be regarded as a single branch line, and the procedure for finding an optimal site is the same as that for a branch line system. If the total demand in the loop is greater than the demand for the rest of the system,

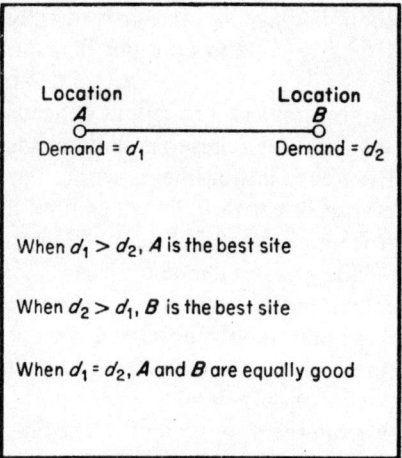

(a)

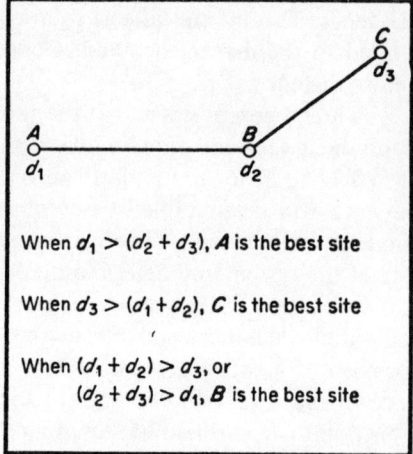

(b)

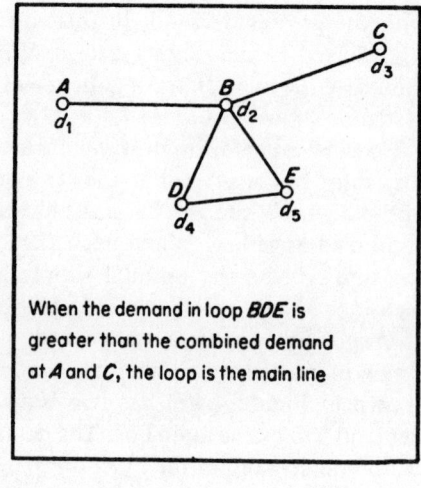

(c)

When the demand in loop **BDE** is greater than the combined demand at **A** and **C**, the loop is the main line

(d)

Figure 4.4   (a) Two demand locations system; (b) three demand locations system; (c) branch line system; (d) loop line system

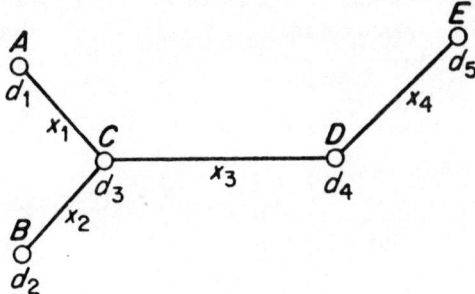

d = demand and *x* = distance

When $d_1(x_1 + x_3) + d_2(x_2 + x_3) + d_3x_3$
is greater than
$d_4x_3 + d_5(x_4 + x_3)$, the best site
is *C*; also, conversely, for *D*

Figure 4.5 Complex distribution system

the supply site will be located along the loop line which must be considered as the main line, and the rest of the system is considered as a branch of it.

SOLVING COMPLEX SITING PROBLEMS

Complex siting problems can be solved with the aid of the line theorem after they have been reduced to one of the basic forms described. When it is impossible to find optimal sites by considering only the demand at locations, distribution costs or distances must be included too. Systems with two or more locations of equal demand can be resolved to give a single supply site by comparing the demand-cost vectors at demand locations. A demand-cost vector is the product of the demand and the cost of delivering it from the supply site. Normally, cost is proportional to distance, and the demand is expressed as weight or volume. Therefore, the demand-cost vector may be defined in units of distance and weight or volume – for example, ton-miles or cubic metre-kilometres.

When two demands are equal, multiplying them by the appropriate supply distance will produce different demand-cost vectors, and enable one of them to be differentiated as the better supply site. Figure 4.5 illustrates such a situation.

In Figure 4.5 the best supply site can be either at location *C* or location *D*, because their demands are equal. The choice between locations of equal demand is decided by comparing their demand-cost vectors. A vector has both magnitude and direction; in the case of distribution vectors, magnitude is the demand for goods as weight, volume or quantity, while direction is the cost or distance for delivering goods to customers.

The choice between locations C and D for the supply site in Figure 4.5 can be resolved by comparing their demand-cost vectors. The optimal site will be at the location of least demand-cost:

1. The demand cost for supplying D from C is:

$$d_4 + d_5(x_4 + x_3).$$

2. The demand cost for supplying C from D is:

$$d_3 x_3 + d(x_1 + x_3) + d_2(x_2 + x_3).$$

When the former is smaller, location C will be the optimal site; conversely, when the latter is smaller, location D will be the optimal site.

Choice with more than two sites

Quite often, more than one supply point is needed for a distribution system, and the vector comparison procedure will be unsuitable for finding optimal sites. Only the demands and the number of sites required are necessary for siting them optimally.

One site of supply will be at the centre of demand, which is at the location of the mean of the total demand. The line network for a system must be constructed, and the demand locations reduced to a single line, then the demand can be cumulated from either end and the optimal site will be at the location where half the demand is reached or just exceeded. Mathematically, the optimal site will occur at the location where the cumulated demand is $D/2n$, when D = total demand and n = number of sites required.

Two supply sites will occur at the locations where the cumulated demand is:

$$\frac{D}{2n} \text{ and } \frac{3D}{2n}$$

More than two sites will be sited optimally at locations where the total demand and number of sites required comply with the following progression:

$$\frac{D}{2n} \quad \frac{3D}{2n} \quad \frac{5D}{2n} \quad \frac{7D}{2n} \quad \frac{9D}{2n} \quad \frac{(2n-1)\,D}{2n}$$

This progression is suitable for cumulated demand locations of a distribution system that has been reduced to a single line. Figure 4.6 shows a system of seven demand locations located equidistantly. Each location requires one van load of goods, and the total demand is seven van loads. The locations for one, two, three and four optimal sites can be calculated with the aid of the progression above:

One site $n = 1$, and the optimal site will occur where the cumulated demand reaches

$$\frac{D}{2n} = \frac{7}{2} \quad \text{van loads.}$$

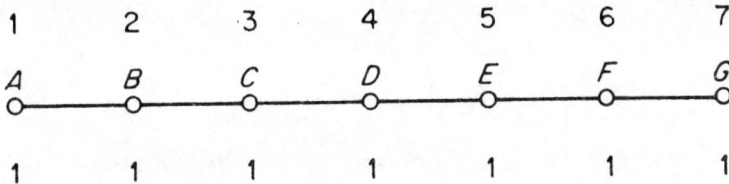

Cumulated demand

The seven demand locations are equidistant

Figure 4.6   More than two supply sites

This cumulated demand is reached at location D.

Two sites $n = 2$, and the optimal sites will occur at locations where the cumulated demand reaches

$$\frac{D}{2n} = \frac{7}{4} \text{ van loads, and } \frac{3D}{2n} = \frac{21}{4} \text{ van loads.}$$

The sites will be at locations B and F.

Three sites $n = 3$, and the optimal sites will occur at locations where the cumulated demand reaches

$$\frac{D}{2n} = \frac{7}{6} \text{ van loads, } \frac{3D}{2n} = \frac{21}{6} \text{ van loads and } \frac{5D}{2n} = \frac{35}{6} \text{ van loads.}$$

These sites will be at locations B, D and F.

Four sites $n = 4$, and the optimal sites will occur at locations where the cumulated demand reaches

$$\frac{D}{2n} = \frac{7}{8}, \frac{3D}{2n} = \frac{21}{8}, \frac{5D}{2n} = \frac{35}{8} \text{ and } \frac{7D}{2n} = \frac{49}{8}$$

van loads. These sites will be at locations A, C, E and G.

Application of the line theorem

Although the different configurations that are explained by the line theorem have been presented in simple terms, practical people find it easier to follow from a practical illustration. Later in the chapter, a real-life case study is used to illustrate the practical advantages of the line theorem. This case study can be adapted to suit many different situations, and it is hoped that distribution managers will find it useful for deciding the best supply sites.

NUMBER OF SUPPLY SITES

The factors that affect the number of supply sites required in a distribution system include the total demand, the customer locations, the warehouse types, the number and sizes of vehicles, the total cost of deliveries and the order lead times available. The number of sites can be found empirically by trial and error, but a systematic approach will help to reduce the number of trials. One of the most important factors in all systems is the order lead time, because it determines the level of service that will be offered to customers.

Order lead time

The difference between the time when a customer places an order and the time that the goods are required is the order lead time. During this time, the following activities have to be performed:

1   Processing the order.
2   Assembling the goods specified by the order.
3   Delivering the goods to the customer.

Each of these activities has a duration that varies with circumstances, but the first two will be fairly stable and the third variable. Therefore, it will be delivery time that most affects the number of supply sites required.

The furthest economic distance that customers can be located from a supply point will depend upon the delivery time in relation to the order lead time. Deciding the number of sites is rather complex, because of the large number of variables which will be pertinent to particular delivery systems.

As an illustration, the economic delivery distance can increase as both the order lead time and the delivery time available increase. When the time that is available for delivering is one day and the transportation method is by road vehicles, the economic distance will be a product of the daily driving time permitted and the average speed of the vehicle. In Britain, the Road Transport Act restricts the driving time of one man to ten hours in 24, and this determines the distance that can be driven in one day. Any customers located outside a radius equivalent to ten hours' driving time from a supply site cannot receive goods with an order lead time of one day. When this sort of situation prevails, alternative delivery methods must be considered, or the service level must be changed, or the site for another supply point must be investigated.

An additional supply point will be necessary when the extra delivery times required are sufficient to justify additional vehicles. There is no standard procedure for deciding the limits of delivery routes from a supply point, and each system must be considered individually. Normally, the time available for deliveries can be converted into distance when the average driving speed is known; route limits can then be fixed fairly accurately on a map.

Total demand

Another criterion for deciding the number of supply sites required is the total demand of a market area. The total demand, divided by the capacity of the largest single transport vehicle that can be operated, will decide the number of vehicles required for maximum efficiency. In practice, it is impossible to operate fully-laden vehicles all the time, due to variable customer requirements. The size of vehicle that should be operated must be the largest possible in order to obtain maximum economy.

Number of vehicles

The conditions for the maximum efficiency and economy of operating vehicles are conflicting, and the optimal number must be a compromise. By and large, the available delivery time will determine the number of journeys required, and the total demand will determine the number of vehicles. However, there must be an acceptable balance between the numbers of journeys and vehicles for the best performance.

Supply areas

It has been shown that order lead times affect operational times; thus delivery times will be instrumental in deciding the size of a market area that can be supplied from a warehouse. Converting the available times into distances will decide the maximum lengths of routes, and a map can then be drawn to show the boundary of each supply area with the customer locations that can be supplied along each feasible route.

Delivery ratios

The factors involved in deciding the best supply sites can be summarized as a set of ratios:

1 *Daily journeys*:
$$\text{Number of journeys} = \frac{\text{total full load delivery distances}}{\text{daily delivery distance}}.$$

2 *Vehicles required*:
$$\text{Number of vehicles} = \frac{\text{total demand for the order period}}{\text{standard vehicle capacity}}.$$

3 *Order cycle*:
$$\text{Number of days} = \frac{\text{number of daily journeys required}}{\text{number of vehicles required}}.$$

When the order cycle is longer than the order lead time, more vehicles will be required in order to reduce the number of days.

Number of journeys

It is advisable to prepare a network for customer locations within the permissible limits of each supply area. The customer drop points can be allocated to routes by starting from the end of each line nearest the boundary. The demand is cumulated at each location, working in towards the supply point, until a full load is obtained. A certain amount of 'give and take' is necessary when compiling loads, but each full load must be sufficient for one vehicle journey. Continuing inwards until all customer demands are satisfied determines the total number of journeys required for the area. Scheduling deliveries will also include the duration of journeys.

The order cycle ratio of journeys to number of vehicles gives the number of delivering days that will be required in order to supply all the customer orders in the area. At the end of each cycle period, the cycle must be repeated as more orders are placed.

THE NUMBER OF SITES AND DISTRIBUTION COSTS

Analysing cannot solve siting problems alone, but it offers a basis for making sound decisions, and helps to optimize the number of sites and their costs. An understanding of how distribution costs vary with warehouse numbers provides guidelines for deciding the best combination of site number and costs. Figure 4.7 presents, in a simplified manner, the general variations of delivery, warehousing and inventory carrying costs with an increasing number of warehouses.

Cost variations

The costs of trunking from factory to warehouse, warehouse operations and inventory increase in steps as the number of warehouses increases, but the costs of local deliveries decreases quite sharply before levelling out under the same conditions. In combination, it is seen that the total distribution cost decreases before rising again when the number of sites increases.

Mathematical analysis

The relationships between warehouse numbers and distribution costs can be clarified by analysing the cost data mathematically. The basic information will be fairly simple, but the large number of combinations that can occur will make calculating the least overall cost a lengthy operation. Repetitive calculations can be reduced when results are expressed graphically, while time can be saved by computerization.

Cost optimization example

The distribution costs of an Australian garden tools manufacturer were becoming excessive and it was decided to review them by mathematical analysis. The annual total distribution cost exceeded the combined asset values of the 12 company-owned depots, and the first suggestion considered was to close down some of the depots.

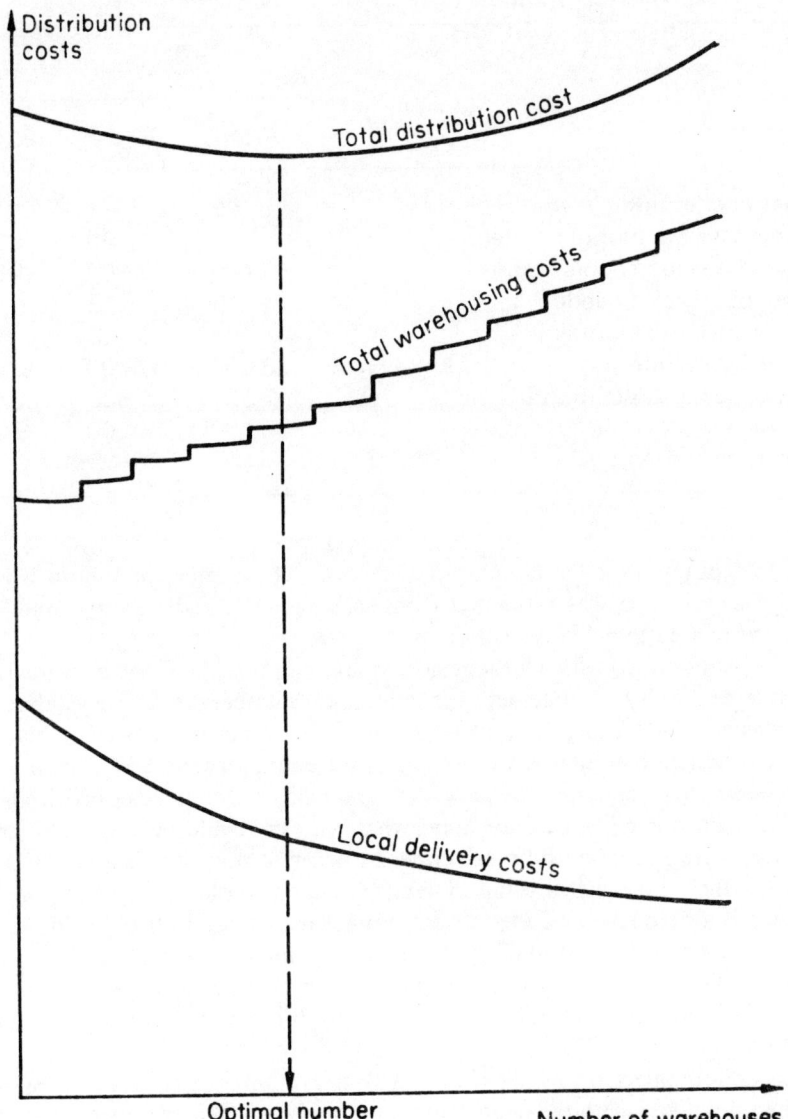

Figure 4.7   Cost variations and the number of warehouses

Mathematical analysis of the distribution system by industrial engineering consultants produced a more satisfactory solution. The analysis started by collecting data on depot investment costs, stockholding costs, labour costs and vehicle operating costs. These costs were tabulated for comparative purposes; a summary of delivery costs is shown in Table 4.8.

Analysing the data collected included costing the vehicle journeys, allocating the demand to depots, revising the depot sites and studying past sales records. The country was divided into supply areas for depots according to demands, and each

Table 4.8   Delivery costs data

Delivery factors	Size of vehicles		
	8-ton	10-ton	20-ton
Journeys per month	85	72	38
Working days per month needed	340	290	150
Total time needed (hours/month)	3 400	2 900	1 500
Number of vehicles needed	15	12	7
Running costs (cents/mile)	6.0	7.0	8.5
Mileage per month	68 000	57 000	30 000
Standing cost ($A per month)	1 500	1 600	1 400
Total cost ($A per month)	15 500	14 200	9 000
Cost per ton carried ($A)	20	18	12

proposed depot was sited at a major market town. The number of annual deliveries needed for each area was estimated from sales records, and then the number of orders was related to delivery lead times.

Routes were studied with a large scale map; pins and pieces of cotton were used to test route feasibility. Altogether, the minimum number of journeys that were required came to 450 using 20-ton trucks, and each journey was costed in relation to its route distance. Different sizes of vehicles were investigated, and 20-ton models proved to be most economic for the orders and delivery frequencies involved.

Similar data was developed for areas where carriers could be employed, and all the figures were processed by a computer in order to find the least costly combination for the whole distribution system. The most economic system computed saved nearly one quarter of the current annual distribution cost. In this optimal system, goods would be trunked from the factory direct to depots with company-owned vehicles, the necessary number of depots would be reduced to seven, and the supplies to local dealers would be delivered by hired vans or public carriers in different areas.

Later, additional savings were obtained by streamlining particular routes, incorporating sales offices with the depots, and establishing vehicle maintenance facilities at strategic points.

A chart showing the distribution costs for different numbers of depots is shown in Figure 4.9.

The capital investment costs in buildings and vehicles rose steadily as the number of depots increased, but operating costs decreased relatively. Combining these costs showed that the optimum, or least total cost, was equivalent to seven depots.

Distribution costs and lead time

The delivery lead time available after an order is placed directly affects the cost of distribution. The longer the lead time available the greater the inventory of goods

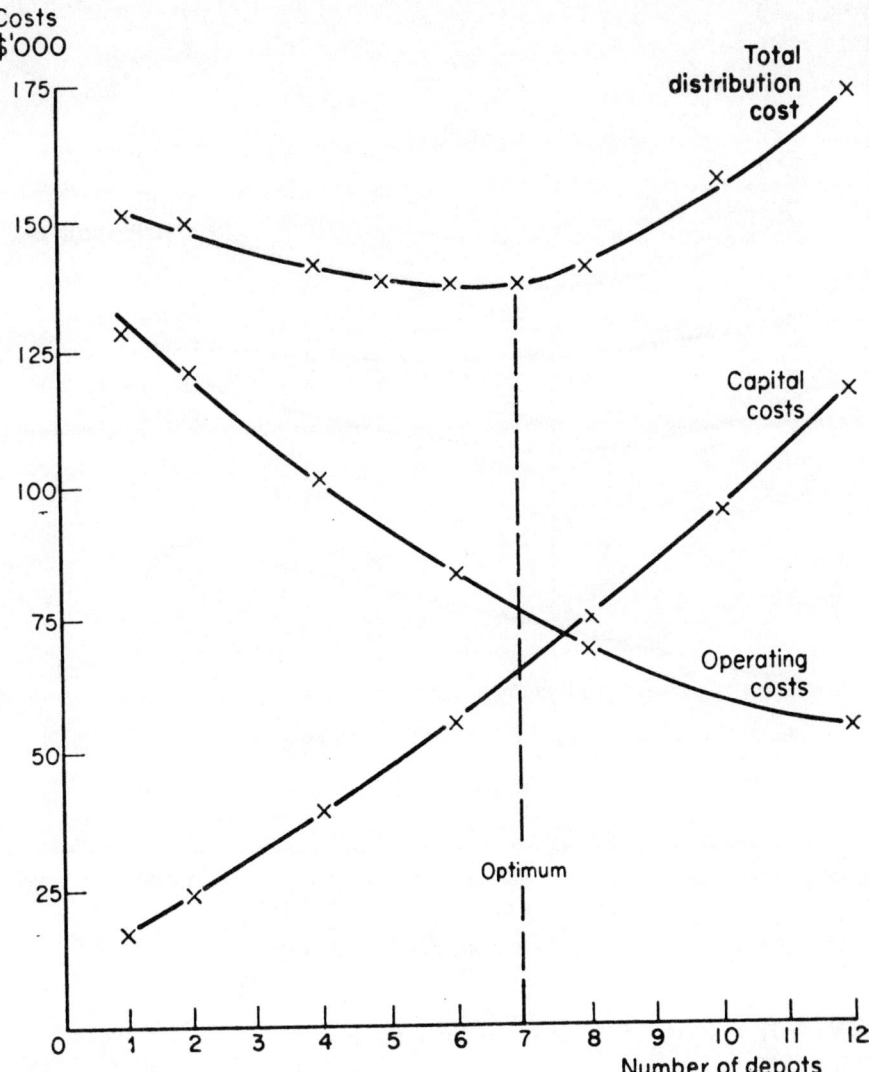

Figure 4.9 Optimizing distribution costs

that has to be held in stock; consequently, distribution costs will rise. Sometimes, a longer lead allows better utilization of the production time, which can reduce production costs. These savings, though, can be wiped out by the cost of carrying extra stock due to the reduced accuracy of forecasting over the longer period.

The relationships between costs and delivery lead times are shown in Figure 4.10. For a particular system there is an optimal lead time when the combined delivery costs, warehouse operating costs and inventory costs are minimal. The optimum varies according to the conditions.

An important factor that is often overlooked is the need for good stock control when trying to reduce distribution costs; it should be realized that stock control can be a tool for controlling distribution costs.

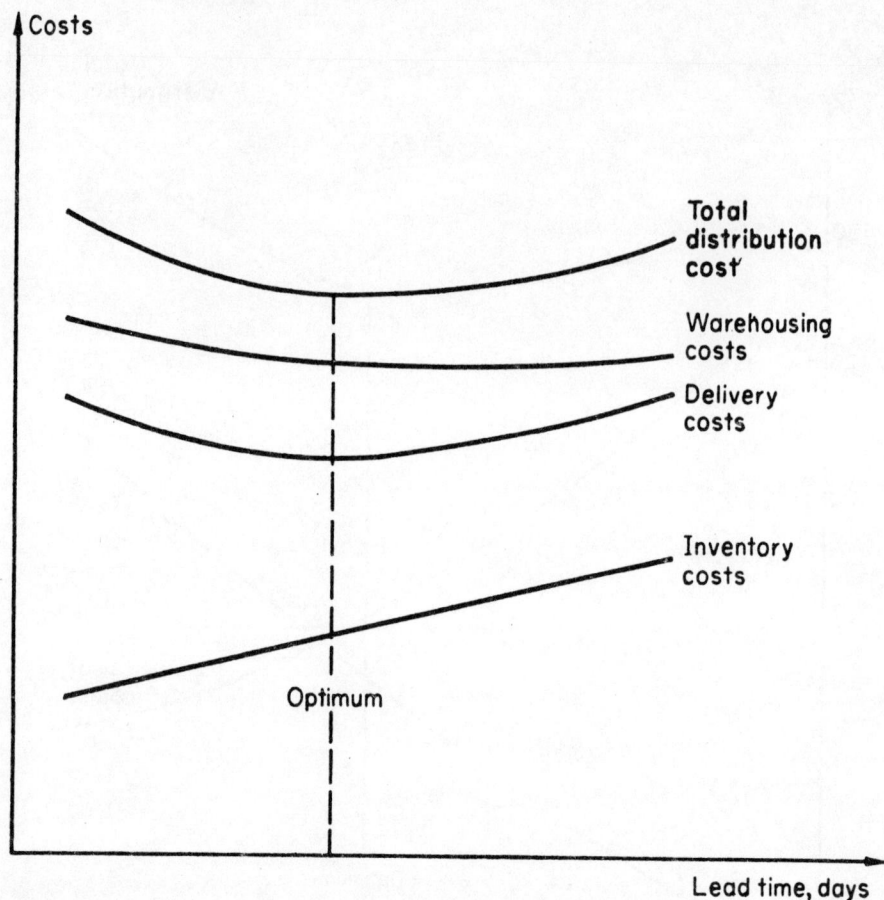

Figure 4.10   Relationships between costs and lead time

VARIABLE FACTORS OF SITING

Until now, the factors of siting have been related to market demand and distribution costs. Both play important parts in deciding the best supply sites, but the best sites may be unavailable or inconvenient, and it will also become necessary to examine other factors. These factors vary from system to system and from site to site. For example, the supply source may be a factory or a regional warehouse, the vehicle types available may differ, or the throughput of goods may fluctuate from time to time.

Effect of plant size on factory siting

The size of a site affects the design of a factory. When a factory is built it has to be designed for a standard production throughput, which sets a limit on the volume of goods that will be stored and the delivery frequency that can be offered. As with other planning aspects, the production potential and the market demand must be balanced in order to optimize the distribution system.

Siting problems

Solutions to problems of siting warehouses can be developed by starting with an appraisal of the requirements of the distribution system and a statement of its objectives. The variable factors that affect the system must be examined at the supply points siting stage. A system may need only one supply point when siting it at the centre of demand for the whole system will be optimal. Regardless of the number of supply points needed, one of them at the centre of total demand will always be necessary.

When more than one site is needed, distance becomes a prime factor, and dividing the distribution region into compact areas with a central supply point will help to keep down costs. Often, it is convenient to make these areas hexagonal in shape, and siting the supply point should be in a town that is both central and well served by roads.

Site location

The location of a supply site will be a focal point when considering changes in marketing policies, new delivery outlets, different transportation routes and other methods of distribution. Correctly sited, an efficient warehouse can improve the overall profitability of a company.

There are five variable factors that carry weight when deciding whether to centralize or decentralize the warehousing function:

1   The type of goods to be handled.
2   The level of service required.
3   The total distribution cost.
4   The method of transportation selected.
5   The degree of control necessary.

Other factors will also have to be taken into account when deciding the best supply site location, and the availability of labour will be quite important in most cases. Different systems or methods should be compared as models in order to assess the effect of different locations on the efficiency and economy of the complete distribution network.

Variations in demand

It is necessary to hold stocks in order to prevent delivery delays when market demand fluctuates. The first buffer stocks will be held at retail outlets as a safeguard against immediate demand variations, and another stock will be necessary at the production end of the system. A third stock must be held near the centre of the system as a buffer against differences that will occur between the market demands and production outputs. These variations will affect the operating efficiency of a distribution system, but not the actual siting of factories and warehouses.

Variations in demand may occur between different distribution areas as a result of factors like sales promotion, customer preferences, product popularity or transport efficiencies. These are minor variations, and the important general ones are now discussed in more detail.

Variation in overhead costs

Overhead costs are incurred regardless of throughputs, operating efficiencies or distribution procedures, and siting has a major effect upon them. The site of a supply source involves overhead cost factors such as rates, rent, building invest-ments and development charges. These overheads are necessary for satisfying pro-duction requirements; consequently, they will increase as the number of production sites increases. On the other hand, unit overhead costs can be reduced by increasing the production throughput which will require more storage facilities. Once again, the optimal solution will be a compromise between the production overheads that increase with the number of sites and the distribution overheads that decrease as a result. The optimum will be the least total cost, which is shown in Figure 4.11 for a varying number of sites.

Obviously, where production overhead costs are high in relation to distribution, such as for precision machinery, increasing the distribution throughput has little effect on total overhead costs. The reverse is the case when distribution costs are relatively high, for example with frozen foods; then the throughput will be critical. The correct siting of supply points is vital, because the total distribution cost is an overhead on products, which can amount to 40% of the price or more.

Variation in transport requirements

The road and rail transport for delivering goods is of two kinds; trunking, and local deliveries. The former influences optimal production sites, and the latter influences depot siting. The requirements of trunking include facilities for loading and parking articulated vehicles, containerization and fully mechanized materials handling at warehouses. Spare trailers enable trunking to be operated independently of local deliveries.

Local deliveries usually need vans, and the depot sites have to be designed for operating them. Goods are delivered from depots directly to customer locations.

A simple transit depot consists of a hard standing for parking the vehicles, a covered area for transferring the goods from trailers to vans, a small office and a warehouse for storing goods. As the number of vehicles required increases, it becomes more economic to provide facilities for their maintenance, bulk storage of goods, rest rooms for drivers, and the like.

Transport variations can be optimized by balancing costs against savings. More depot sites means that fewer vans but more bulk-carrying vehicles will be required. It can be shown graphically that the best general balance is obtained with one central supply site and about ten regional depots. Below ten depots, costs rise quite sharply, and above this number the costs rise only slowly.

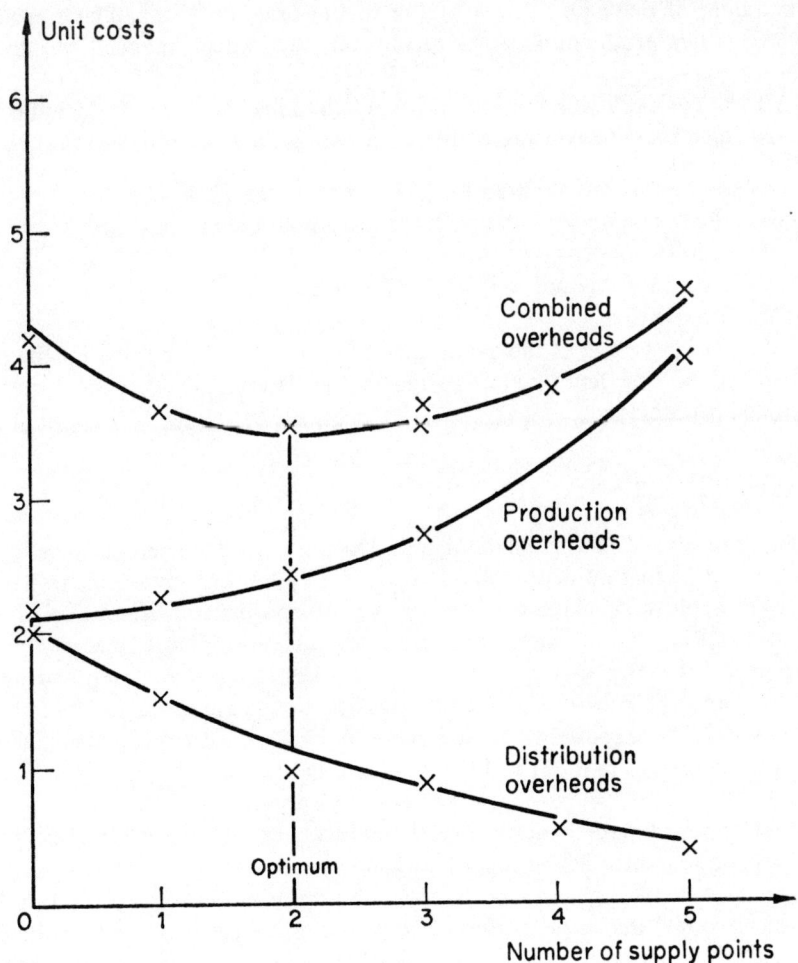

Figure 4.11 Optimizing overhead costs

Variation in production outputs

Distribution throughputs are specific to production outputs; therefore, the throughput of a distribution system must be planned to suit particular production requirements. Unfortunately, production outputs are uncontrollable in some industries. Minimizing distribution costs according to variations in production outputs requires the combination of several cost/throughput graphs which may become complicated at times.

DEPOT SITING

A distribution system must be planned as an integrated whole, so that each function is related to the others and there are no duplications. In this way, the best utilization of time and equipment is ensured. The siting of depots, the routing of vehicles and the scheduling of deliveries all contribute to the price of goods. These costs are indirect to either production or marketing, but they affect financial profitability directly.

Depots are basically warehouses for local deliveries and there are a number of questions which must be considered before selecting the site for a depot:

1   How many depots are required for providing the service level necessary?
2   Where will they be sited, strategically, in relation to land values, labour resources and distribution costs?
3   What is the range of goods that will be stocked at each depot for supplying to its distribution area?
4   What must be the size of the depot, and how much land is needed for the site?
5   What will be the depot requirements in the future, and can the system be modified if necessary?

Deciding depot sites

The best method for deciding the number and locations of depot sites is to start from the position of having no depots at all. Then it is comparatively simple to site one depot at the centre of demand with the aid of coordinates; the value of each coordinate will be equated in terms of its costs and service level. Two depots can then be sited optimally, assuming that each will be responsible for approximately half the demand. This process of siting continues for the estimated total number of depot sites. The overall cost and service level of each site must be evaluated, and they can then be compared in order to find the best. The site with the least total cost for providing the service level desired will be the one chosen.

When the approximate location for a depot has been decided, its practical implications must be examined. The cost of land may be important in a built-up area, or the optimal site may apply to a fairly wide area. In addition to differences in land prices, there is the interest on capital to be considered as well as the availability of labour. However, these variations are small when compared with overall warehousing and delivering costs.

The service level offered to customers may be a measure of the goods ordered or the time for delivery, and both are incorporated in the order lead time. Multiplying order quantity by delivery time or distance has the effect of giving greatest importance to large orders.

The steps that must be followed in order to optimize the siting of a depot are shown in Figure 4.12; additionally, they can be used for formulating the structure of any distribution system. The schematic diagram is a general concept that becomes specific when operational data is included. It is very useful for showing the factors that have to be considered when deciding the best sites for depots, because it develops an understanding of the interplay between the different variable factors that make distribution a dynamic function.

Depot siting example

A British clothing manufacturer had factories in Bradford and London with five regional warehouses in Newcastle, Liverpool, Birmingham, Swindon and London

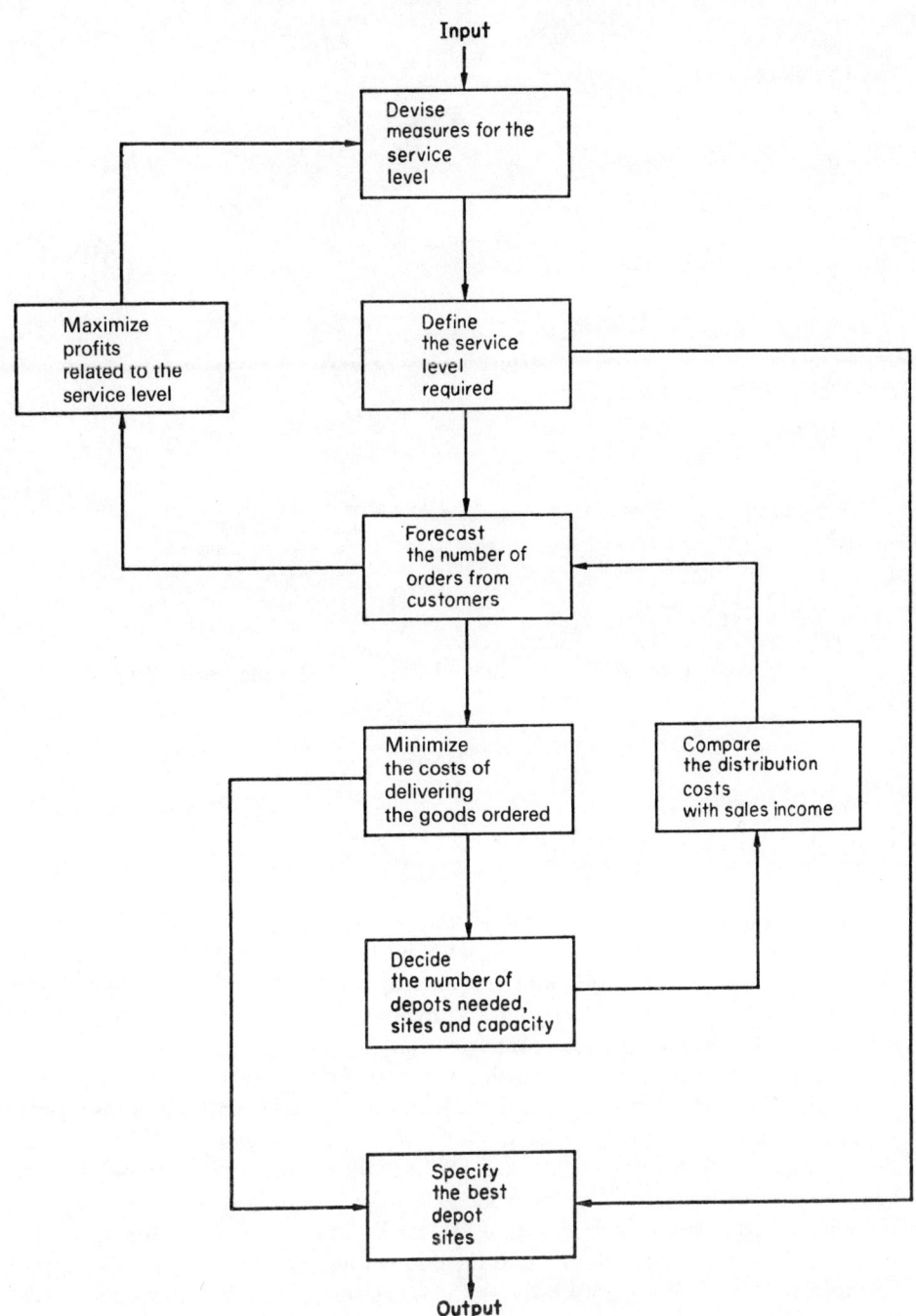

Figure 4.12   Depot siting procedure

Total sales volume

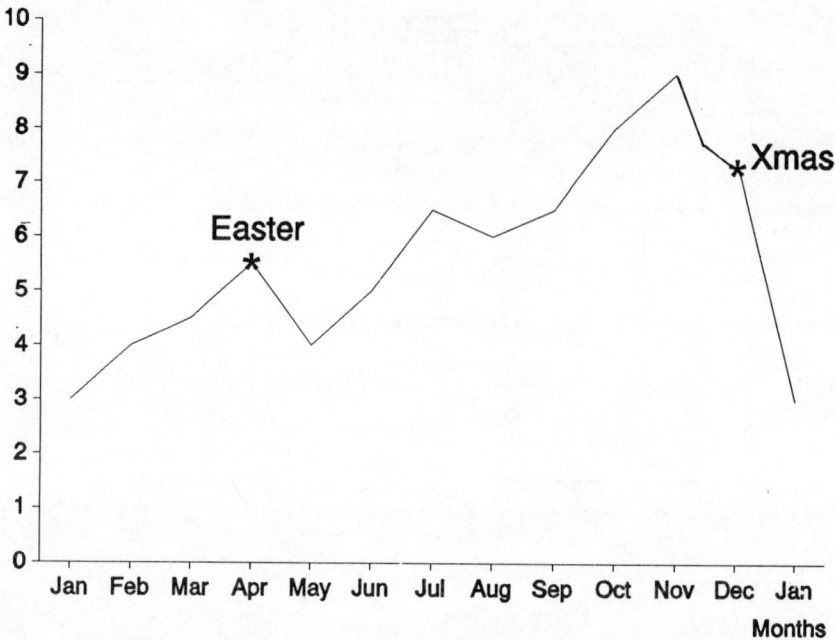

Figure 4.13   Seasonal clothing sales

which were supplied in bulk from both of the factories. The clothes were delivered to retail outlets on a regular basis along standard routes; therefore, it was easy to collect data and to compile it into a model of the system. The objective of this exercise was to optimize the number and locations of the warehouses in order to satisfy the total demand for ready-made clothes.

The distribution model included the distances from warehouses to shops, and they were acceptable as measures of the delivery costs. Since hundreds of shops were supplied, a computer program was designed to prepare a distribution network from the distances recorded in the vehicles' logbooks. Next, figures for customer demand over recent years were analysed in order to look for trends; a seasonal sales pattern was discovered (illustrated in Figure 4.13). Peak sales occurred just before Christmas, which was followed by a rapid decline before picking up again late in the spring. Sales then fell off until May and climbed again throughout the rest of the year.

Trunking costs to the warehouses were based on supplying the stocks needed to satisfy all local sales. Delivery costs were based on the vehicle operating costs per mile, and they were used to find the contribution made by each retail shop annually;

this was done by multiplying the delivery distance to a shop by the mileage costs and the number of visits in a year. When a number of shops were supplied during one trip, the total cost was shared between them.

Warehousing costs included operating costs and inventory-carrying costs; they were allocated to the shops according to the value of the clothing supplied to them each year. The total distribution costs had to be computed with the objective of deciding the optimal numbers and locations of the warehouses for the least total cost. The computer model assumed that trunking and delivering costs were linear with distance and warehousing costs were linear with throughput.

Then the model was tested in practice, first with the existing five warehouses followed by permutations of different numbers, up to the five, then, with an additional warehouse at Glasgow, Hull, Norwich or Brighton.

Results

All the computations were analysed in order to discover any positive or negative savings from the new combinations of warehouses compared with the existing system; the results are presented in Table 4.14. It is obvious that the present number of warehouses was too large, because savings decreased with increasing warehouse numbers. This suggested that warehousing costs contributed most to the total distribution costs. Generally speaking, three warehouses in different parts of Britain offered the best potential savings, although reducing them to two, strategically sited at Newcastle and London, could produce the greatest savings overall.

The final choice lay between two warehouses at Newcastle and London, or three at Newcastle, Birmingham and London. Estimations of the services offered by these two combinations, in terms of the waiting times after customers placed orders for clothing, came out in favour of the three warehouse system, and this was chosen.

Before implementing the new distribution system, its sensitivity to external changes was investigated, including the effect of increased demands, different delivery costs and changes in the resale values of the surplus warehouse sites. The chosen system was found to be robust and feasible for variations in the demand. Finally, this exercise showed up the advantages of looking closely at operations which had previously been taken for granted, particularly when some could be improved or eliminated. It was a case of stock-taking in more ways than one!

Table 4.14 Warehouse savings

Warehouse number and combination	Savings over existing combination (%)
Existing combination: 5 warehouses at:	
+ Newcastle, Liverpool, Birmingham,	0
Swindon and London (Leytonstone)	
4 Warehouses at:	
— Newcastle, Liverpool, Birmingham, Swindon	− 5.67
— Newcastle, Liverpool, Birmingham, London	− 2.42
— Newcastle, Liverpool, Swindon, London	+ 1.58
— Newcastle, Birmingham, Swindon, London	+ 3.16
— Liverpool, Birmingham, Swindon, London	− 1.88
3 Warehouses at:	
— Newcastle, Liverpool	− 1.0
— Newcastle, Liverpool, Swindon	− 0.53
— Newcastle, Liverpool, London	+ 5.91
— Newcastle, Birmingham, Swindon	+ 3.22
— Newcastle, Birmingham, London	+ 9.89
— Liverpool, Birmingham, Swindon	+ 2.37
— Liverpool, Birmingham, London	+ 6.92
— Birmingham, Swindon, London	+ 5.71
2 Warehouses at:	
— Newcastle, Liverpool	− 7.63
— Newcastle, Birmingham	− 5.20
— Newcastle, Swindon	− 3.38
— Newcastle, London	+ 12.56
— Liverpool, Birmingham	− 0.75
— Liverpool, Swindon	+ 1.98
— Liverpool, London	+ 6.43
— Birmingham, Swindon	− 0.26
— Birmingham, London	+ 3.55
— Swindon, London	+ 3.01
6 Warehouses, with the additional at:	
— Glasgow	+ 2.17
— Hull	− 1.84
— Norwich	− 2.36
— Brighton	− 1.12

5   Logistics of warehousing

Warehouses are used to store goods for varying lengths of time in such a way that the goods can be retrieved easily to satisfy orders from customers. Thus, the logistics of warehousing largely concerns the movement of goods in and out, the costs of storing goods and the control of related operations. The goods in a warehouse are actually part of a distribution system between the producer and the customer; consequently, a warehouse is an expensive intermediary stage in the system, and stress has to be placed on the rapid movement of goods through the warehouse.

Storage, however, is passive, and stock held in a warehouse is not earning. The dynamic part of warehousing is making the goods more accessible to customers. Rarely do the needs of production and consumption coincide; often, the former covers a long period of the year while the latter has a short season. For example, Christmas decorations may be produced throughout the year, but they will be sold only in November and December. At the other extreme, strawberries for canning are only available in summertime, although customers want them all the year round.

The function of a warehouse, therefore, is nearly always marketing-orientated; sometimes however, it may be production-orientated for storing raw materials, or for storing items for internal use in another part of the organization. Whatever its function, a warehouse is a cost centre and a target for improving efficiency by reducing costs.

CHOICE OF WAREHOUSE

There are probably as many reasons for having a warehouse as there are different products to be warehoused. There are three general reasons that override others: economic, operational and service reasons:

Economically, warehouses provide the opportunity to purchase in bulk or at a time when prices are favourable. At the warehouse, goods can be stored until they are required in different quantities by the customers.

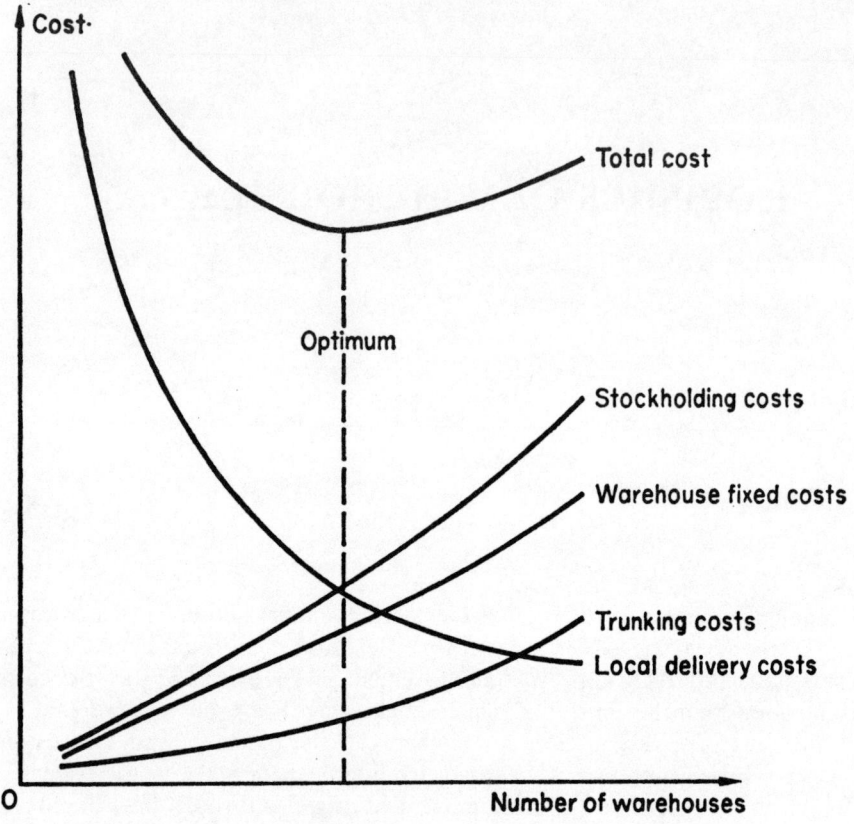

Figure 5.1   Total cost of distribution

Operationally, the goods stored provide a buffer against fluctuations in demand, and the warehouse provides the facilities for processing orders according to demand.

Service is provided by warehouses, since the goods are held at places that allow delivery times to comply with the requirements of customers.

Total cost of distribution

Distribution is a complex function that includes the number, sites and sizes of warehouses, vehicle routes and schedules, resource investments and control activities. Each element can be designed singly, but it is better to plan them in unison because the interactions between them must be coordinated for successful implementation.

The total cost of distribution is illustrated graphically in Figure 5.1, showing component costs that include warehouse fixed costs, warehouse stockholding costs, trunking costs and local delivery costs. The requirement for the least cost of the first three components is fewer warehouses, but local delivery costs are minimal with more warehouses. The optimum will be the least total distribution cost.

The least total cost can be improved by streamlining local deliveries, by building less expensive warehouses, by holding fewer stocks or by reducing the number of trunking deliveries. The slopes of lines in Figure 5.1 depend upon specific costs, but this shows a method for comparing costs in order to optimize the total cost of distribution.

Warehousing siting

The optimal site for a warehouse depends upon the number and locations of other warehouses in the distribution system, upon the locations of customers allocated to each warehouse and upon the total cost of handling goods. The practical approach allows each of these factors to be considered both singly and together for a number of different sites. It has the advantage of considering a number of known sites, and compares the ones that satisfy the cost and service limits feasibly.

The chief disadvantage is the extra work involved in considering sites that may not be feasible. An alternative approach is the theoretical one which assumes that a warehouse can be sited anywhere within the distribution area under consideration. This is a flexible approach, but specific costs have to be examined later.

Collecting data

Starting with customers, demand data is needed for reducing the number of customers to manageable limits in terms of the vehicles and delivery times. The market demand is dynamic, and sales forecasts are more valuable than sales records. Examining the market helps to establish the service levels required.

Cost data that is relevant to the service levels must be collected. Warehousing costs are fixed or variable, and they depend upon the warehouse location and its throughput of goods. Delivery costs include both trunking and local delivery costs.

Developing plans

When there is a choice of known sites for a warehouse, the alternative advantages and disadvantages can be compared by simulation. Simulation allows many different factors to be examined in potential rather than in fact. Interactions cause fluctuations in cost and service level so that their effects have to be optimized.

A useful method for developing warehouse siting plans involves heuristic programming. Heuristics are a set of rules for attaining objectives feasibly, but not necessarily optimally. The use of practical knowledge and commonsense heuristically can produce good warehouse locations quickly and economically.

Implementation

Plans for warehouse sites have to be implemented effectively for successful distribution, and it is important to study all reactions to the plans beforehand. This is the

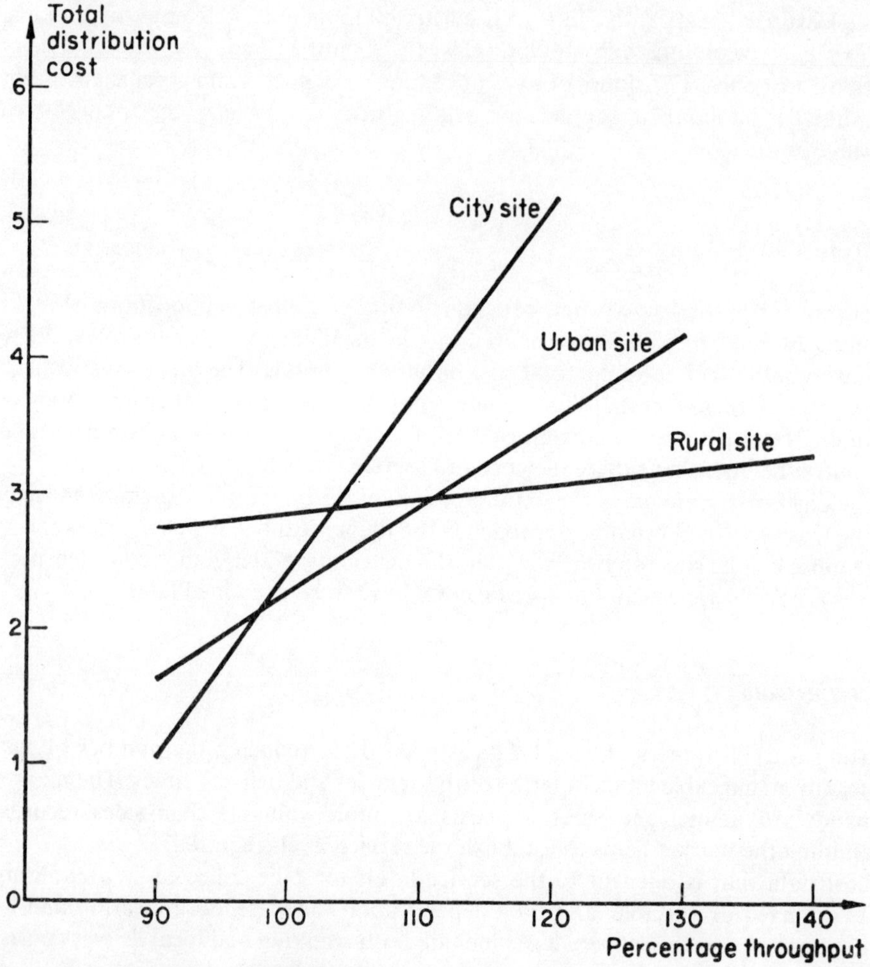

Figure 5.2   Sensitivity analysis chart

essence of strategic planning, because a plan is tested for robustness under different conditions. Testing for robustness is sometimes called *sensitivity analysis*.

An illustration of the reaction of the total distribution cost to differences in warehouse site is shown in Figure 5.2 The least costly site depends upon the throughput, and each site is optimal for different throughput ranges.

The sensitivity analysis chart in Figure 5.2 covers a single time span, but graphs also have to be prepared for other times in order to plan dynamically. A decision to select a particular warehouse site is far reaching, possibly for 20 years or more, and it is wise to estimate the future costs when studying the reactions within the system. Different variable factors can be compared with the sensitivity analysis chart; for example, different delivery vehicles or routes on a unit cost or a time basis.

In the chart, the total distribution cost is relative, and the throughput is expressed as percentages of the current volume. It can be seen that a city site is preferable if throughput is declining, but a rise of 10 to 20% favours an urban site, and above this increase a rural site should be selected.

Dynamic planning

Distribution parameters change with time, and it is necessary to determine the length of the planning period in order to prepare dynamic plans.

The time span depends upon the cost of setting up and closing down a warehouse, and upon the accuracy of the forecasts. Decisions to change the site of a warehouse cost least money if the establishment time is short. After a short while, property depreciates least and the cost of improvements is small. When forecasts are good or future conditions seem fairly certain, the time span for strategic plans can be longer, and they will be more accurate than when forecasting is poor or conditions are uncertain.

The data required for dynamic planning is similar to that already described, but information for forecasting the delivery resources for the length of the plan is needed in addition to current data. Estimates will also be required of the costs involved in setting up and closing down warehouses. Comparisons are more relevant if these additional costs are discounted back to the current time, so that interest costs and appreciation values are included.

The dynamic siting method starts by deciding the current optimal size for a warehouse. The cash flows for successive years can then be calculated, and the total distribution cost for the period determined. Next, the optimal cost sites for the changes forecast throughout the period need to be analysed in the same way. Alternative total costs for the planning period must be compared in order to decide which is the best.

Successful warehouse siting

The best sites for warehouses provide the best service to customers in terms of delivery times and the least cost for delivering goods.

Making sound decisions requires careful planning which has been based upon good forecasts and relevant experience. However, a knowledge of scientific planning methods ensures that the practical expertise available is guided to produce optimal plans.

TYPES OF WAREHOUSE

A common distinction between warehouses relates to whether they are public or private. The goods held in a public warehouse belong to other parties, but the owner's own goods are stored in a private warehouse. Public warehouses are used when their facilities cannot be justified in a private company, or when they provide flexibility in terms of available space and location. They require no private capital investment and space is rented as required.

The following services are offered by public warehouses:

1 Bonded storage for goods that are subject to import duties.
2 Publicity display areas for the firms that rent the warehouses to store much of their inventory.
3 Integrated data-processing equipment for incorporating public warehouse information into private plans.

4   Inventory level maintenance is delegated outside the private company.
5   Local deliveries are undertaken in some instances.
6   Unpacking, testing and order assembling operations may be available.
7   Delivery records are provided which are useful for controlling customers' orders.
8   Improved protection from pilferage and natural hazards.

Private warehouses are more suitable for *just-in-time* distribution systems which only hold goods in transit, thereby reducing the amount of inventory being held at any one time. Such a system requires the supplies to be closer to the production plant and the goods nearer the markets. The most common users of private warehouses are the retail chain stores which handle huge volumes of merchandise in an integrated system. Usually, it is advisable for them to have a central warehouse that stocks a wide range of items before supplying them to specialized depots.

Warehouse design and layout

Throughput is a measure of the volume of goods passing through a warehouse in a given time period, and it affects the design and layout. For example, a low throughput requires maximum space utilization for storage, while a high throughput must be capable of rapid information processing and materials handling. Trade-offs must balance the disadvantages against the advantages of providing more or less space, mechanization and turnover of stocks. Space may be an advantage at times, but not when long retrieval distances are involved; likewise, the choice between vertical and horizontal storage racks will vary according to the throughput.

Layout must take into account the type of materials handling equipment to be used, whether order-picking and stock-replenishing have to occur at the same time, how arrivals and departures are organized, or whether operations are labour intensive or suitable for automation. In any case, a modern warehouse needs to be designed so that it can benefit from computerized controls.

Computers in warehousing

Proliferation of computers into all walks of life has virtually revolutionized management, and distribution is no exception. Programs have been written for both mainframe computers and small personal computers so that the costs of operating warehouses and transport vehicles can be analysed quickly with a view to improving their efficiency.

Inputs for an analysis of warehousing data include the volume of stocks and orders received, their storage times, the manpower and machine times needed, as well as the inventory values and safety levels. Data has to be processed by a computer according to a program that satisfies the desired objective and outputs. One standard program deals with the storage function and decides the number of pallets, items per pallet, weights and the heights of stacked pallets. Another program which is suitable for microcomputers is called *The Inventory Clerk*, and it is used for recording stocks according to customers' orders, stock descriptions and codes, packaging records, batch sizes, storage locations, balances in hand and freight classifications.

Private warehouses tend to need a sophisticated data-processing system because they handle a variety of standardized products under particular conditions and use specialized storage and handling procedures. When some of the equipment has already been programmed by computers, it can be linked to other places through a central control. An example of a computerized order print out is shown in Figure 5.3.

It shows the codes for supplier/customer and storage location, as well as details of the goods which are often read by a scanner. Scanners placed adjacent to conveyor belts can recognize data printed on cartons in order to provide the computer input that produces warehouse records or allocates items to different locations. Once the goods are in storage, they can be checked with small scanning torches in order to compare the data with inventory schedules.

CENTRALIZED WAREHOUSING

Although there are many textbooks dealing with the choice of location, type and functions of warehouses, we have found none covering the centralization of them. No ready source of information was therefore available, so this part of the chapter has been based solely on experience in industry. Though the companies described are based in The Netherlands and Great Britain, the lessons learned are applicable throughout Europe, and indeed almost anywhere in the world. They are all multi-national organizations, and have distribution systems covering most European countries, so account has been taken of national boundaries and customs. Although the term multi-national is used, it is done so in the literal sense and not in the current euphemism meaning a large corporation.

The question of whether or not to centralize the warehousing function within a distribution system is currently being given a considerable amount of attention in industry, due to the need to reduce costs to a minimum and improve efficiency. As the distribution system has to be seen as a complete entity in itself, it is almost impossible to separate the warehousing function from within it. As a result, any centralization or decentralization of the warehousing function will mean a similar move for the rest of the system, and many of the factors outlined in the chapter are also equally applicable to transport.

The aim of this section is to identify the factors that influence decisions regarding the warehousing function within a distribution system, and to show how they can be controlled.

Definitions

Definitions of centralization, and its converse decentralization, are required at this point to clarify their objectives. Two conventions exist, therefore, the concept can be confusing: both conventions are considered below:

1   *The single basket definition* – this applies primarily to smaller companies whose distribution systems are national rather than international. A single warehouse serves the entire company's distribution system. Several factors may supply the warehouse through a trunking operation or daily rail deliveries. The output from the warehouse goes to regional depots or directly to the customer's own ware-house. An example of this system is the Rowntree MacIntosh distribution

RELEASE REPORT/PACKING-LIST/ORDERPICKLIST/
PRO-FORMA INVOICE/SHIPPING ORDER

03/04/91   PAGE
1

12796000   CBN CORPORATION, DALE STREET, NORTHBR ILL. 60062

DATE OF ORDER: 03-04-91
SHIP TO: CBN JAPAN KK AYA KUDAN BLDG6F
          2-3-27 KUDAN MINAMI CHIYODAKU
          TOKYO 102
          JAPAN
SHIP VIA: OCEAN
MARKS: ADDRESS

CBN 'S ORDER NO.: GB8106
WASSING'S REG. NO.: W000955
SOLD TO: 000031
          CBN JAPAN KK AYA KUDAN BLDG6F
          2-3-27 KUDAN MINAMI CHIYODAKU
          TOKYO 102
          JAPAN
TERMS: CASH ON RECEIPT OF GOODS

SPECIAL INSTRUCTIONS: CIF TOKYO

PRODUCT CODE	DESCRIPTION	QUANTITY PIECES	BOXES	UNIT PRICE	TOTAL AMOUNT	WEIGHT	VOLUME	PURCHASE ORDER NO.	PRODUCT GROUP
1132850	SUREBIND STRIPS- A4 BLACK 1"	15000	150	0.18	2700.00	210.00	1500	J-4063	02007
		LOKATIES	150	c 06 04 4	07/03/91				
TOTAL LAND OF ORIGIN 007					2700.00	210.00	1500		
TOTAL DOCUMENT COM					2700.00	210.00	1500		
TOTAL ORDER					2700.00	210.00	1500		

Figure 5.3 Computerized order printout

system outlined amongst the case studies. The depots in such a system are break-bulk stores catering for rapid delivery and high throughput, so they do not really count as warehouses.

2 *Semi-centralized or single hub definition* – this is not strictly a true centralized system such as the single basket system. It is a cross between the centralized and decentralized systems illustrated above; the factories support a single central warehouse, but this in turn supports a series of regional depots. The function of these depots is local delivery; they may break the bulk to the customers' requirements, but they do not carry out other functions of a warehouse beyond that.

The warehouse function

The warehousing function relates to the storage of goods and not just to the actual building which is where the activities are carried out. This point is made as many companies produce goods that are unaffected by the weather, and storage can be provided by a fenced area; the warehousing function, however, is still being carried out by gathering the goods into one place and storing them for a period of time. Examples of this are raw materials such as sand, timber and ores, or finished goods such as cars, glass products and pipes. The function is storage before, during and after production, which may also be carried out at various points along the distribution chain before the point of sale. Examples of this are the systems used by Volvo Cars and by Philips Glass Division, both of which are described in more detail later.

As stated above, the warehousing function may be carried out at various points within the distribution system; this is particularly relevant where deliveries have to cross international borders and the trunking transport system gives way to national or local distribution. The diagram in Figure 5.4 illustrates this in its simplest form, and is the system that will be used throughout the chapter:

The warehousing function is carried out to a greater or lesser degree at each store, depot or shed. This figure is only diagrammatic: in a more complex system, there may be additional stores at regional level and products may leave the factory directly to finished goods stores in the neighbouring regions or elsewhere in the same country.

Having identified the function of a warehouse, the next logical step is to question why that function needs to be carried out. If the function can be eliminated then there will be obvious cost savings for a company. Storage facilities are required to hold inventory as a buffer against foreseen and unforeseen circumstances.

Inventory management

This is an activity that concerns the stock within the warehouse rather than a function of the warehouse itself. However, it is relevant to the warehousing objectives that follow. Inventory management covers the following objectives:

1 To allow management to express inventory policies in quantitative terms allowing consistency in the warehouse operations.
2 To reduce inventory operating costs to a minimum.
3 To provide a desired level of service to customers.

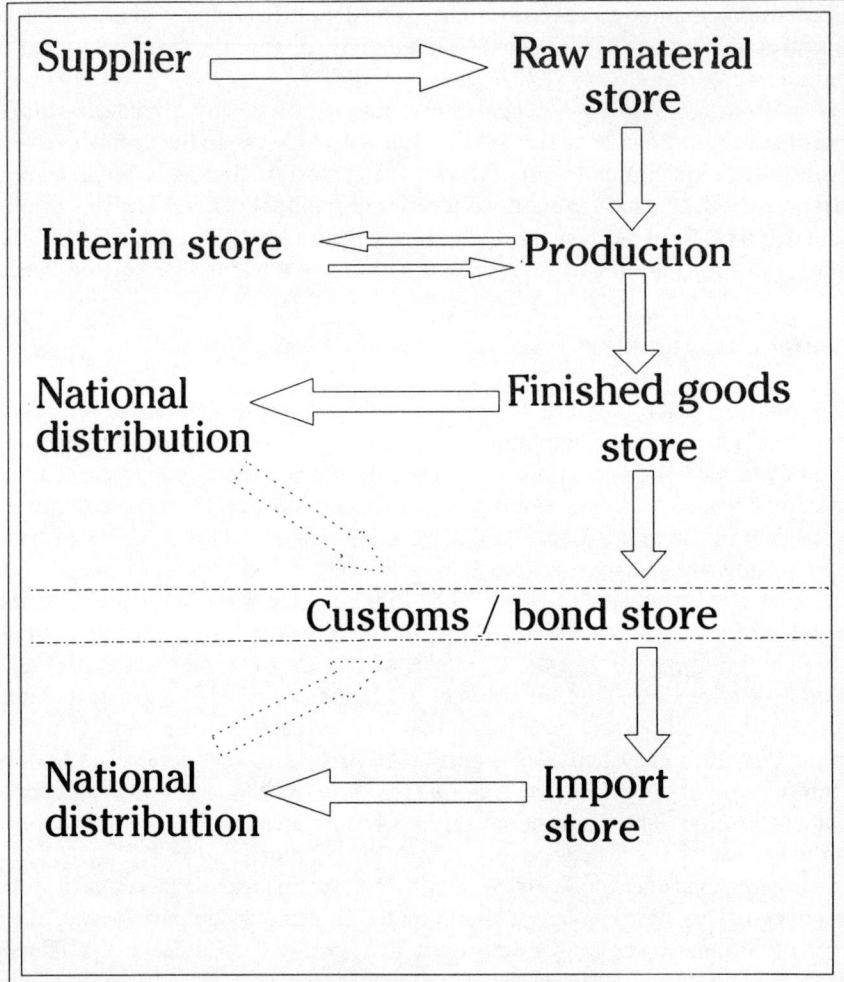

Figure 5.4   International distribution

4   To report promptly about exceptions and non-routine situations for manage-
    ment decision and action.
5   To carry stocks in order to cover delays due to transportation and delivery
    times where the distribution chain is very long or complex and production
    cannot be held up waiting for distribution. In the case of raw materials, it could
    be the converse when incoming supplies cause a build up of stocks before
    production can use them.
6   To hold stocks awaiting pre-delivery inspection or administration. This is
    particularly applicable to automobiles which have to be stored whilst awaiting
    type approval, homologation or sales paperwork.
7   To overcome general *hiccups* in the manufacturing process where production
    does not match sales either, because sales are unpredictably low for a period, or
    stocks are held to cover breakdowns on the production line.
8   To cover for expected industrial actions in companies with poor industrial

relations, a prime example of this was the Central Electricity Board having to stockpile coal prior to the 1984/5 miners' strike in the UK.

9 To retain stocks left over from an extended production run is often necessary when it is deemed more economic to over-run than to halt production.

10 To maintain stocks of spare parts for customers from the date of production until many years after their production has ended. It is clearly uneconomic to open up production every time a customer requires a slow moving part. In the motor trade very large numbers of parts have to be held in stock; for example, DAF Trucks' spare parts division at the Eindhoven factory carries 60 000 parts, of which only 1800 account for 80% of the turnover. Some replacements are being held for vehicles up to 15 years old.

11 To build up seasonal stocks which are produced over a six to nine month period before sales take place. Once sufficient stocks have been built up, production switches to a different line thereby, maintaining an even production output. Rowntree MacIntosh make Easter eggs from September to March and Christmas chocolates from April to August.

A logical deduction from this is that the size of the storage facility has to be linked to the objectives listed above; therefore, this becomes another point in favour of centralization, otherwise costs will go up as the company guards against stock-outs. However, there comes a point in larger companies when the storage facilities required become so large that it is not possible to centralize in one place.

The final point to be covered under the types of warehouse concerns their facilities. In ascending order of complexity they are:

1 *Simple* – a simple warehouse is an open stores where stock is sorted and picked by hand; stocks will normally be dumped on the ground, although low level shelving could be used.

2 *Mechanized* – a mechanized warehouse is one in which stock-handling is done with manually operated machines; for example, turret trucks. By implication, the stock will be palletized for machine-handling, and it will be stored on racking to a height capable of being reached by the machines, typically up to 7 metres. In the case of ISO container parks at ports, though, the stacks may be up to six boxes high (i.e. 4 metres).

3 *Automated* – an automated warehouse is one in which the stock-handling machines are unmanned, and are controlled by a central computer. This computer controls the placement and picking of items from the racking which may be 12 to 15 pallets high. Details of the Rowntree MacIntosh centralized finished goods store at York are included in the case studies at the end of this book.

Figure 5.5 shows the relationship between different types of warehouse and the cost of running them. The fixed cost is the same for any warehouse occupying one site, and it includes charges for rent, rates and other elements that are related to the land that the warehouse stands on; running costs such as electricity, gas and water are not included. Due to the capital costs increasing as the warehouse becomes more automated, clear cut-off points between the cost effectiveness of each type can be calculated, which makes the choice of warehouse type easier.

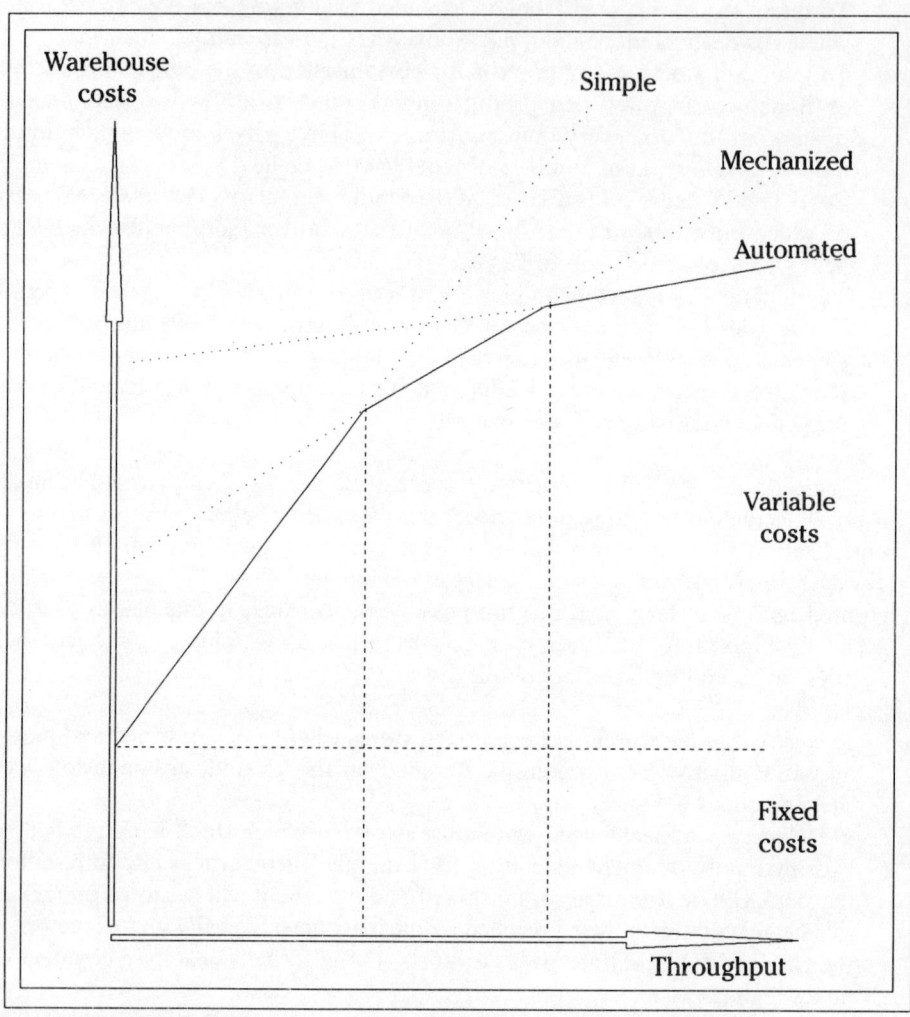

Figure 5.5   Cost comparison of different types of warehouse

WAREHOUSE LOCATION

The possible locations for warehouses within a distribution network were outlined earlier; however, choosing the precise location of a warehouse can be a key reason for centralization or decentralization of the activities. Much of this section deals with computer modelling of warehouse locations, giving detailed formulae and explaining the principles behind them. The most common method of choosing the optimum was developed by Keefer in 1934. This method is best described by imagining a sheet of plywood mounted vertically and covered by a map of the distribution area. Each customer or terminal of the distribution network is marked by a pin or small nail. A weight scale is then decided and a weight allocated to each customer in proportion to the annual tonnage of goods that are delivered to him. A length of fine twine is cut for each customer and the end tied to a small ring, the customer's weights are attached to the other ends of the lengths of twine and they are hung over the appropriate pins. When this exercise has been completed the ring will settle at the optimum location for a central warehouse that will achieve a balanced distribution throughout the network (see Figure 5.6).

Various factors must be taken into account when using the Keefer, or Ton-centre method. Any manufacturing plants within the region must be included with weights equivalent to their production outputs; if the outputs are not entirely delivered within the region, then the point at which they leave the distribution network or the region must also be included. It may be convenient to look upon a factory as the point of export from a region, and consider the trunking operations to other warehouses as a separate model.

For a large multi-national company, the area covered may be a whole continent, thereby making it impossible to model around a single warehouse using this method. The next level of modelling, as suggested earlier, would then be to construct a model of the international distribution network and superimpose it onto each national, regional and area model, so building up a superimposed card index system that represents the whole distribution system. As the network becomes more complex it ceases to be practical to make a physical model for the warehouse locations, but expensive computer models are available for complex systems. Using them, it is possible to model a series of situations covering both centralized and decentralized distribution systems. The larger computer models can produce a variety of information for differing situations as the parameters are altered, the most common output is cost effectiveness as warehouses are moved from the original to more suitable locations. It will be appreciated that this modelling system produces an optimum and not the most suitable location for the distribution centre; it is not uncommon for models of the London area to produce a warehouse location in Buckingham Palace gardens which is patently an unsuitable location! The jargon for this type of modelling is called *What-if* games.

Modelling is a planning tool that is merely a guide to be followed when considering a series of options. A particular model produces the answer for a given period of time; as customers change their requirements, the model becomes out of date. Once the initial model is built it has to be provided with data such as tonnages which can only be chosen with a crystal ball based upon market trends. The answers can, however, be usefully balanced against other decision factors in order to produce a compromise solution. The following are some of the factors to be considered when siting a warehouse:

1 *The land available for sites*, probably land already owned by the company.
2 *Location grants* which can offset much of the building and running costs; these are normally only available in areas of high unemployment, often far from the optimum location.
3 *Local taxes or rates* on buildings, and land in areas where grants are not available.

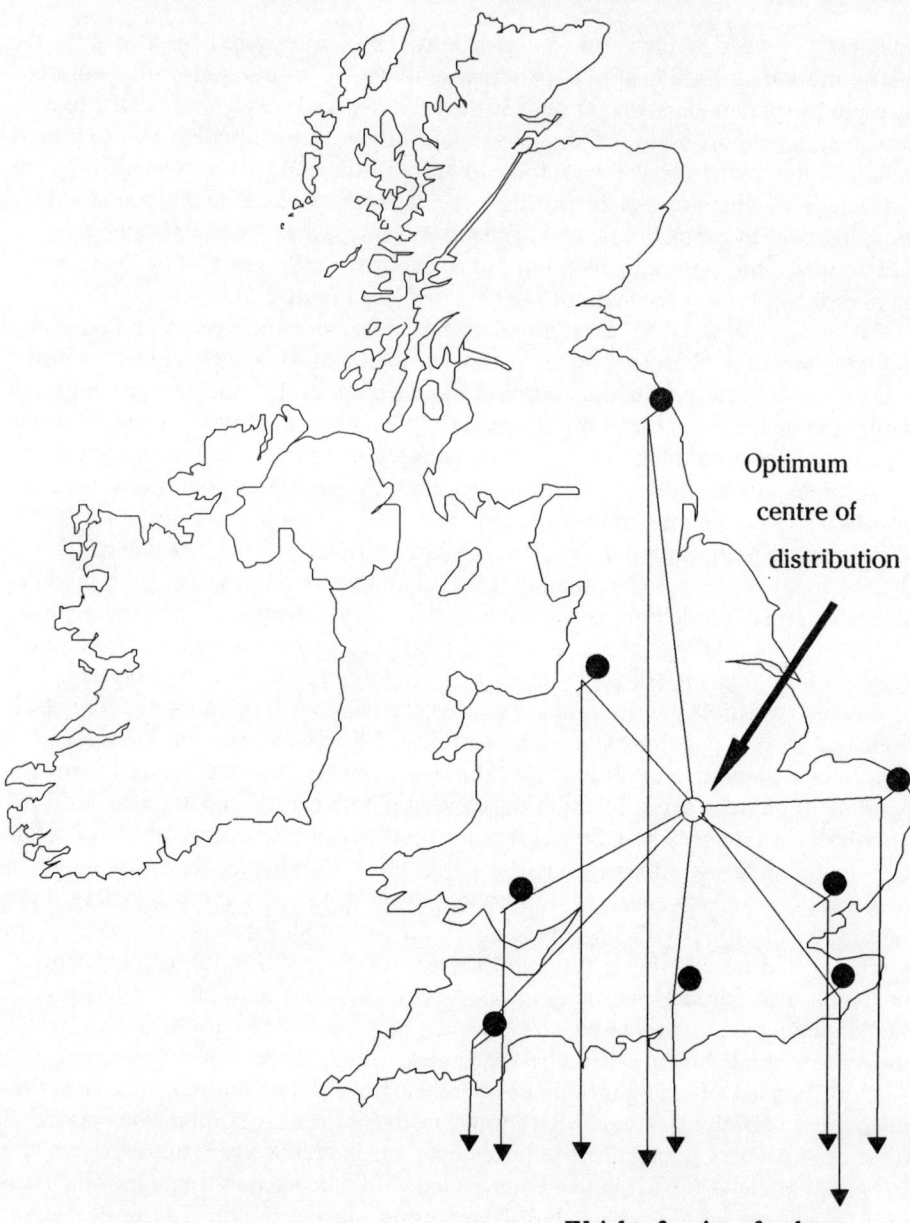

Optimum
centre of
distribution

Weights for size of orders

Figure 5.6   Keefer's central location method

4   *Customer relations* – the location may be chosen to attract a particular segment
of the market or to retain certain customers.
5   *Competition* may force a company to locate its warehouse and delivery system in
an area that is some considerable distance from the optimum location.
6   *Service industries* which support a distribution system may make it unwise to
select a location far away from that support.
7   *Access* is probably the most important factor affecting a warehouse location,

because transport must be able to collect and deliver easily the goods stored there.

The next stage in deciding upon the location and whether to centralize or decentralize is to consider the future in more depth. An allowance must be made for expansion and modernization, the latter is often disregarded in the early planning stage which can result in the whole process having to be repeated later at greater cost. Previously, the model was adapted to allow for changes in the market, but at this stage, allowance must be made for the physical size of the facility. A site must be chosen to allow expansion of perhaps 40% over a ten year period; this also applies to the design of the warehouse selected. It is unlikely that any but the largest companies can afford to include excess space for expansion in the initial building, so allowance must be made for an extension of the structure and the handling facilities within it. An automated warehouse is considerably more difficult and expensive to expand. Finally, the consideration given to future expansion could be the deciding factor in favour of a decentralized system, because it allows room for growth into other market segments.

GEOPOLITICAL FACTORS

This section discusses factors having an indirect influence on distribution decision areas which cannot be altered or moulded to meet the company's needs. Some of the geopolitical factors were mentioned in the previous section, but the following are considered here:

1   National and international economics.
2   Population, industry and wealth distribution.
3   Transportation policies and facilities.
4   Resources.

Each of these areas affects either the national or global situation, and some complex computer models have been designed to predict future movements in these areas. However, unlike the warehouse location models they come within the public domain, and copies of the results can be purchased; sometimes universities will run the programs for companies in order to predict movements directly relevant to their areas of interest.

The economic factors which have to be considered are the distribution of wealth and economic aid, the latter having already been mentioned in passing. Figure 5.7 shows the relative distribution of wealth within the EEC, and is based on 1985 statistics.

The distribution of wealth will affect the location of the warehouses within a distribution system, because the wealthy areas are the ones where the most profit can be made, therefore, ensuring the future of the company as a whole. For the majority of companies, between 70 and 90% of their sales will be in those areas, thus influencing the composition of the distribution network. The optimum location for a centralized European warehouse would seem to be in the southern part of Germany; while a decentralized system would be spread along a corridor between Birmingham and Turin. As suggested earlier, economic aid is the antithesis of wealth, and grants

■   Centres of wealth

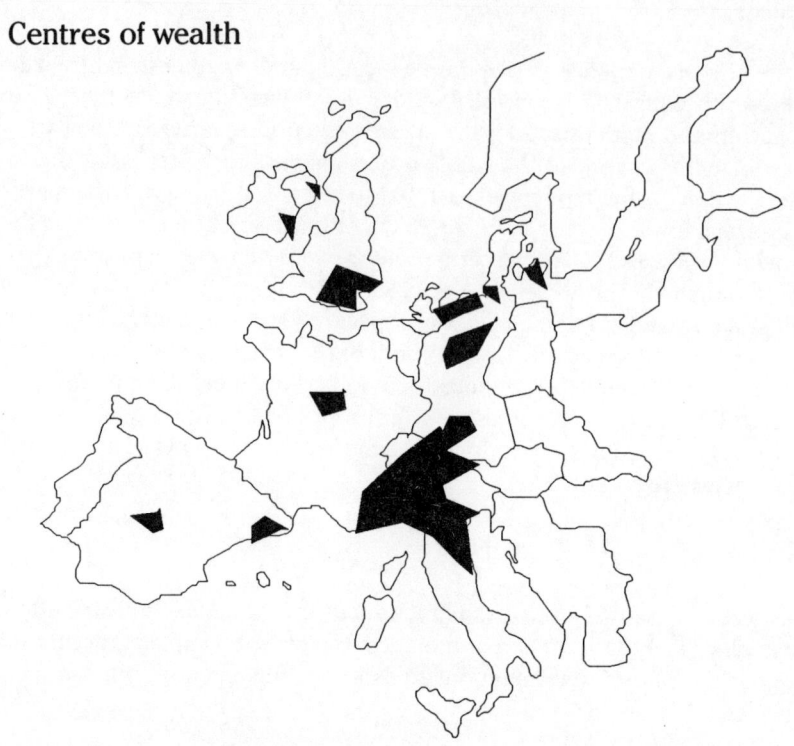

Figure 5.7   Distribution of wealth in Europe 1985

have to be given to attract industry to the poorer regions of Europe. When developing an entirely new company, its probable layout should have the plant in one of the poorer areas and the warehouses for deliveries in the richer areas; this will lead naturally to a decentralized system, due to the need to have a finished goods store near to the factory. The allocation of EC grants and aid is shown in Figure 5.8.

The industrial distribution in Europe follows the corridor indicated in Figure 5.7, and so does the population distribution, because industry, its workforce and wealth are all linked. Figure 5.9 illustrates this.

However, with the change from traditional industry to high technology and finance-related industries, wealth is beginning to spread away from the corridor, and with it manufacturing and population. This illustrates the need for complex computer models and accurate forecasting when planning a new company or factory. It is quite possible for a factory to become stranded with long distribution chains which make it uneconomic to continue manufacturing after only 10 to 15 years of existence. Economic aid can also direct factories to areas where they will later become isolated; the Londonderry and Antrim areas of Northern Ireland are examples of this. Markets have moved away from those areas due to the hostilities, and the cost of distributing goods has escalated to the point where some textile

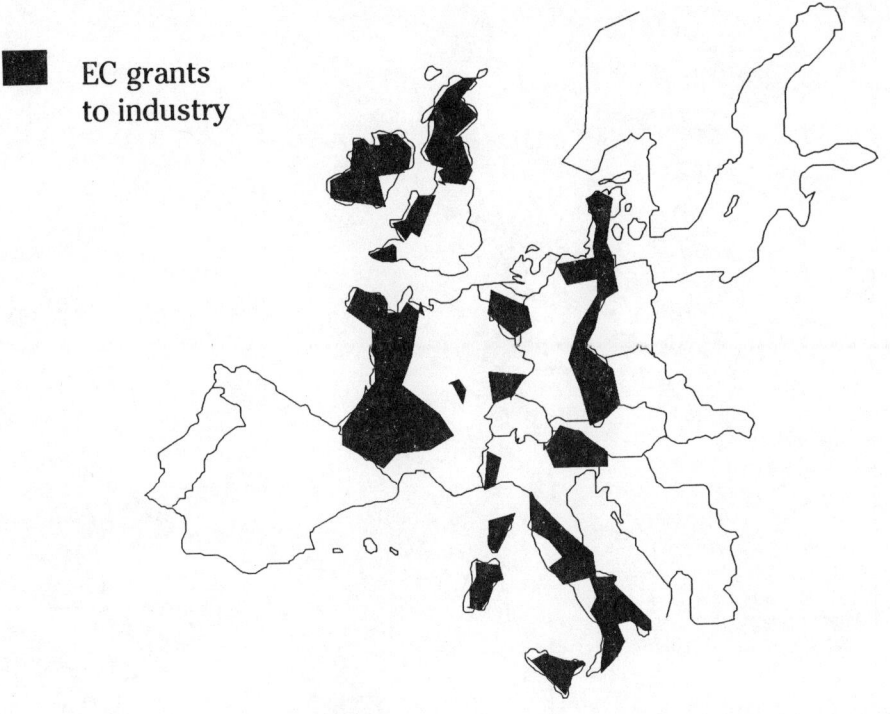

EC grants
to industry

Figure 5.8   Allocation of EC grants to industry

factories such as British Enkalon and Courtaulds have had to shut down, while the De Lorean automobile venture failed completely.

Due to the location of the sources of materials and energy, companies needing the same manufacturing resources often tend to be located in close proximity to one another. This means that the competition is faced with similar distribution costs and problems. When the raw materials are found close to the manufacturing site, the supply distribution costs are at a minimum, but that often stretches the delivery distribution network to the point where a centralized system cannot cope. An example of this is the Rexel Cumberland pencil factory at Keswick in North West England, an area noted for its isolation and rugged countryside, and with a particularly poor transport access. However, the graphite mines in Borrowdale 10 km away and a thriving local forestry industry for the wood made the site attractive for making pencils. Unfortunately, the mines are no longer productive, and the forests are dwindling so that the wood has to be imported from Canada; the site has now become a distribution nightmare. Due to the availability of plentiful skilled labour locally in Keswick, plus the high cost of moving production to another site, the company's problems will remain for many years to come.

The importation of iron ore has drawn industry to seaports rather than near the

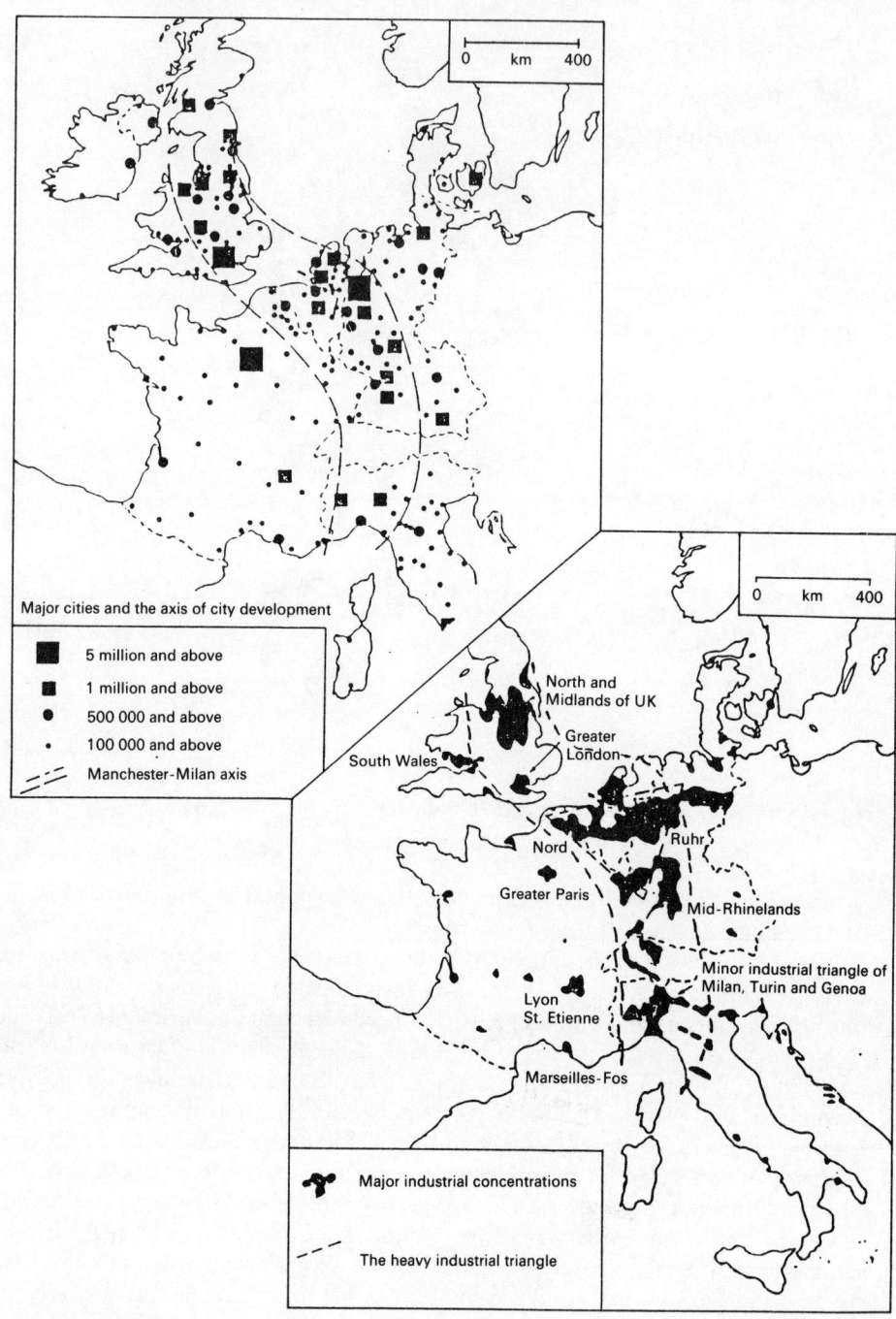

Figure 5.9   Links between industry, population and wealth

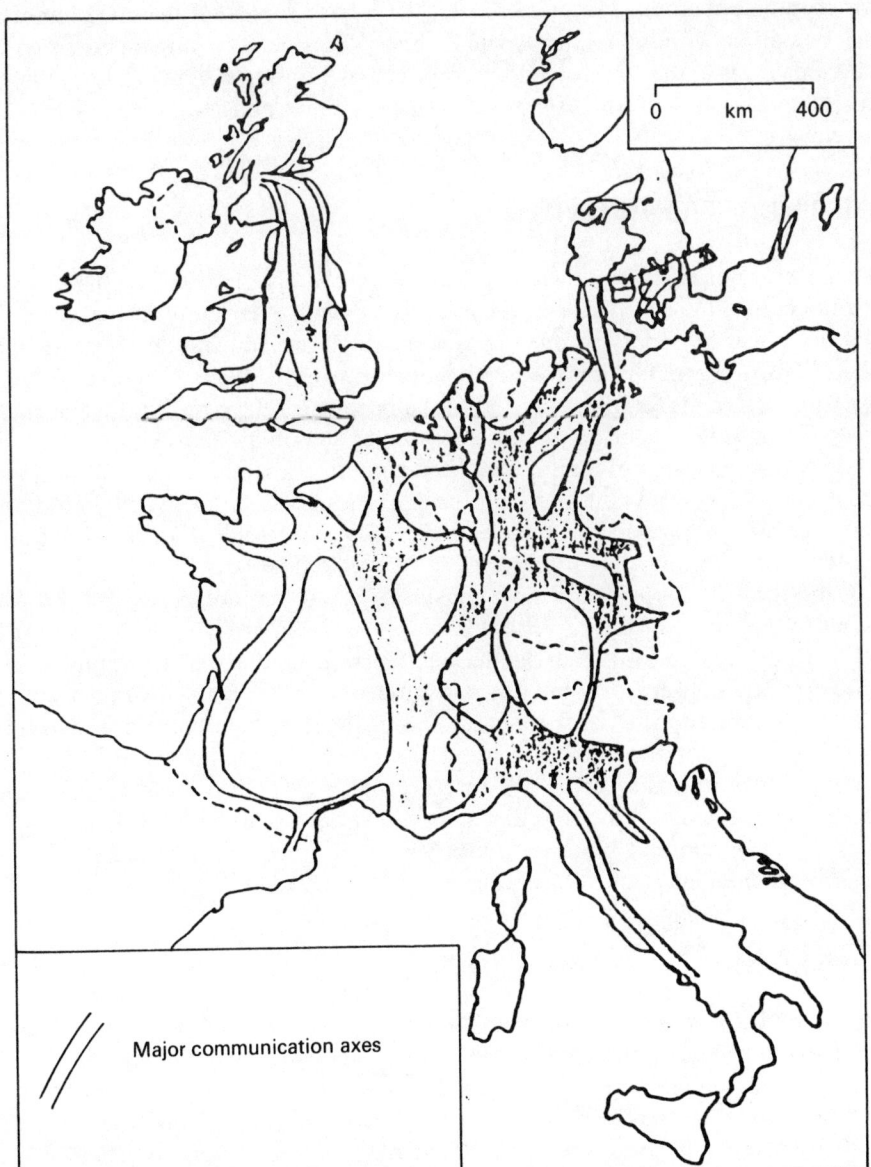

Figure 5.10   European transport networks

former mines, so the European steel industry is gradually moving away from traditional areas such as Sheffield, the Ruhr and Turin to Port Talbot, Bremerhaven and Genoa. As distribution costs become more significant, industry has moved towards motorways and other efficient transport networks. Again, the main European road, rail and canal systems are concentrated in and around the corridor of population and industry, as shown in Figure 5.10.

Geopolitical factors are moulding the shape of the European distribution network for economic reasons. The main routes, the labour force and the most important markets all lie within a relatively small area of Europe. The long narrow shape of that area leads to the need for a decentralized warehousing system in a line along the corridor. This will make best use of transport times and reduce the distribution pipeline.

DISTRIBUTION COSTS

The pressure of rising costs will affect all aspects of distribution, whether it be the manufacturer, the distributor or the retailer. In 1965, Peter Drucker remarked that 'Physical distribution is the one big area in which one can still do anything about costs.' Distribution, including warehousing, is one of the major cost areas in industry, and it accounts for an average 30% of a product's total cost. It is for this reason that so much effort is being placed on trimming distribution costs. Manufacturing costs have been pared to a minimum in most industries, and so any future savings must come from warehousing and transportation. The latter is being constantly reviewed with regard to the vehicles used; so warehousing is currently the main target for cost cutting operations.

Centralization is one of the main considerations for cutting costs, and this is the solution that most of the supermarket stores have adopted. Centralization of the retail trade will be looked at in the next section. As far as the manufacturing industries are concerned, some centralization took place many years ago, in that warehouses were located at the factory end of the distribution chain. When transport was slower and less efficient, warehouses were located further away from the factory and nearer the customers; that decentralized system allowed loads to be moved progressively away from the factory, town by town. It had its advantages as far as distribution and transport times were concerned, but it was not very cost effective in manpower, therefore wage bills were very high.

CENTRAL WAREHOUSING

Retail food stores such as Sainsburys and the Co-op are Britain's leaders in centralized warehousing, so this section is based on experiences from retail trade. In this field, the advantages are savings in warehouse costs and bigger discounts from manufacturers for bulk deliveries to a single destination. The big disadvantage is higher delivery charges to the retail outlets due to the need for more road vehicles and drivers. The financial balance between these two factors is very fine. In more detail, the advantages and disadvantages of centralized warehousing are:

1   *Easier central management control* over operations using computers, but this can also apply to some decentralized operations.
2   *The total stock level* is lower, except for fast-moving items which can account for a large percentage of the overall stock.
3   *By locating the central warehouse* in a low cost area, storage costs are less despite the much larger size of the central stores which may increase the overall cost above that of several small decentralized warehouses.
4   *In the retail industry*, storage space at retail outlets is released for selling goods.

This, however, increases the range of products carried and, therefore, increases the size of the central warehouse required.

5 *Delivery from manufacturers* directly to depots can be unpredictable, since many vehicles from different suppliers often arrive at the same time, or a supplier may be late in delivering a particular line, leading to stock-outs. Good scheduling of deliveries is easier from a central warehouse using owned vehicles.

6 *Administrative costs* involved in dealing with customers' orders and suppliers' delivery notes and invoices should be lower; however, it is a well-known fact that a centralized administration has a habit of escalating its own costs and importance! Therefore, centralization is only an advantage when tight control is kept over system operations.

7 *In the retail trades*, the centralization of warehousing also helps centralization of related activities such as pricing, packaging and merchandising.

The decision to centralize warehousing activities is a complex one, as the cost savings are not achieved automatically; they come from improved efficiency and tighter controls. Often, the deciding factor is obscure, only applies to one particular industry and cannot be transferred to another easily. At Rowntree MacIntosh, the deciding factor to centralize was the need for conditioned stores for chocolate products, particularly seasonal lines such as Easter Eggs. Due to the high volume of sales in a short period, manufacturing had to begin several months before sales could start, and that necessitated a large storage facility with air-conditioning. The cost of building such storage facilities at all the factories out-weighed the cost of building a single massive store in York. All the vehicles were insulated for delivering chocolate as a matter of course, so that the additional transport costs could be kept to a minimum.

The increased size of articulated vehicles allowed on British roads was also a factor in favour of centralized warehousing. The increase from 32 tons to 38 tons meant that a trunking vehicle could carry an extra six tons which, in terms of weight, was an additional delivery van load. As retail chains were beginning to opt more for central warehousing, this increase in size meant that a supermarket which normally took an articulated truck load of goods every day now required three or four loads a week, which reduced the transport costs by roughly the same amount as centralizing the warehouse increased the transport bill.

Where owned transport vehicles are not involved, the balance is in favour of centralized warehousing. Transport costs are still high, but the larger independent transport operators have depots at key points around the country, allowing them to swap trailer bodies between tractor units and to change the drivers. This precludes the need to site manufacturers' depots in positions that serve the customer directly. The emergence of Red Star in Britain and overnight delivery services has meant that, for small- and medium-sized loads, the customer is getting a faster service from a central warehouse than previously was possible with small loads from regional warehouses.

DECENTRALIZED WAREHOUSE SYSTEMS

Transportation costs can be calculated for any given distribution area using a computer model. A list and brief details of some of the software that is available are

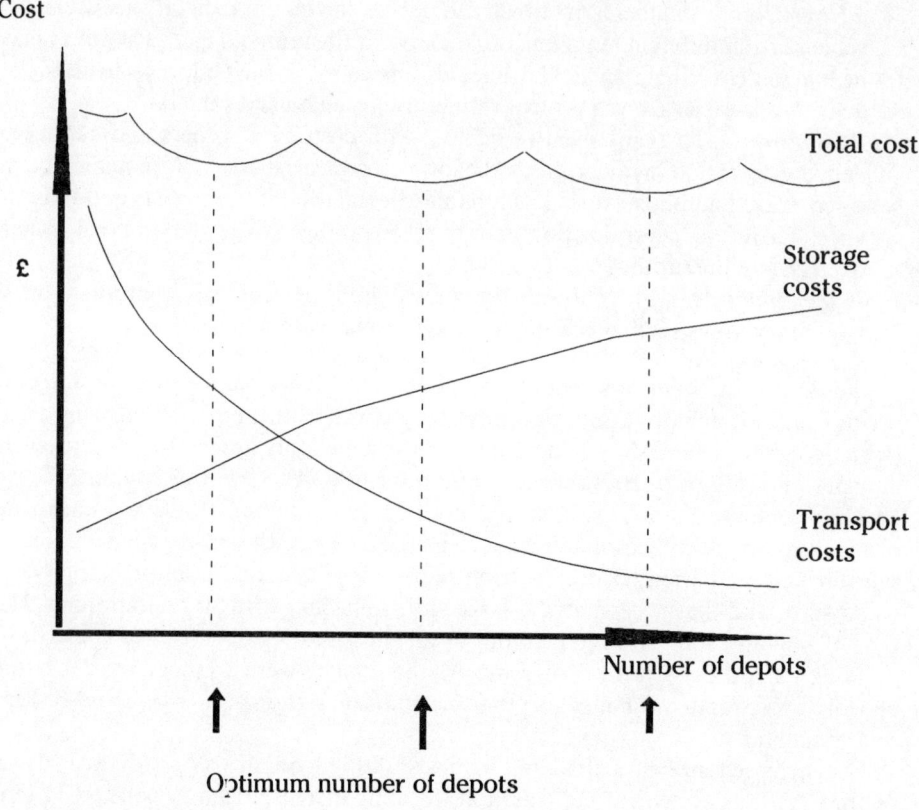

Figure 5.11 Transportation costs

included in Appendix 2. One of the most useful outputs from such models are graphs showing *What-if* answers. With respect to decentralized warehousing, the most important is the correlation between numbers of warehouses and cost effectiveness. That model can plot transport costs against increases in the number of warehouses on a graph to produce a concave curve. A second curve can then be drawn on the same graph to show the cost of warehousing against the number of warehouses; this produces a convex curve, and the two curves can then be averaged to give the graph shown in Figure 5.11. It indicates that the decentralized system has distinct cost advantages. The optimum is obviously where the two lines cross, but in some instances this cannot be achieved because the cost differential between warehousing and transport does not allow the curves to be drawn on the same piece of graph paper. If this does happen, several warehouses should be considered together, or centralizing a single warehouse. The lower line is experimental during the early planning stages until the best solution is found because, once construction has started, things cannot be readily changed.

The primary advantage of decentralized warehousing concerns the support given to customers; this is particularly important in the retail trade, where deliveries are to independent shops. The decentralized warehouse, being closer to the customer, is able to respond more quickly to changes in the customers' requirements. Such changes are inevitable at the last moment, particularly when the customer discovers that a certain item has been forgotten, or increased sales requires a larger order. In some businesses where competition is fierce, the ability to respond quickly can mean an increased market share for the manufacturer. Increased sales can be the deciding factor between centralizing or not; potential savings against costs must be balanced in order to arrive at the best decision.

Decentralization does offer a degree of security, because all a company's eggs are spread over different baskets. In the past there have been a number of cases where central warehousing has cost companies dearly, both operationally and through lost trade. The British Army and Nissan/Datsun have both had major fires in their central warehouses that resulted in reduced capacity for 12 to 24 months while stocks were built up in a new warehouse. Rowntree MacIntosh have suffered software problems with a new central finished-goods store, the basic problem being the computer refusing to issue stocks once the overall stock level had dropped to 30%. As fate would have it, the problem only came to light during the Christmas rush when customers were demanding large quantities of confectionery and the factories were running down for the holiday period. The result was a week of crisis management and the loss of several orders to competitors.

INTER-DEPARTMENTAL CONFLICTS

This section can be split into two parts depending on the size of the company. First, a conflict between different departments (such as purchasing and production) is part of life in every company. Second, in larger corporations, such a conflict may extend to different divisions or the whole organization. Inter-departmental conflicts occur when differing requirements are needed from the distribution system, especially when goals differ. For instance, bulk purchases may produce additional discounts, but make more work for other departments. Table 5.12 shows some of these conflicts and their effects; the table is by no means complete, but illustrates the points raised. When planning a distribution system and, in particular, the warehousing element within it, consideration must be given to conflicting relationships. It is apparent that in industry, department heads wear blinkers too often and look inward convinced that the rest of the firm will not be affected. The need for good communications between all personnel is essential for the efficient running of a company.

The departmental requirements which should be remembered when considering a centralized distribution system that involves more than one department are also shown in Table 5.12.

The second chart in Table 5.12 shows secondary goals in order to illustrate the need to consider this line of thought when developing a new warehousing system or modifying an existing one. Taking each of the goals in turn, it will be seen that bulk purchasing suggests the need for a decentralized system, particularly if more than one factory is involved. A raw materials warehouse will be needed at each factory.

Table 5.12   Departmental differences

ATTITUDE TO DISTRIBUTION

Required	Executive	Marketing	Production	Finance
Transport	Overall efficiency	Customer priority–delivery when, what and how he wants.	Priority is collection of raw material to clear production lines.	Cheapest option – transport is non-productive
Warehouse	Minimum size to do the job.	Large so goods always in stock.	Geared to raw materials.	None
Raw material stock	Enough to give production 2–4 weeks work.	Can the raw materials be sold at a profit.	Large stock	Capital tied up, so minimize.
Finished goods stock	Enough to meet customer orders.	Large so customers never kept waiting.	Just keep the lines clear.	Minimize unsold stock.

ATTITUDE TO MANAGEMENT OF DISTRIBUTION

	Centralized system	Decentralized
Bulk purchasing of raw materials	Production can't wait for delivery to outlying factories but ideal for bulk buying.	Stock required at each factory, so bulk purchasing is more difficult.
Long production runs	Large warehouse needed to hold large orders. But don't want to stop production waiting for lines to be cleared.	Large orders are dispersed around all factory sites. But production lines cleared to store on site.
Wide product range	Ability to supply all items to customers from one site in single delivery.	Deliveries of individual items from each site to single customer.
Delivery time	Longer to small customers but better for bulk buyers.	Better customer relations at High Street level.
Transport fleet	Small and single type of large vehicles.	Large fleet with a wide range of types of vehicle.
Warehousing	Pallet level storage.	Item level storage.

Long production runs indicate a similar solution, but for the finished goods. The broad range of products, based on cost, suggests that a centralized system could reduce the overall stock of each item. Reducing the delivery time can only be achieved by placing the warehouses nearer the customer or operating more delivery vehicles; in the long term, the former is the less costly solution. Finally, unit loads are a warehouse manager's dream; they are also ideal for a large automated central warehouse. The decision to centralize the warehousing function depends largely on the outcome of balancing the objectives of different departments.

OTHER SITING FACTORS

As well as the factors already considered, it is useful to look at the real reasons why companies adopted their warehouse layouts in practice. All of them carried out a cost benefit study along the lines already indicated, to a greater or lesser degree, and were guided by the findings. As an example, Van Gend and Loos the Dutch national distributors, decided to centralize their express parcels traffic using a single warehouse and sorting office. They carried out a cost benefit study and made models of the existing system in order to arrive at the conclusion that the optimum location would be very close to one of their existing depots. However, this depot was rented and a decision had to be taken whether to use it or a company-owned site. However, the money was not available to construct a new depot or to buy the existing one. The final outcome was to locate the centralized distribution network some 80 km further east, at a depot the company owned. Several other companies, have had to adopt a current warehouse as the central location, because it was owned by them and needed to be fully utilized.

Another reason for keeping the current distribution system is typical of the older family firms where a reluctance to change exists, despite the considerable cost savings that can be made. Fortunately, this attitude is becoming less common, but an old fashioned layout still affects any decision on changing to a new system. The over-riding factor is often land, because prime sites are hard to find and expensive to buy. The natural tendency is to modernize existing buildings on old sites. Very few companies have taken the Rowntree MacIntosh line and sold their old sites to lower the cost of huge central warehouses. The higher potential gain expected from selling the sites in the future being preferred to cash in hand now. This may be for tax relief or other reasons, but it does inhibit the growth of an efficient distribution system.

WAREHOUSING DECISIONS

Factors for and against centralization of warehousing vary from company to company, and also with time and circumstances. This section concentrates on those factors that influence decision-making when starting with a clean sheet of paper. We hope that the established companies will pick out the points that refer specifically to their situations. The fixed factors include types of warehouse and the functions that they perform. Centralization has been defined in two ways, but the essence of such a system is that all the warehousing functions are situated in a single place within the distribution system, although it does allow some warehousing activities to be performed elsewhere in the system.

Factors that affect selecting an optimal location for a warehouse have been covered based around modelling the network and then adapting it to comply with forecasts of future production and markets. This applies to both centralized and decentralized systems. Other factors that can alter the optimum locations are land prices, transfer grants, competition and the need to be seen in a market.

Geopolitical factors will also affect decisions such as the effects of population, wealth and industrial concentrations. The movement of population occurs gradually over many years, but should be considered in long-term forecasting.

Costs are the over-riding factors that decide which system to adopt and operate. The more depots and warehouses in a distribution network, the lower the vehicle operating costs, but naturally, warehousing costs will go up directly with their number. A balance lies somewhere between the two, dependent on the type of company running the system. This balance will probably shift after taking into account a cost/benefit analysis of both centralization and decentralization. The factors in favour or central warehousing are:

1   Easier management control.
2   Lower stock levels per commodity.
3   Lower administration costs.
4   Better use of bigger vehicles.
5   Increased facilities at retail outlets.

On the other hand, the factors in favour of a decentralized system are:

1   Reduced transport costs.
2   Better customer service.
3   Greater safety of stocks and fewer losses if the central warehouse burns down.

The final selection must consider inter-departmental conflicts and the need to maintain a balance between the requirements of different departments. Conflicts occur in groups of companies, between the different divisional distribution requirements. Having considered the various implications in practice, many companies opt to modernize their existing systems because they have worked well until now, so they resist change. They give little consideration to long-term potential savings in manpower and money, but fortunately this line of thinking is gradually changing as markets become more competitive and it is necessary to trim costs in order to stay in business. There is no single condition that says all companies must centralize their warehousing function; each company has its own requirements and must work out its own solution.

6 Logistics of inventory

Customer service can be measured in terms of the availability of goods ordered and the timeliness of deliveries. Delivery times can be reduced by carrying more inventory particularly by increasing the number and sizes of warehouses. However, investments in inventory increase disproportionately with improvements in customer service levels. It has been known for an inventory to double in size when trying to reduce customer delivery times by 10%.

INVENTORY CONTROL

Reductions in inventory-carrying costs can be quite large in relation to savings from other distribution activities. Although the general description of distribution is the movement and storage of goods, an American interpretation is the strategic replacement and utilization of inventories.

Inventories represent capital tied up for varying lengths of time, and the investment costs of doing so will contribute to the total cost of distribution. For many years, companies have charged the investment in stocks at the bank lending rate plus 1%. Recent opinions think that it should be charged according to the *opportunity cost* of capital investments. For example, it is more economic to invest in other company projects if they produce interest rates of 20% or more, than investing in a distribution improvement that will give a return of 10% or less.

Economically, inventory reductions are important, but those savings have to be balanced against the cost of losing a customer if the goods ordered are not available. In practice, it is difficult to rank one above the other; they are interrelated and must be tackled together in the light of current circumstances.

Inventory costs

Inventories are stocks of goods that are held in readiness for delivering to other places, and they tie up capital according to the amount of goods lying idle in

109

warehouses; consequently, inventory-carrying costs can be high, even though the stocks themselves appear to be assets on the balance sheet. Unfortunately, stocks will be seen as *loss-making assets* unless they are controlled in order to improve sales by offering a reliable delivery service. Like everything in business, there are both advantages and disadvantages to carrying inventories, and balancing one against the other is the essence of inventory control.

Controlling inventory costs starts with identifying what they are:

1 *Storage costs* – related to the building space occupied by stocks in a warehouse or depot.
2 *Handling costs* – depend upon the nature of goods and the method of storage.
3 *Insurance costs* – protect stored goods from losses due to fire, flood, theft and other perils.
4 *Shrinkage costs* – include deterioration, accidental damage and misappropriation of stocks.
5 *Depreciation costs* – cover the fact that stocks become obsolescent or unsaleable with time.
6 *Interest charges* – are levied on the money invested in stocks that produce no income.

These inventory-carrying costs when added together amount to roughly 25% of the value of the stocks, which is substantial, especially when comparing it with the profit margins that will be made on those stocks themselves.

The costs involved are a major disadvantage of carrying inventory, and the first question that comes to mind is 'Why not dispense with stocks?' That would be too easy, because *no stocks often means no sales!* It would be better to keep stocks to a bare minimum to prevent a stock-out, which occurs when stocks are exhausted.

Stock-outs

A stock-out often means a lost sale because an item is not available when required, but it can also mean a lost customer; at best it is a delayed sale. Market research has shown that a lost sale occurs in 67% of stock-outs, a lost customer in 23% of stock-outs and a delayed sale in 10% of them.

Lost sales

The cost of a stock-out can be quantified from these percentages for an example of the inventory for a shop that sells electrical toasters at a price of £100 each.

1 *A delayed sale* means no loss of income, although it will occur 0.10 or 10% of the time: – the average loss = £0 × 0.10 = £0.
2 *A lost sale* means a loss of 15% profit on a toaster, namely £15, and it will occur 0.67 or 67% of the time:
   – the average loss + £15 × 0.67 = £10.
3 *A lost customer* means a recurring loss of sales, and it will be assumed in this case that each customer lost would make three more purchases, to which must be

Figure 6.1 Optimal buffer stock level

Buffer stock		Inventory costs (25%) for one extra batch‡ (£)	No. of stock-outs† prevented by one extra batch	Savings from holding one extra batch (£)
Safety No. of units*	Value (£)			
10	1 000	250	15	360
20	2 000	250	12	288
30	3 000	250	9	216
40	4 000	250	7	163

*Value of one unit = £100
†Cost of one stock-out = £79
‡Size of batch = 10 units

added a share of the sales promotion costs which could be equivalent to another lost sale, making four lost in total. A lost customer occurs 0.23 or 23% of the time:
– the average loss = 4 × £15 × 0.23 = £14.

The full value of a lost sale is the sum of these average losses which amounts to £24. It is easy to see that a stock-out which prevents a batch of ten toasters being sold will lose the company £240 in income ... and it seems to be a fact of life that the number of stock-outs tends to escalate after the first one!

Buffer stocks

Maintaining buffer stocks is an assurance against stock-outs and lost sales; however, holding buffer stocks costs money. Incrementally, the savings fall off as the size of the buffer stock increases, so that there is an optimal size for the buffer stock where the savings per extra batch is less than the extra cost of carrying that batch.

Using the example of the electric toaster sales, an incremental analysis of the costs and savings is shown in Table 6.1. The smallest economic size of a batch is taken to be ten toasters worth £1 000, therefore at 25% of its value the inventory-carrying cost of an extra batch is £250. The savings from preventing one stock-out is £24.

The break-even point for the largest size of buffer stock occurs when the carrying cost of an extra batch, £250, exceeds the savings from an extra batch.

From Table 6.1 it can be seen that the break-even point is a buffer stock of between 20 and 30 toasters. A buffer stock of 20 toasters will ensure savings of at least £288 per batch for a carrying cost of £250, but increasing the buffer stock to 30 toasters will reduce the savings to £216 per batch. Since the electric toasters are supplied in batches of ten, the optimal size of the buffer stock is two batches; any more will cost more than permitting nine stock-outs during the year.

This example concerns only one item, but you can imagine what it would be like for a depot that stocked 200 items!

Replenishments

It has been said that a buffer stock needs to be carried for the sake of safety so that stock-outs will not occur; however, the buffer stock has to be kept to a minimum economic level. When this level is reached, that is the time to replenish the stocks. Deciding how much to order for replenishing the stocks is a compromise between a number of conflicting factors:

1   Inventory-carrying costs.
2   Re-ordering costs.
3   Batch size.
4   Lost sales due to stock-outs.
5   Buffer stock costs.
6   Risks of obsolescence, deterioration, or declining prices.

The replenishment quantity will be a balance between the extra costs and the loss of sales. Here is an example of the conflicts that can occur; small orders are cheap, inventory-carrying costs are reduced, and there will be fewer risks, but re-ordering costs will increase and a larger buffer stock will be required. If throughputs are regular, the size of the buffer is easy to calculate, because it will be the number of items used in the time it takes to obtain replenishments.

Economic order quantity

The economic order quantity (EOQ) can be calculated when you know the annual throughput (A units), the replenishment costs (B), the unit value (C) and the inventory-carrying costs (I). It is expressed as:

$$EOQ = \sqrt{2\frac{AB}{CI}} \text{ units}$$

For example, assuming that the warehouse throughput of electric toasters worth £100 each was 2 500 units annually, the replenishment costs were £326, and the inventory-carrying cost was 25% of the sales value, then:

$$EOQ = \sqrt{\frac{2 \times 3000 \times £326}{£100 \times 0.25}} \text{ units}$$
$$= \sqrt{78,400 \text{ units}}$$
$$= 280 \text{ units}$$

Re-order point

The time to replenish stocks in a warehouse will depend upon the throughput, the size of the buffer stock and the time to replenish an order. The re-order point will occur when the stock in hand plus the stock on order equals the EOQ plus the safety stock. In the electric toaster example, the EOQ is 280 units, the throughput is 60 units per week and the time to replenish stocks is two weeks; therefore, the re-ordere

Figure 6.2 **'That Logisticon automatic replenishment and stock control system sure works!'** (With acknowledgement to the Logisticon Systems Company of the U.S.A.)

cycle is as shown in Figure 6.3. The safety stock must never be used, except in an emergency.

In a replenishment time of two weeks, the throughput will be $2 \times 60 = 120$ units, and this must be the safety stock level which prevents a stock-out before the replenishments arrive. The replenishment level will be $120 + 120 = 240$ units, and the full inventory level will be the EOQ plus the safety stock, or $280 + 120 = 400$ units.

In Figure 6.3, it is assumed that the warehouse has a full inventory (A) of electric toasters at the end of the first week, but it will fall to the replenishment level (B) of 240 units in

$$\frac{400 - 240}{160} = 2.7 \text{ weeks}$$

at a throughput of 60 units per week. When after 4.7 weeks the replenishments arrive (C), only the safety stock of toasters will remain in the warehouse, then the full inventory is restored (D).

If the throughput now increases from 60 units to 100 units per week, the re-order level will be reached in

$$\frac{400 - 200}{100} = 1.6 \text{ weeks}$$

and stocks will have fallen to the safety level (E) before the replenishments arrive this time. This will be an emergency where the safety stocks have to be used and, fortunately, they will last until the replenishments do arrive (F), but the stock will be down to 50 units. However, the stock level will rise to 330 units (G) instead of 400 units, and the cycle time has reduced to 3.6 weeks; thus, the next re-order point will occur only 1.6 weeks later (H), but the cycle will be back to normal afterwards.

Another kind of emergency is a supply delay so that replenishments do not arrive on time. For example, with a full inventory at (I), the next replenishments are due after 4.7 weeks as usual, but a breakdown delays them for another week; consequently, some safety stock has been used and it will have fallen to 60 units (K). Replenishing the stock brings the level up to 340 units (L) and the full inventory (N) will be restored 3.4 weeks later (M).

Using this economic replenishment procedure shows how it copes with variations in demand and supply, but it is important to monitor the warehouse inventory constantly. When the re-order point is reached, the EOQ is ordered from the supplier. A computer can monitor the system and inform the warehouse manager when to re-order, if its memory includes the re-order and safety stock levels. Also, it can handle other items stocked at the same time, as well as print out the appropriate re-ordering documents.

Regular ordering

When the throughput is regular for particular stock items, they can also be re-ordered at regular intervals. How much stock to order is found by subtracting the

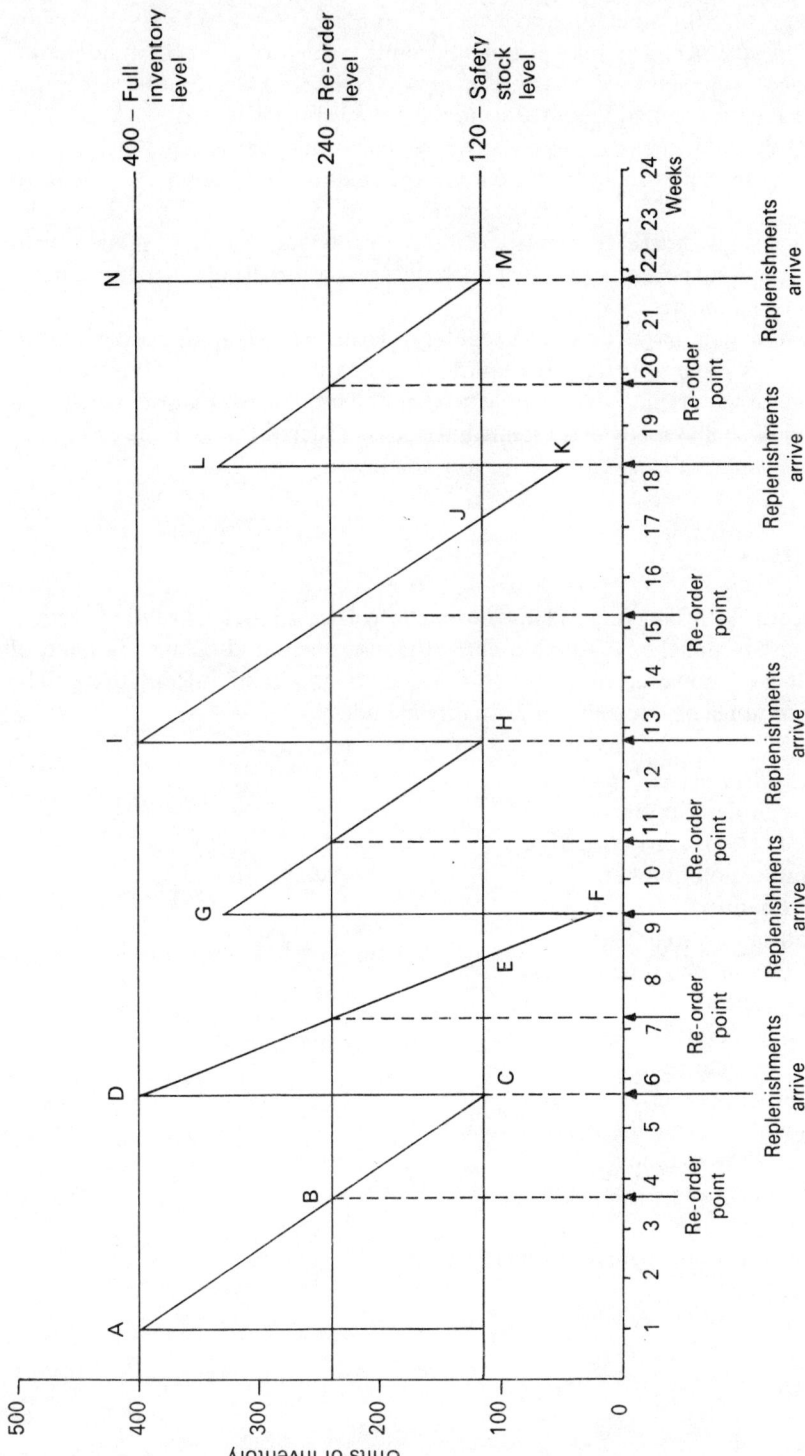

Figure 6.3   Re-order cycle for economic replenishments

stock on hand plus the stock already ordered from an *imprest* stock level which is determined in advance. The replenishment quantity will vary, but the time period between orders is constant. Normally, the *imprest stock level* has to be large enough to cover the greatest demand likely during the replenishment period.

Regular ordering is most appropriate where *many items* are ordered at the same time, *savings* from bulk orders are based on the size of the total order, or *significant advantages* can be had from ordering separate items in large quantities. Examples include replenishing stocks at depots from a central warehouse and taking advantage of cheaper transport charges for bulk deliveries, or ordering a variety of items from the same supplier.

A similar application that combines regular ordering with economic order quantities is known as *group ordering*. It requires items to be coded according to EOQ levels, and stocks are replenished regularly when the total order quantity reaches an imprest level. Usually, a few extra items have to be ordered to reach the EOQ, but the savings outweigh the inventory-carrying costs.

Stock records

Keeping records is the key to good inventory control. Continuous inventory records usually consist of punched cards that show the movement and balance in hand of each item stocked; however, the paperwork needed to obtain this information can be complex. The range of information probably includes:

1   *Item identification*:
    - name or description;
    - specifications for re-ordering;
    - identification number;
    - unit quantity;
    - location in warehouse;
    - remarks on handling and loading;
2   *Inventory control*:
    - re-order point;
    - re-order quantity;
    - buffer stock level;
    - cumulative throughput;
    - replenishment time;
    - unit value;
3   *Movements*:
    - date of last order and customer;
    - order quantity;
    - date of last replenishment;
    - wastage details;
    - balance in hand;
    - stock on order.

A typical stock-balance record and replenishment stocklist are illustrated by Figures 6.4 and 6.5.

```
ROW 1   OWA050 MT    HISTORICAL REPORT STOCKCHANGES FROM COMPANY: WASSING BV    01/05/91                    PAGE  1

    2   DEBTOR. 127960/00          CBN CORPORATION, DALE STREET,          NORTHBR.  ILL. 60
                                                                          UNTIL DATE 30-04-91
```

ROW	DATE	DOCNR.	NAME SHIP/CONS	ADDRESS	PLACE	QUANTITY	STOCK	QUANT. SRT	STOCK
4	PROD.CODE:	1100419		16 BD BINDER					36
5	030491	GB7704	CBN FRANCE SA ZAC LES MAR	44 RUE MAURICE DE BROGLIE	93600 AULNAY SOV	9	27	9 U	27
6	040491	GB7407	CBN DEUTSCHLAND GMBH	BOSCH STRASSE 1	D-8901 KONIGSBRU	1	26	1 U	26
7	050491	GB7605	CBN NEDERLAND NV	GRAFTERMEERSTRAAT 36-38	HOOFDDORP 2131 A	2	24	2 U	24
8	050491	GB7605	CBN NEDERLAND NV	GRAFTERMEERSTRAAT 36-38	HOOFDDORP 2131 A	2	22	2 U	22
9	120491	GB7408	CBN DEUTSCHLAND GMBH	BOSCH STRASSE 1	D-3901 KONIGSBRU	1	21	1 U	21
10	170491	W963	CBN NORTHBR			10	31	10 I	31
11	PROD. CODE:	1101667		9 LA HAND SLOT PUNCHES					17
12	030491	GB7704	CBN FRANCE SA ZAC LES MAR	44 RUE MAURICE DE BROGLIE	93600 AULNAY SOV	5	12	5 U	12
13	050491	GB7605	CBN NEDERLAND NV	GRAFTERMEERSTRAAT 36-38	HOOFDDORP 2131 A	2	10	2 U	10
14	050491	GB7605	CBN NEDERLAND NV	GRAFTERMEERSTRAAT 36-38	HOOFDDORP 2131 A	8	2	8 U	2

This example of a stock movement sheet for goods stored in a warehouse on behalf of different clients provides a record of the stock changes, both inwards and outwards. Such a report was prepared by the storage company (Wassing **BV**) and it records stock changes numerically and chronologically according to products, suppliers and customers. Explanation row by row:

Row 1: Title and company (Wassing BV)
Row 2: Account no., Client name and address (CBN Corporation)
Row 3: Headings
Row 4: Product code (1100419) and description (16DB Binder); stock in hand (36 pieces).
Row 6: Date (04.04.1991), customer (Deutschland GMBH), issues (9 pieces), new stock balance (31 pieces) and movement summary.
Row 10: Date (17.04.1991), suppliers (CBN Northbrand factory), receipts (10 pieces), new stock balance (31 pieces) and movement summary.
Row 11: Another product (code no. 1101667).

Figure 6.4   Computer printout of stock balance

OWA050 MT   STOCKLIST FROM COMPANY: WASSING BV   01/05/91 14:19 PAGE   7

DEBTOR.   127960/00 CBN CORPORATION   NORTHBR ILL. 60062

PROD. CODE	DESCRIPTION	TOTAL STOCK	MINIMUM STOCK	MAXIMUM STOCK	REMARKS	STOCK PIECES	TOTAL WEIGHT	CHARGEABLE PALLETS	RESERVED STOCK
2519912≠	1 STEP COVER 1.5 MM BEIGE	160				4000	160		
2519914≠	1 STEP COVER 1.5 MM BORDEAUX	60				1500	60		
2519915≠	1 STEP COVER P WHITE	18				450	13		
2519916≠	1 STEP COVER P PARCHMENT	12				300	12		
2519917E	1 STEP COVERS ⅛" P NAVY	19				475	19		
2519918≠	1 STEP COVER ⅛"P BURGUNDY								
2519919≠	1 STEP COVER W WHITE	10				250	10		
2519921≠	1 STEP COVER W NAVY	6				150	6		
2519922≠	1 STEP COVER ⅛" BURGUNDY	10				250	10		
4500584≠	REGENCY SHEETS BLACK	9529				9529	953		
4500585≠	REGENCY SHEETS BLUE	8179				8179	818		
4500585E	REGENCY SHEETS BLUE	17				1700	306		
4500587≠	REGENCY SHEET WHITE	7174				7174	717		
4823184B	CERLOX BLANKS ¼ BLACK 84R								

This example shows part of a list of the items stocked in a warehous by a storage company (Wassing BV), but it does not record details of their movements, only giving the total number of packages, the number of pieces and their weights.

Figure 6.5   Computer printout of warehouse stocklist

Checking the inventory

Effective control means continually checking the inventory in a warehouse. A check may be made by counting, weighing, measuring or estimating, and it will prevent the extra costs of stock-outs, or disposing of surplus or obsolete items. Regular stock checks improve inventory control and the proficiency of warehouse staff.

INVENTORY MANAGEMENT

It is important to manage the inventory of a warehouse well, because carrying it will cost about 25% of its value. Those costs depend upon the items stocked and the type of warehouse, but they include the following:

1 *Inventory-carrying costs* or the costs of owning the stocks.
   (i) *Commercial costs*:
        * interest on capital;
        * insurance;
        * investment;
   (ii) *Storage costs*:
        * building;
        * materials handling;
        * staff;
   (iii) *Risk costs*:
        * obsolescence;
        * deterioration;
        * wastage;
        * reduced replacement value;
        * reduced throughput;
   (iv) *Opportunity costs*:
        * losses due to tied-up capital;
        * reduced dividends;
        * restricted expansions.
2 *Ordering costs* which depend upon the number of orders.
   * administration;
   * handling;
   * uneconomic quantities.
3 *Stock-out costs* due to the inability to satisfy orders.
   * loss of profit on sales;
   * loss of investment in the development of customers;
   * emergency expenses;
   * extra promotional expenses.
4 *Inventory management costs* arising from controlling the inventory.
   * staff recruitment;
   * staff training;
   * personnel;
   * updating information.

Managing inventory

In practice, the purpose of carrying inventory is exactly the same as that of distribution itself; namely, reducing costs while improving customer service. Good inventory management can save over 10% of the total inventory costs, and it can decrease the capital and space invested in the inventory, as well as prevent stock-outs.

Successful inventory management requires objective planning, effective control and practical organization. The objective of planning is to prepare information for calculating economic order quantities, determining the most profitable buffer stocks and minimizing the time that an item is held in stock. Effective control must have good records in order to keep delivery dates, to avoid duplications and to optimize inventory costs. In practice, the organization must improve inventory control and reduce costs, but it needs a wide experience and management skills.

From a cost-reduction point of view, managing inventory offers a wide scope for innovation, and its success will bring the rewards of customer service satisfaction and increased company profits.

JUST-IN-TIME INVENTORY

The basic principle of a *just-in-time* system is to reduce the waiting time to an absolute minimum, because time is money, as managers know only too well. This concept originated in Japan, where it is known as *Kanban*, but it is now being used widely in Europe and America. The just-in-time (JIT) inventory system is related to regular ordering in which orders for supplies are placed at fixed intervals but order quantities vary each time. However, fixed internal ordering does not take advantage of economic order quantities (EOQ), because discounts are greater from suppliers who prefer regular orders. On the other hand, JIT is related to the EOQ system, because ordering costs are assumed to be negligible, as inventory carrying costs are minimized by ordering frequently and *just-in-time*.

Although JIT is considered to be a modern concept introduced from Japan, it was conceived by Henry Ford when he integrated production with assembly plants for manufacturing automobiles in the 1920s. Iron ore for the plant arrived by barges before smelting it into steel and stamping or casting it into components ready for assembly within two or three days. Ford said 'Waste is stocks in excess of requirements.' Unfortunately, this truth was ignored in the affluent times that followed, but Japanese industry had to start from scratch after the Second World War, and the Toyota Motor Company went back to Ford's concept and vigorously implemented its own version which it called *Kanban*.

Kanban system

Kanban means 'card', and the system uses two cards which convey instructions – rather like those used by a football referee! One card is the *move card* which is used for workers on the assembly line as a message to the controller that they are running low on components. The necessary components are then brought to the assembly line from a nearby stock in a container that has a *production card* attached to it. This card is removed and sent back to the controller who re-orders some of those components so that they arrive just before the next *move card* is expected.

There are differences between just-in-time and its counterpart Kanban. JIT in the West considers inventory to be an *insurance*; whereas Kanban in Japan looks upon inventory as *waste*. The Japanese believe that the key to reducing inventory is to see the supplier as part of the production process; while Americans tend to view suppliers as competitors who should be played one against the other! Therefore, in America, multiple suppliers for multiple components are common, but in Japan, all components of a similar nature come from one supplier. Thus, Toyota has 250 suppliers compared with General Motors' 4000 in Detroit.

The advantages of a Kanban system apply to production systems more than distribution, particularly of products made from standard parts; but the system must be subject to very good control, otherwise production will stop when a batch of faulty parts arrives just-in-time!

Contrary to what is claimed, only a limited number of computer software packages are capable of controlling JIT systems. For that reason, few people have the 'know-how' or experience of combining JIT order processing; in any case, the few suitable packages are not very advanced.

JIT and delivery

Road delivery vehicles are most suited to relatively small but frequent deliveries, because they provide superior service in terms of *in-time* pick-ups and deliveries. They are smaller than railway wagons, barges or aircraft, and they operate *door-to-door* in less time. However, air cargo is quicker for delivering over longer distances, but it is therefore not suitable for JIT, which needs adjacent supplies in order to reduce inventory-carrying costs. Some automobile assembly plants overseas benefit from both lower labour costs locally and lower mass production costs in the home country when they freight assembly components in bulk by air.

JIT and warehouse siting

As said earlier, timely deliveries require supplies to be sited near to where they are wanted, and the same applies to warehouses when quick replenishments are the order of the day. This is particularly important for fresh goods and vegetables – Albert Heijn is the biggest supermarket chain in the Netherlands, selling mainly its 'own-brand' groceries so as to reduce the time between manufacture and marketing, but they necessitate daily deliveries of both the supplies to warehouses and the requirements of supermarkets. Storage space in supermarkets is very limited, therefore the warehouses must be sited in all the local markets in order to ensure JIT delivering. Of course, the cost of operating such a distribution system is high – Albert Heijn reckons on 45% of the gross margin – so a high turnover of goods is essential to counter the reduced profits.

INVENTORY LEVELS

The inventory function

The participants in a distribution system are interdependent; consequently, each affects the others, but warehousing is 'the pig in the middle'. On one hand, fluctuating production outputs mean that warehouses have to be capable of holding ever-changing stocks, and on the other hand, market demands rarely coincide with the stock changes. This makes it very difficult to control inventory in order to reduce costs, unless the distribution system is very flexible and its records are kept up-to-date.

The simplest way to keep track of inventory is to use a blackboard and chalk, or a clipboard with pencil and rubber. All the different items are listed on the left hand side and a mark is made against each item every time a certain number or batch is received. A mark is rubbed off every time that number or batch goes out. The tally of marks represents the stocks on hand which can be checked physically from time to time. Also, this is a convenient way for sales representatives to check what items are in stock.

Nowadays, large warehouses use exactly the same procedure, but with computers for greater speed and accuracy. In seconds, a computer can show the quantity and location of any item in stock. Another recent innovation has been the use of bar codes and electronic scanners that can be connected directly to a computer. This system started with groceries and has become fairly universal since.

After a scanner reads the bar code of an item, a computer translates the information into product price and description, as well as recording inventory levels cumulatively and comparing them with safety or re-order levels plus any other information that may be useful.

Seasonal inventory levels

A fundamental aim of carrying inventory is to absorb differences between demand patterns and production patterns, so the design of a logistics system for seasonal fluctuations must be quite flexible. It must allow short-term plans to be made that balance inventory costs against production and market savings. Models for determining capacities and costs must include factors for seasonality – the larger models will also include the time dimension. Seasonal stock requirements can be determined after satisfying the basic demands, and a separate mathematical program can then be used to optimize the capacities.

Linear programming is useful for analysing the balances between estimated costs and demands. Production outputs will be one set of constraints, and the problem is solved for several different outputs and demand constraints rather than treating the output level as a direct variable in the optimization process. This approach makes the form of an analysis simpler, and allows the process to be seen from another perspective.

Seasonal stocks can be viewed as a means of conserving production time, so it is desirable to concentrate on those items with a low inventory-carrying cost relative to the handling and processing time: similarly, to concentrate high throughput items in seasonal stocks in order to smoothe out throughput when demand is difficult to forecast far in advance. It is advisable to site seasonal stocks close to the manufacturing plant rather than dispersing them around outlying depots.

DECIDING INVENTORY CONTROLS

Variable stocks

One of the more complex decisions that have to be made by warehouse managers is that of deciding the safety stock levels for a range of items. A tedious solution, for which a computer is really useful, is to calculate the safety stock for each item and add them together; however, the use of statistical lognormal graphs can give estimates of all these safety stocks in less time. A graph of the standard deviations of the demands for a number of items can provide an estimate of how a single item will vary. Such an estimate can then be used as the base number for determining the safety stock required for any particular segment of the range.

Using statistical lognormal distribution graphs in this way makes it easier to estimate quickly both the volume throughput and the safety stock level under different circumstances, as well as the low-volume items to be consolidated and the standards of customer service expected.

Another way that the lognormal graph can be used is for estimating the demand for each item in a mixed range, or for calculating specific delivery volumes and the size of inventory needed to support them. Alternative policies for service availability and inventory costs can be compared in terms of their objectives.

ABC stock control

Worthwhile savings have been reported by companies that prefer commonsense inventory control to the statistical methods just mentioned. One example is the ABC method which is used to keep the attention given to stocked items proportional to their values. The importance of a product is determined by its useful value over the period of time required to replenish its stocks, or the cost of a stock-out. Usually, the bulk of an inventory investment comprises a very few expensive items, and they are labelled as Class A. Special care is needed to keep accurate records of such items, and to see that delivery dates are met, because a big proportion of the inventory-carrying cost will be tied up in these few items.

Items of average value are classed B, and they will receive an average amount of attention; they are intermediate between the few expensive items and the large number of cheap items in Class C. The latter class is relatively unimportant, although well over half of the items stocked usually belong to this class. Generally, their total value is small compared with their numbers; being mass-produced, the cost of stocking them is less than the cost of closely controlling their safety levels, re-order levels or order quantities. Inventory controls for items in Class C need to be no more than a simple two-bin system.

The warehouse manager must have a plan for controlling the total inventory costs, it will be based on his experience in a particular field. Various techniques and formulae are available, and commonsense should play an important role in dealing with new problems, because usually they will be variations of standard ones that already have recognized solutions.

Computerized inventory control

A series of computer models for inventory control has been investigated at the Cranfield Institute for Technology in the UK; the packages contain a number of different options that allow them to be 'tuned into' individual requirements, and they include optimization of ordering, demand patterns, forecasting and deciding inventory levels. Figure 6.6 gives an outline of how these computer modules can be built into a total control system.

Market variables

Despite the fact that inventory costs are reduced by carrying smaller stocks, market situations may make such a decision undesirable. In boom times, buyers' markets will create shortages as a result. However, if stockpiling follows as a precaution against future shortages, high costs of inventory-carrying can force retailers out of business. A slump results and orders fall off, which reduces warehouse throughputs.

This is just an indication of the paradox of market variables that affects inventory management. Inventory control is most important when interest rates and inflation run high, but empty warehouses jeopardize future profits. Keeping just the right amount of inventory is neither simple nor painless. The only solution is to maintain a proper balance between too much stock and too little – logistics models are useful tools for this balance, but *maintaining* the balance also means having a *sense* of balance!

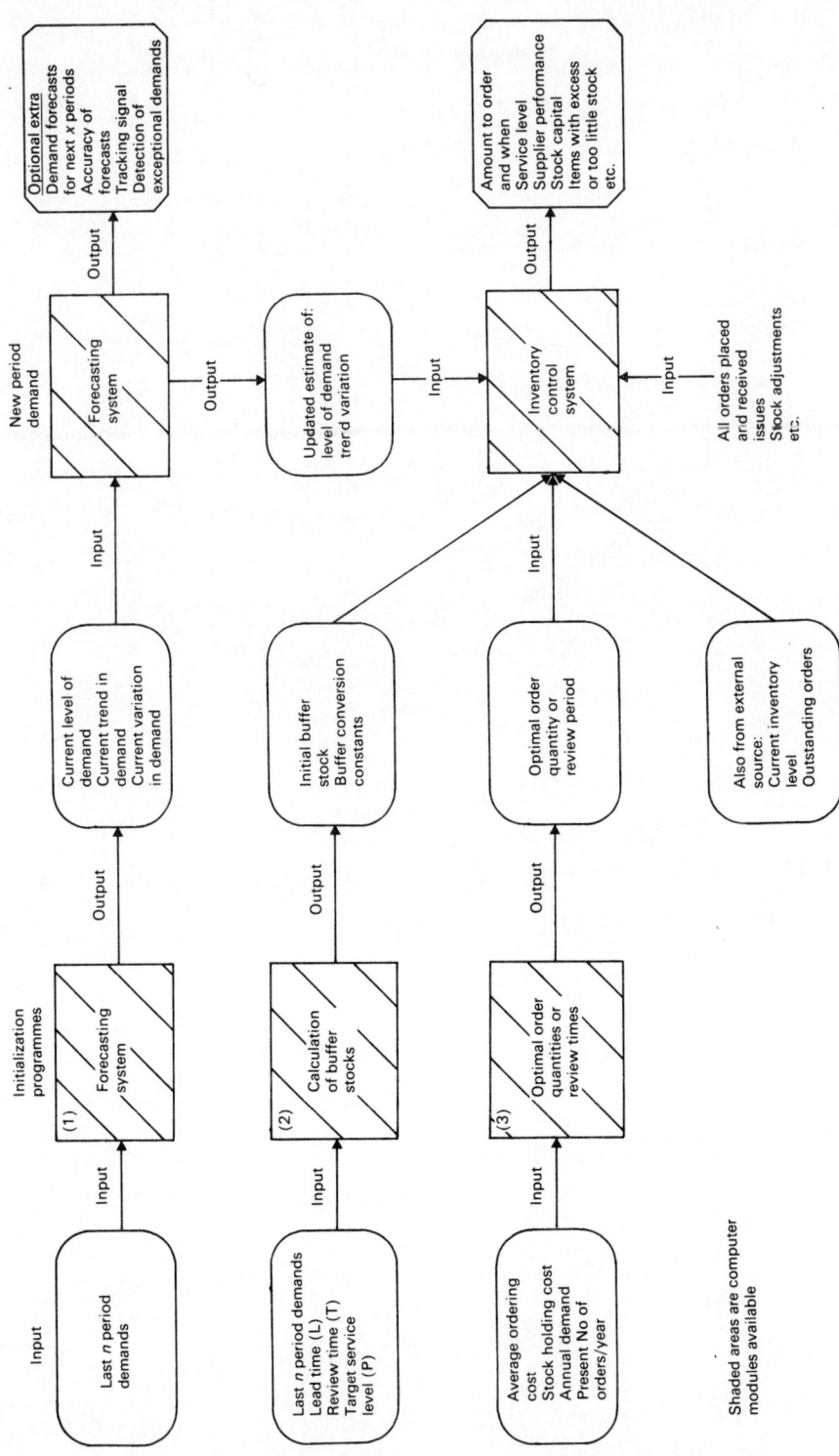

Figure 6.6 Inventory control system

7   Materials handling

Since warehouses exist for the storage of materials, usually in the form of industrial or consumer goods, materials handling plays an important role in the logistics of warehousing. Within the warehouse, goods are moved by a variety of machines which are controlled either manually or automatically, while the goods themselves may be moved individually or grouped into cartons, pallets or containers. Whatever method is chosen, the numbers of items and distances moved provide the data for logistics models that simulate materials handling operations.

It is not surprising, therefore, to learn that materials handling is responsible for a large slice of the labour costs in distribution, but improving its efficiency is a question of saving time and effort, as well as money. Savings are the objectives for analysing the materials handling operations logistically in order to improve them, and the techniques available are work study, value analysis and standard costing.

WORK STUDY

Materials handling in distribution requires manual or mechanical effort to move goods into and out of storage, to assemble goods according to customer orders and to load them onto or unload them from delivery vehicles. These movements can be measured in terms of time and effort using work study measurements that can be converted into standard costs to analyse their value with a view to making savings.

Warehouse layout

In the warehouse, work study must start with flow charting so that the best layouts can be developed with the least wastage of space and movements while giving the greatest throughputs. A conventional single storey warehouse has many advantages, because forklift trucks can operate more easily on the same floor while lifting pallet loads to heights up to six or seven metres. Although it is possible to stack pallets on

Table 7.1   Truck movement average times

	Movement in the storage area		Movement from store to vehicle	
Type of forklift truck	Min/pallet	Min/yd or m	Min/pallet	Min/yd or m
1 Rider truck (*RT*)	1.02	0.018	1.35	0.018
2 Steer truck (*ST*)	0.43	0.025	0.77	0.025
3 Pallet truck (*PT*)	0.79	0.027	1.08	0.027

top of each other, the lowest pallet is always the last to leave despite being the first to arrive!

Hence, steel racks are better, because each pallet sits on its own shelf and can be moved without disturbing the others. With high-rise racks, the aisle width can be kept to a minimum, either for mechanical trucks or automatic picking from a conveyor belt.

Remember at all times that the layout of a warehouse determines to a large extent how efficiently the operations will be performed, because the layout affects the flow of materials, the flow times, the handling effort and safety of the work done.

Forklift truck operating times

Comparing three different types of forklift truck in order to choose the most suitable for moving pallet loads from a store and loading them into vehicles was the subject of a study by C.G. Chantrill and Partners. The total time for handling one pallet was built up from the individual times for the various work elements. The elemental times were obtained from different studies in the warehouse.

Different forklift trucks

The three trucks for handling goods on wooden pallets were all powered by electric batteries, but their costs differed according to the type of control:

1   *Rider truck*: an expensive, fully automated truck with provision for a riding operator who has foot and hand controls.
2   *Steer truck*: an intermediary type of truck with a pedestrian operator who can stand and ride when a hinged platform was dropped at the rear. Hand controls.
3   *Pallet truck*: a simple, hand-operated truck with a pedestrian operator.

A summary of the movement times for these trucks is presented in Table 7.1.

The trucks are compared in terms of the minutes for loading a pallet and minutes for transporting a pallet 1 yard (1 m). Elemental times are shown in Table 7.2 for the complete activity of loading a pallet in the store, transporting it to a vehicle, unloading the pallet into the vehicle and returning empty for another pallet. As expected, the most expensive truck completed the activity most quickly, but economically the intermediary truck proved most suitable for this particular activity.

Table 7.2   Truck handling and movement times

	Description of movement	Operational minutes			Remarks
		RT	ST	PT	
1	Manoeuvre truck to pallet	0.20	0.07		Working in the
				0.27	storage area.
2	Lift pallet load	0.09	0.05		Times affected
					by layout of
3	Remove pallet from stack	0.07			the area and
			0.05	0.17	truck handling
4	Prepare to transport	0.15			ability
5	Take pallet to the vehicle at the loading bay	0.90	1.25	1.35	Transport distance was 50 yd/m
6	Manoeuvre to unload pallet	0.32	0.14	0.17	
7	Lower pallet to floor	0.08	0.08		Unloading the
				0.20	pallet into a
8	Withdraw truck forks	0.07			vehicle
			0.06		
9	Prepare to return to store	0.07			
10	Return empty to the stack of pallets in store	0.72	1.11	1.22	Transport distance was 50 yd/m
	Total time per pallet	2.67	2.81	3.38	

The total time for transporting a pallet was the sum of the minutes to load a pallet and the distance moved multiplied by the speed. An example of this calculation is collecting a pallet from the store with a rider truck and loading it into a vehicle 50 yards (metres) away.

$$\text{Minutes per pallet} = 1.35$$
$$\text{Transport minutes} = 0.018 \times 50$$
$$= 0.90$$
$$\text{Total time per pallet} = 2.25 \text{ minutes}$$

Pallet handling times

Work operations with the three forklift trucks were studied and standard times were established for each element. These times are given in Table 7.2, and they were used for preparing synthetic times for different methods of handling goods in the warehouse. In this way, different flow lines, stacking areas and trucks could be compared.

Table 7.3   Additional handling times

Work element	Minutes per occurrence	Remarks
1 Await instructions about goods to be moved	0.63	Times depended upon the degree of
2 Discuss schedule with helper	0.28	understanding and teamwork between the
3 Locate the goods to be moved	0.42	forklift truck operator and helper
4 Decide the goods loading sequence	0.24	
5 Wait for pallet to be cleared for loading on truck	0.10	
6 Check contents of pallet load	0.15	
7 Wait while the pallet is secured in the vehicle	0.24	

Additional work elements

In addition to the operational times tabulated, time was needed for issuing instructions to the operator, searching for the correct pallet, and other minor jobs. These times have been excluded from the truck handling and movement times, but they are summarized in Table 7.3.

Schematic procedure

Just as work activities can be broken down into elements, a complete process can be broken down into individual activities and operations. When standard times are available for the elements, work contents of different processes can be compiled and compared for planning purposes. A schematic diagram of the warehousing system is presented in Figure 7.4.

Whenever a new method is devised, it should be analysed into activities and elements so that operational times can be developed. According to the accuracy of the standard times, the overall work times can be synthesized in order to assist decision-making.

MATERIALS HANDLING LOGISTICS

Bulk materials and mass-produced goods lend themselves admirably to the computerized control of handling operations. The concerns with most experience in these two fields are the railways and the post office; both have developed really sophisticated systems. In many cases, it will pay to take advantage of these professional organizations which have made distribution and materials handling into a fine art.

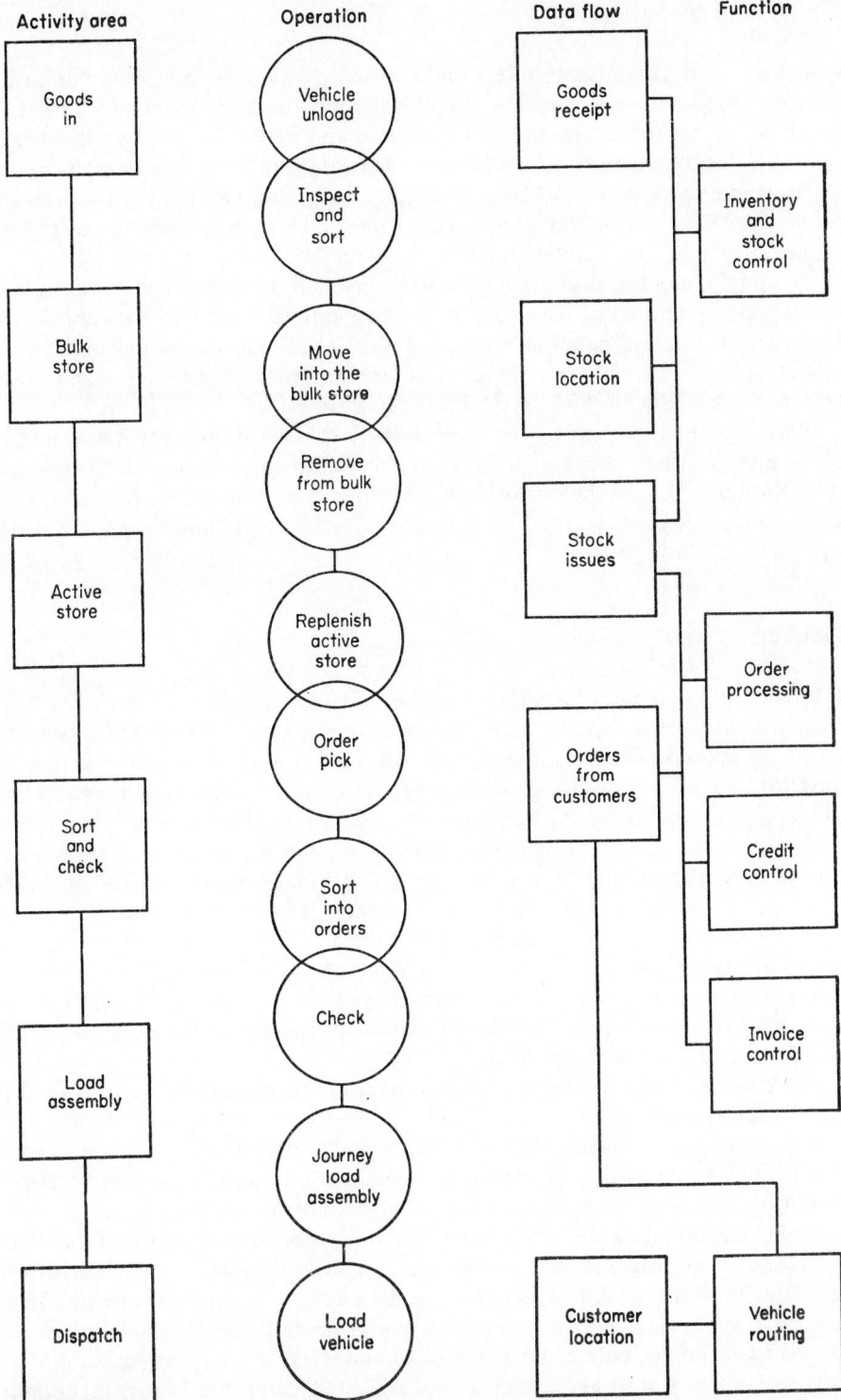

Figure 7.4   Schematic warehouse materials handling

Delivering by rail

Countries with the strongest economies usually have the best communication systems, especially when it comes to delivering the goods. A country like the UK, which has a large percentage of small businesses and a good roads network, relies on road vehicles for much of its distribution delivering; the Dutch geography makes canals viable, the size of America favours air freight; but Germany encourages rail deliveries: 20% of its international freight is moved by railways, as opposed to 10% in the US, 5% in The Netherlands and 2% in the UK.

The development of faster materials handling equipment is no advantage unless the delivery system keeps pace with it. The new railway tracks on the continent of Europe are capable of handling *high-speed trains* at 160 km/h or more, and they are attracting increasing volumes of materials for transportation between seaports and industrial areas. Such railway systems are highly organized and efficient.

When the Channel Tunnel is completed, the UK railway system will become part of the European network, and all countries in the European Economic Community (EEC) will be selling in the market on equal terms. Therefore, less order officialdom and excellent rail connections should lead to reduced distribution costs for exported goods.

Delivering mail

The Dutch PTT handles 17 million letters a day, collecting them from 17 000 post boxes and delivering them to six million addresses; for this, it uses 4 000 vans that travel 100 million kilometres a year; to which must be added ten million kilometres travelled with its own trains. Using computerized logistics, the PTT aims at a *one-day* service for delivering letters, despite the colossal number involved.

Operating such a large distribution system requires first-class organization and control; The Netherlands is divided into 12 distribution regions which are subdivided into 206 delivery areas. The postcode system is based upon these regions and areas – a six digit code is used comprising four numbers and two letters. The first two numbers represent the regions and the last two numbers the areas, while the letters refer to streets. Distribution between the regional collecting centres is by trains which travel five times in 24 hours. Automatic readers at these centres sort the mail for the 206 area sorting offices.

The UK's postcode system is explained later in this chapter, where it is used to plan local deliveries.

Each sorting office also consigns the Dutch mail to the 206 areas, each of which is handled by one post office. In this way, the mail is sorted twice into 206 × 206 = 42 400 street walks or bags. The addresses are read by an optical scanner.

At the time that they are sorted, the letters are franked and the value of the stamp is checked with ultraviolet light. If both the address and the stamp value are correct, the letter is stamped with a red index code which is a kind of barcode. Then, automatic sorters allocate the coded mail to the 206 destinations; when the address and postcode do not tally, a letter is rejected and it has to be sorted by hand.

The advantages of this system are its speed (35 000 letters can be sorted per hour) and its flexibility (42 400 delivery bags). December is the busiest month, and during this period in 1990 over half of the six million addresses in the country received a postal delivery in the Netherlands.

Computers for controlling materials handling

For obvious reasons, the computerized control of materials movements is more appropriate to large distribution systems; however, a growing popularity of the personal computer has led to the development of simple software programs for everyday use. The first large-scale distribution computer programs were developed for costing operations in American public warehouses, costs being analysed from inputs of data from incoming goods, stocking, handling, order filling, packing, checking and despatching. Later, programs became adapted for the flow of materials using standard times; now, PC programs are available for storage-rate analysis with pallets in order to make space utilization more economic.

Scheduling materials handling trucks lends itself to control with a PC, particularly where a range of products have to be handled in different batches. In one study of an assembly plant, it was discovered that the trucks were running empty almost 40% of the time, and it was obvious that better monitoring and assigning of their loads would improve efficiency.

Forklift truck scheduling

The success of using a microcomputer for scheduling forklift trucks rests upon the data collected on a continuous basis, which can be inserted into the program. The most important data includes: the loads to be moved (products, locations, order numbers and packing areas) and the trucks themselves (types, locations and availability). In this study, a *central microcomputer* was connected with data terminals on the trucks by means of radio-frequency signals. A *printer* on each truck gave its driver the move orders. Also, each terminal had a *visual display screen* and a *keyboard* linked to a *radio transmitter-receiver* on the overhead guard of the truck. Signals were received from a personal computer which had a 128 K memory, two disk drives and a printer. The warehouse was divided into *racking areas* for specific products that had to be transferred to order despatching bays. The PC database contained information about each of the trucks such as truck number, type, capacity, maximum speed, lifting height, distance travelled and maintenance schedules. Information about the *materials movements* included despatch bay numbers, storage rack numbers, distances between bays and racks, and stock levels.

Once the computer had received the data, the program took over and allocated trucks to different orders before transmitting instructions to the printers about the respective trucks. The driver then picked the containers required, took them to the assigned despatch bay, attached the *move order* to the load and informed the computer that the job had been completed.

The advantages of such a system are numerous: paperwork is simplified, truck utilization is improved, the number of trucks is reduced, movement and order-packing times are minimized, operating costs are smaller, and control of the system is improved.

A program that incorporates a heuristic algorithm is probably the best for this sort of situation; it proceeds sequentially, assigning one load at a time to a particular route and testing it against truck availability. Routes involving 50 storage racks and despatch bays can be processed in about one minute with a PC in order to provide results that otherwise would have needed many months of experience!

PLANNING TRUNKING DELIVERIES

A wholesale groceries distributor in northern France supplied provisions to supermarkets from two depots, one at Reims and one at Lille. The objective for trunking deliveries was to supply bulk goods so that local deliveries could be made with vans.

Preparing the overall plan commenced with an analysis of the market demand in order to calculate the volume of goods to be handled. First, the number of vans required at depots had to be determined in order to plan the schedule for supplying the goods.

Number of vans

An examination of the demands showed that a minimum of 21 van journeys per week would be needed from the Reims depot and 29 from Lille. Each journey required a full van load of goods, and it would take a whole day to deliver it. A five-day week was worked at the depots.

The ideal number of vans needed for local deliveries was calculated by dividing the number of journeys per week by the five days per working week. This number would provide full time operation of the vans:

Reims depot: 21 journeys per week ÷ 5 = 4.2 vans per week.
Lille depot: 29 journeys per week ÷ 5 = 5.8 vans per week.

These numbers of vans were impractical and they had to be rounded up to five and six with corresponding reductions in the time utilization efficiencies.

Routing the vans

Improving the van time utilization was possible if the routes were rearranged and the allocation of retail outlets to depots was altered slightly. Reallocating 0.2 of a van load per week from Reims to Lille reduced the number of vans needed from eleven to ten – that is, four at Reims and six at Lille.

Trunking to depots

Local delivery costs were reduced by optimizing the number of vans needed, and trunking costs could be kept down by operating the smallest feasible number of container vehicles. Each container vehicle comprised a tractor unit and a trailer. Consequently, a tractor could operate independently of a number of different trailers.

Conditions for making trunking deliveries were summarized and incorporated in the distribution objectives:

Depot	Factors	Initial resources	Week one					Week two					Week three				
			M	T	W	Th	F	M	T	W	Th	F	M	T	W	Th	F
R E I M S	Trailers	(15)		(0)	(15)	(0)	(15)			(0)	(15)					(0)	(15)
	Deliveries	4 vans	4	8	12	16	20	24	28	32	36	40	44	48	52	56	60
	Stock	15	11	7	18	14	25	21	17	13	9	20	16	12	8	4	15
L I L L E	Trailers	(15)	(0)	(15)	(0)	(15)		(0)	(15)	(0)	(15)		(0)	(15)	(0)	(15)	
	Deliveries	6 vans	6	12	18	24	30	36	42	48	54	60	66	72	78	84	90
	Stock	15	9	18	12	21	15	9	18	12	21	15	9	18	12	21	15
Number of trailers needed			3	4	4	4	4	4	4	4	4	4	4	4	4	4	2
Loaded trailers in transit				1	1	1	1		1		1	1		1		1	

15 = Trailer arriving with a loaded container

0 = Trailer going to central warehouse with an empty container

Figure 7.5 Scheduling chart

1   One tractor unit is allocated to each of the depots.
2   The minimum number of trailers is independent of the two tractors.
3   One trailer only can be loaded at a time in the central warehouse.
4   Tractor drivers must be at their base depot for weekends.
5   One container can hold sufficient goods for fifteen van loads.
6   There are two depots with ten local delivery vans between them.
7   All deliveries must be made within a five-day working week.
8   One delivery van load is equivalent to one journey-day.
9   Local delivery vans set out early each morning.
10   Each van delivers standard loads each week to customers along fixed routes.

Scheduling bulk deliveries

The articulated container vehicles had to operate with a minimum number of trailers which would be determined by preparing a scheduling chart. One tractor unit was assigned to each depot and the information that was needed for scheduling them included the containers to be supplied in depots, vehicle movements, the daily deliveries of goods by vans and the stock in hand at each depot. The scheduling chart used is shown in Figure 7.5.

Each scheduling chart should cover one complete trunking supply cycle which could be found by relating the volume of goods supplied to the depots that delivered them locally:

Trunking supplies = local deliveries
Trunking supplies = container loads per week × container capacity (van loads)
Local deliveries = length of cycle (weeks) × weekly deliveries (van loads)

The relationship between supplies and deliveries could be expressed as a simple mathematical equation:

$$15T = WV$$

where:

15 = container capacity as van loads
T = number of trailers required
W = number of weeks for a complete cycle
V = volume of weekly deliveries as van loads.

In addition to the container capacity of 15 van loads, the volume of weekly deliveries at each depot was known in advance. The number of trailers required and the length of the trunking cycle could be found by converting the equation into a ratio:

$$Delivery\ ratio = \frac{T}{W} = \frac{van\ loads\ delivered\ per\ week}{15}$$

Inserting the number of van loads to be delivered from each depot allowed the ratio to show the number of containers that would be needed for the cycle duration.

Cycle duration

The number of van journeys at Reims was 20, with 30 at Lille, after adjusting the delivery areas for maximum time utilization:

At Reims: $\dfrac{T}{W} = \dfrac{20}{15} = \dfrac{4}{3}$, i.e. four container loads every 3 weeks

At Lille: $\dfrac{T}{W} = \dfrac{30}{15} = \dfrac{2}{1}$, i.e. two container loads every week

The length of the trunking cycle for both depots together would be three weeks, in which time four container loads would be supplied to the Reims depot and six to Lille. Before installing the cycle, one container load would be needed at each depot in order to provide initial stocks.

Scheduling chart

Three factors were scheduled on the chart for each depot, namely, the movement of trailers, the cumulated deliveries and the stock on hand at the end of each day. The final stock on hand should be the same as it was at the beginning of the cycle.

The scheduling chart was useful for controlling the deliveries, but a set of rules was necessary in order to keep the operations in line with the trunking conditions:

1 The number of van loads delivered is cumulated day by day throughout the full cycle.
2 The stock on hand is calculated by subtracting the number of van loads delivered each day and adding the number received in containers.
3 Whenever the stock level falls below the number of van loads needed for two days' work, the tractor has to take a trailer and an empty container to the central warehouse for a new supply of goods.
4 An empty container cannot be loaded at the warehouse if one is already loading there, and the schedule has to be advanced or retarded in order to correct this situation.
5 The stock on hand at a depot at the end of a cycle must be the same as the stock at the beginning.
6 The number of trailers needed each day is shown at the bottom of the chart, along with the number of trailer containers supplied to the depots.
7 The stock on hand at a depot cannot exceed one container load, because the containers are used as transit warehouses.

Solution: in order to comply with the trunking conditions for the system, the optimal number of vans was ten and the number of container trailers was four. These numbers were determined with the aid of a scheduling chart. There would be two trailers with containers and one tractor unit at each depot. In this way, goods could be supplied to the four vans at Reims and the six at Lille for making local deliveries.

The scheduling rules ensured that the resources needed were minimal and the time utilized was maximal.

LOCAL DELIVERIES PLANNING

The second type of delivering found in a distribution system is local deliveries from depots to customers. The quantities of goods required by customers are specific and orders differ from time to time; consequently, planning local deliveries must place greater emphasis on the service level than the cost of delivering. Keeping down costs is important, but customers' orders are the lifeblood of a distribution system.

Planning local deliveries follows siting the depots and planning the bulk deliveries to them. Then it is necessary to prepare plans for the local delivery resources, for the number and size of vehicles required, the delivery routes and the drops per vehicle journey.

Example of distributing cased goods

A British distribution company operated with five depots that were sited strategically around the country, but the resources in each region for making local deliveries to customers had to be planned economically and efficiently. The depot at Birmingham for distributing cased goods in the Midlands region of England was being reorganized. The cases varied in size and volume; therefore, deliveries had to be standardized by loading the cases onto pallets and installing mechanical handling equipment. Most orders were large, usually full pallet-loads, but some were small and local deliveries had to be planned so that all orders were delivered efficiently.

Objective

The distribution planning objective was to calculate the number of vehicles and their load carrying capacities that would be required for delivering cased goods locally from the Birmingham depot.

Developing strategies for deliveries

The number of vehicles would depend upon the number, the frequency and the size of the drops, because these factors would determine the routes, the number of journeys and the capacities of the vehicle. Initial strategies would be vague until more information had been collected. However, there were three basic alternatives:

1   To own and operate a fleet of vehicles.
2   To hire vehicles on contract.
3   To employ carriers to deliver the goods.

First, owning the vehicles was suitable when delivery areas were concentrated ensuring full employment; second, the vehicles could be hired if capital for purchasing them was not available; and third, carriers would be employed most economically in remote areas. The choice of strategy for making the deliveries would depend upon the information that was collected with respect to the driving times and distances involved, the drop sizes and frequencies and their different costs.

Planning deliveries

Information was collected in the form of delivery records, and it soon became obvious that there was a peak period for deliveries in November when retailers stocked up for Christmas. Vehicle requirements had to be based upon two types of deliveries, in the peak period and during the rest of the year.

Delivery areas

It was decided to divide the Birmingham distribution region into 12 areas using Post Office postcodes, as the majority of orders were received by mail. The customer drop points were grouped according to geographical delivery areas, and the orders were classified according to size and frequency; consequently, the number of deliveries required per drop per month could be calculated.

Delivery frequency

The frequency of deliveries to the different drop points affected the planning of routes and schedules which were based upon planning standard times. Calculations assumed that the average delay between order receipt and order delivery should be one day. The delivery frequency for different areas determined the type of vehicles that would be required, and the minimum delivery frequency to an area depended upon the maximum number of deliveries required by any one customer each month.

Delivery distances and time

The total distance driven along any journey route comprised the distance to and from the delivery area and the distance driven while delivering to customers.

The straight line distance in crow-miles to an area boundary and back was taken as being double the distance from the depot to the nearest point on its boundary. The driving speed varied according to road conditions and average speed, as follows:

(a)   Central urban roads (12 mph or 20 km/h).
(b)   Urban roads (16 mph or 25 km/h).
(c)   Country roads (26 mph or 40 km/h).
(d)   Motorways (45 mph or 70 km/h).

In order to convert distances into times when preparing the planning standards, estimated distances in crow-miles were expressed as minutes

Planning standard minutes =

$$\frac{road\ distance\ (crow\text{-}miles)\ \times\ 600\ mins\ (daily\ working\ time)}{average\ speed\ (mph)}$$

The average driving time between drop points inside a delivery area was calculated from the estimated mileage, the road conditions and the average speed. Empirically, the planning standard minutes (PSM) between drop points could be obtained with the following formula for the time:

Internal delivery time (PSM) = Average crow-miles per drop × average minutes per mile for the road conditions × number of drop points

$$= 1.2\ (\frac{delivery\ area,\ square\ miles}{number\ of\ drops})\ \times\ (\frac{60\ min}{average\ speed,\ mph})\ \times\ number\ of\ drops$$

Note that 1.2 is the factor needed to convert crow-miles into road miles.

Delivery routes

Some routes were restricted in length by the time available and others by the capacity of vehicles. The maximum time legally available per day including overtime was 600 minutes, and for half a day, a journey time limit of 270 minutes was assumed. A five-day week comprised 50 hours or 3 000 minutes, and it was recommended that the vehicles should start from the depot by 07.30 hours so that deliveries could be made during customers' working hours.

Unloading time

The time for off-loading the cases at stop points varied with the number of cases to be delivered, and they were classified into numerical groups so that standard times

Table 7.6   Standard off-loading times

Group	Unloading method	Order size (cases)	PSM (minutes)
1	By hand	0–12	4.2
2	By hand	12–24	6.2
3	By hand	25–50	11.2
4	By hand	51–300	25.0
5	Pallet loads	51–300	22.5
6	Pallet loads	over 300	36.0

Table 7.7   Vehicle capacities

Vehicle capacity	30-cwt	8-ton	12-ton	16-ton
Average no. of cases	80	260	400	1000

could be allocated according to the work study analysis (see Table 7.6). The total unloading time for all the orders to be delivered in an area at one time could be calculated in this way, or the average unloading time per order could be obtained by dividing the total time by the number of orders.

Vehicle capacities

The capacities of different vehicles were expressed in terms of cases, and they were used as planning standards. The types of vehicles were designated by their weight capacities, but converting capacities into volumes enabled them to be expressed in cases (see Table 7.7).

On several routes the maximum vehicle weight was restricted to 8 tons by bridge load limits, and the vehicle size was limited by the turning radius required at drop points. The maximum capacity of a delivery vehicle was 8 tons, and the number needed had to be determined for each area. Those considered are shown in Table 7.7.

Vehicles required

In order to illustrate the procedure for planning the number of vehicles required for local deliveries, three different adjoining areas will be considered. However, it is wrong to think of an area on its own in practice, because efficiency and economy can be improved by combining areas or routes. Only vehicles with a capacity of 8 tons or less were considered in this case.

Procedure for planning local delivery resources

In order to obtain an effective solution, the objective had to be defined clearly; then planning the strategies could proceed after collecting the basic information. The first

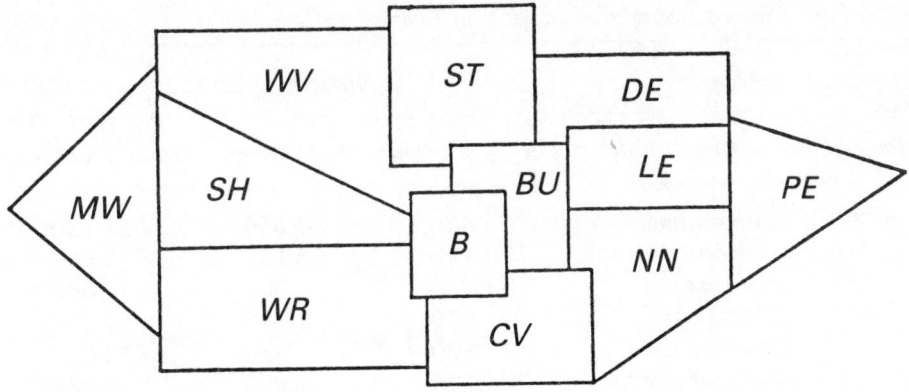

Figure 7.8   Post-coded delivery areas in the Midlands

step was to investigate the distribution system as a whole, and then to consider each depot in turn. This particular problem concerned the Birmingham regional depot only, which distributed cased goods to the Midlands; the region was divided into delivery areas according to the Post Office postcodes (see Figure 7.8).

Delivery areas

The Midlands region was divided into areas approximately 400 miles^2 in size, each based upon a postcode which was a convenient form of classification. Basically, there were 12 delivery areas with varying trade intensities, the greatest intensity being in the centre around the Birmingham depot site. The areas were designated by their Post Office postcodes, and are shown as a schematic map of the region in Figure 7.8.

Collecting information

In order to calculate the number and size of vehicles to be operated, it was necessary to collect information about the current deliveries in the regions, and also about expected trends. Sources of information were vehicle and customer records and sales forecasts. The number of cases delivered throughout the year varied little, except for a peak in the month of November. Distribution volumes were fairly constant during the off-peak months, but the volume nearly trebled in the peak period. The annual volume of cases for delivery could be estimated mathematically:

Annual volume (cases) = (peak month (cases)) + (11 × off-peak month (cases))

If the cases ratio for peak month/off-peak month was P and the number of cases delivered in an off-peak month was Q, an estimate of the annual volume would be $11Q + PQ$ cases, that is an annual volume equal to $Q(11 + P)$ cases.

The expected numbers of cases to be delivered in the 12 Midlands areas were tabulated, and they are shown for the off-peak and peak months of 1990 in Table 7.9.

Table 7.9   Cases delivered to the region in 1990

Area		Number of cases		
Postcode	Main town	Off-peak month	Peak month	Annual volume
B	Birmingham	1 480	4 950	21 230
BU	Burton-on-Trent	1 120	3 180	15 500
CV	Coventry	1 240	4 200	17 840
WR	Worcester	870	1 840	11 410
SH	Shrewsbury	830	1 650	10 560
WV	Wolverhampton	1 220	3 690	17 110
MW	Welshpool	200	740	2 940
ST	Stafford	1 050	2 210	13 760
DE	Derby	1 190	2 400	15 490
LE	Leicester	1 070	2 350	14 120
NN	Northampton	1 280	2 560	16 640
PE	Peterborough	930	2 020	12 250
	Whole region	12 480	31 790	168 850

The equation for estimating the annual volume in cases delivered was tested with these figures:

$$P = (\frac{peak\ month\ cases}{off\text{-}peak\ month\ cases})$$
$$= \frac{31,790}{12,480}$$
$$= 2.55$$

The actual volume delivered in January was 12 310 cases; therefore, the annual volume could be estimated:

$$\text{Estimated annual volume} = Q(11 + P)\text{ cases}$$
$$= 12,310 \times 13.55$$
$$= 166,700 \text{ cases}$$

An error of less than 2% was achieved by this estimate when comparing it with the actual volume for the previous year.

The sales forecasts for the delivery areas in the coming year were used in connection with the planning standards for calculating future vehicle requirements; the estimates are shown in Table 7.10.

Planning standards

When calculating the number and sizes of vehicles in each delivery area, planning standards were used. In this way, standardization helped to simplify the work

Table 7.10 *Estimated cases for delivery in 1991*

Area	Number of cases		
Postcode	Off-peak month	Peak month	Annual volume
B	1 520	5 030	21 750
BU	1 130	3 220	15 650
CV	1 250	4 270	18 020
WR	870	1 860	11 430
SH	830	1 680	10 810
WV	1 240	3 720	17 360
MW	210	750	3 060
ST	1 070	2 250	14 020
DE	1 210	2 460	15 770
LE	1 100	2 390	14 490
NN	1 320	2 610	17 130
PE	950	2 080	12 530
Region	12 700	32 320	172 020

involved. The planning standards had been tested in practice and were acceptable. They were expressed as elements of vehicle operations according to the elapsed time expressed in minutes. The planning standards for vehicle operations when delivering cased goods are shown in Table 7.11.

A preliminary examination of the road conditions in the region showed that it was impossible to operate standard vehicles in excess of 8-tons capacity due to road restrictions. Since vehicles had to be covered in order to protect the cased goods, vans were selected and the alternative capacities considered were 30-cwt, 5-tons and 8-tons.

The accuracy of time estimates based upon planning standards would be affected by the variations that occurred when unloading the vehicles; therefore, mean times were used for calculating the delivery standard times.

Location of customers in the delivery areas were defined by sticking coloured pins into a map of the region according to the locations of drop points.

Methods of planning deliveries for different customers will be shown with reference to one delivery area only. However, all deliveries can be calculated in the same way and the total vehicle requirements used to optimize the system. The area chosen for illustrating the calculations is coded SH, and has Shrewsbury as its main town (see Figure 7.12).

Customer order sizes varied only slightly from month to month in the off-peak period, and it was decided to cater for the maximum off-peak monthly requirement. The estimated monthly requirement for next year is represented for the eight customer locations in the SH area in Table 7.13.

Customer order frequencies depended upon storage facilities at the drop points. The maximum order frequency in the off-peak period was twice a month and, in the

Table 7.11 Delivery planning standards

Planning standard	Minutes		
1 Variable unloading time	Varies from 4 to 36 min according to the number of cases dropped Mean drop time = 10 min		
2 Variable journey time	In towns: 6.0 min per crow-mile Urban roads: 4.5 min per crow-mile Rural roads: 2.75 min per crow-mile Motorways: 1.6 min per crow-mile		

Vehicle capacity	30-cwt	5-tons	8-tons
3 Variable loading time	15 min	10 min	15 min
4 Constant unloading time	4 min	5 min	5 min
5 Constant journey time:			
(i) Pre-delivery check	10 min	12 min	12 min
(ii) In-transit allowance	5%	5%	5%
(iii) Post-delivery check	15 min	15 min	15 min
6 Load capacity (cases)	80	260	400

peak period, four times per month. These were used as the minimum delivery frequencies for this area.

Load capacities of vehicles were determined in terms of the average number of cases for each of the vehicle sizes. Considering the monthly customer requirements and the case capacity of the largest vehicle (8 tons), there had to be slightly more than two trips in an off-peak month and four in the peak month. This complied with the order frequencies, and it was used as a basis for the vehicle journey calculations.

Vehicle journey calculations

The number of journeys depended upon the number of vehicles required, the customer order sizes and frequencies, the vehicle capacities and the delivery routes.

The Midlands region was about 10 000 square miles in area, and it was sub-divided into 12 areas according to their postcodes. Customers' orders were grouped into the areas according to:

1 Drop point location.
2 Number of cases ordered.
. 3 Delivery frequency.
4 Average size of drops delivered (cases).
5 Total number of cases delivered each month.

Elements of vehicle operations were expressed as times which were used as planning

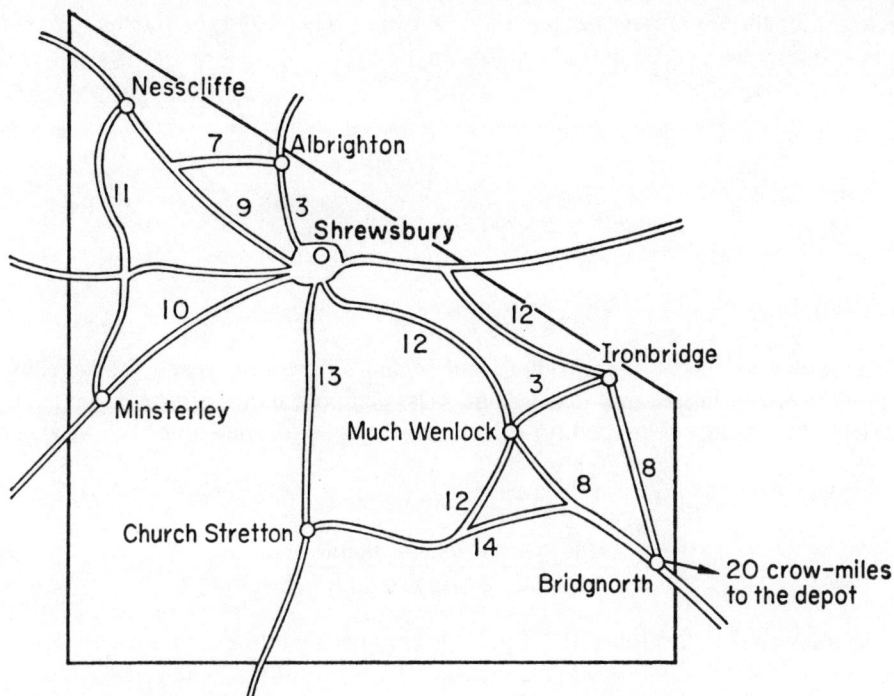

○ Customer location Distances in road miles

Figure 7.12 Delivery area SH

Table 7.13 Estimated monthly requirements

Customer location	Order size (as cases per month)	
	Off-peak	Peak
Bridgnorth	160	300
Ironbridge	80	150
Much Wenlock	50	100
Church Stretton	80	160
Shrewsbury	220	450
Albrighton	100	210
Nesscliffe	60	120
Minsterley	80	190
Delivery area total	830	1680

standards. The largest size of vehicle had an average capacity of 400 cases. The average number of journeys per month in each area depended upon the number and sizes of orders divided by the vehicle capacity:

$$Off\text{-}peak\ monthly\ journey\ frequency\ =\ \frac{830}{400}\ =\ 2.1$$

$$Peak\ monthly\ journey\ frequency\ =\ \frac{1680}{400}\ =\ 4.2$$

Journey times

Each journey comprised the travelling time to and from the delivery area, travelling within the area, plus the non-driving time. The planning standards are presented in Table 7.11, and they were used for calculating the total journey time:

1 Driving time to and from the area =

$$\frac{2(60\ \times\ crow\text{-}miles)\ minutes}{average\ miles\ per\ hour}$$

2 Journey constants applied to all the delivery areas, and they comprised:

    (a)   Time at depot for loading a vehicle
    (b)   Time for performing pre-delivery checks
    (c)   In-transit time allowances
    (d)   Time for performing post-delivery checks

3 Driving time within an area depended upon the average road speed, the number of drop points and the distances between them.
    A simple equation was developed for the planning standard total time within an area after measuring its area in crow-miles:

$$PSM\ =\ number\ of\ drops\ \times\ 1.2\ \sqrt{\frac{area}{number\ of\ drops}}\ \times\ average\ speed$$
$$=\ 1.2\ \sqrt{number\ of\ drops\ \times\ area}\ \times\ average\ speed\ (minutes\ per\ crow\ mile)$$

4 Unloading times at drop points varied with the number of cases off-loaded, but it was found that a mean time of 10 minutes per drop was acceptable overall.
5 The maximum time that was available for each daily journey was obtained by deduction:

    Total working time per day = 600 min.
    Minus driving time to and from the area.
    Minus journey constants.
    Minus internal driving time.
    Minus unloading times.

When planning the delivery schedule, the variable times to be considered were the internal driving and unloading times. A composite equation was evolved for calculating these times:

Time available = 600 minutes − time to and from area − constant times
              = internal driving time + unloading time + (15 × no. of drops)
              = 1.2 $\sqrt{\textit{number of drops} \times \textit{area} \times \textit{speed}}$

Therefore, the feasible number of drops per day (N) was given by the following equation:

$$N = \left(\frac{M}{12R\sqrt{A}}\right)^{2/3}$$

where N = number of drops per day, M = time available in minutes,

R = average road speed in minutes per crow-mile, and A = area in square crow-miles.

The number of journeys per month in the area could be obtained by dividing the number of drop points by the monthly journey frequency (F):

$$\textit{Journeys per month (J)} = \sum \textit{drop points} \times \frac{F}{N}$$

The capacity of a vehicle was decided by dividing the monthly total number of cases by journeys per month (J):

$$\textit{Vehicle capacity per journey} = \frac{\Sigma \ \textit{cases per month}}{J}$$

Summary of vehicle journey calculations

1   Determine the load capacities of vehicles.
2   Determine the planning standard times.
3   Calculate the period journey frequency.
4   Calculate the journey times.
5   Determine the number of drops per day.
6   Determine the number of journeys required.
7   Decide the vehicle capacities.

Applying the vehicle journey calculations to the problem

1   *Vehicle load capacities*
    30-cwt van = 80 cases
    5-ton van = 260 cases
    8-ton van = 400 cases

2   *Planning standard times for 8-ton van*

Variable loading time	15 mins per journey
Constant unloading time	5 mins per drop
Average unloading time	10 mins per drop
Average road speed	3.5 mins per crow-mile for mixed urban and country roads

Constant journey times per day:

Pre-delivery checks	12 mins
In-transit allowance	30 mins
Post-delivery checks	15 mins

3   *Monthly journey frequencies*

Off-peak	2.1 journeys
Peak	4.2 journeys

4   *Journey times*

Driving to and from the area

$$= \frac{2(60 \text{ min} \times 20 \text{ } crow\text{-}miles)}{21 \text{ } miles/hr}$$

	$= 115$ mins
Constant journey times	$= 12 + 30 + 15 = 57$ mins
Loading time (8-ton van)	$= 15$ mins
Time available for deliveries	$= 600 - 15 - 57 - 15$
	$= 413$ mins
Time required for deliveries	= internal driving time + unloading time
Number of drop points	$= 8$
Internal driving time	$= 1.2 \sqrt{number \ of \ drops \times area \times speed}$
	$= 1.2 \times \sqrt{8 \times 400} \times 3.5$
	$= 238$ mins
Unloading time	= number of drops $\times$ 15 mins $= 8 \times 15$
	$= 120$ mins
Total time required for deliveries	
	$= 238 + 120$ mins
	$= 358$ mins
Time available for deliveries	$= 413$ mins
Surplus time per day	$= 55$ mins

Vehicle requirements

The actual journey time utilized by one 8-ton van was $600 - 55 = 545$ minutes for the eight drop points; therefore, one day would be required for delivering to all customers in the SH area. The time frequency for daily journeys to the area could be expressed as 1.0, and it was calculated that the load frequency for an off-peak month was 2.1 for one 8-ton vehicle. Therefore, the combined journey frequencies were $1.0 \times 2.1 = 2.1$ journey days with an 8-ton load.

 · Journey frequencies for 8-ton vans were converted into whole numbers by considering smaller vans with a fractional capacity of an 8-ton van for the surplus amounts. That is:

8-ton van = 1.00 journey load
5-ton van = 0.65 journey load
30-cwt van = 0.20 journey load

It followed that the requirement for area SH in an off-peak month was 2.1 ×
8-ton van days or two 8-ton van days and one 30-cwt van day.
Equation for estimating 8-ton van days required

Monthly 8-ton van days = journey frequency × 8-ton van load frequency

where: one 5-ton van day = 0.65 × 8-ton van day
one 30-cwt van day = 0.2 × 8-ton van day
one 30-cwt van day = 0.325 × 5-ton van day

Examination of the delivery area SH showed that there would be half a day's
work in an off-peak month for the 30-cwt van if it only delivered goods to the Much
Wenlock customer. As a result, the planning times were corrected for this revision,
and they are given in Table 7.14 below.

Table 7.14   Local delivery vehicles is area SH

Vehicle requirement	Number of drop points	Corrected journey time	Utilization		Journeys per month	
			% time	% load	Off-peak	Peak
One 8-ton van	7	515 min	86	97	2	4
One 30-cwt van	1	286 min	100	63	½	1

Vehicle requirements for the areas

When considering the SH, WV and MW areas together, the theoretical number of
journeys could be reduced by combining journeys in practice. In an off-peak month
five van days were required anyway, but the additional deliveries could be made in
one day by a single 5-ton van without any 30-cwt vans at all. Ten extra 8-ton van
days would be necessary in the peak month, when delivering to the three areas
together. This is summarized in Table 7.15.

Journey days for the whole region

The total number of journey days required for delivering to the whole of the
Midlands region would be reduced by combining small van journeys into larger
ones. The actual number of journey days required for each area are shown in Tables
7.16 and 7.17; calculations were based upon estimated distances and corrected
journey times:

Number of 8-ton van days = journey time frequency × load frequency.

Table 7.15   Vehicle requirements for the three areas

| Area | Main town | Off-peak month | | | | Peak month | | | | Ratio of off-peak to peak |
| | | Total cases | Journey days | | | Total cases | Journey days | | | |
			30-cwt	5-ton	8-ton		30-cwt	5-ton	8-ton	
SH	Shrewsbury	830	1	–	2	1680	1	–	4	½
WV	Wolverhampton	1240	1	–	3	3720	–	1	9	⅓
MW	Welshpool	210	–	1	–	750	–	–	2	⅓
All areas theoretical		2280	2	1	5	6150	1	1	15	⅔
All areas practical		2280	–	1	5	6150	–	1	15	⅔

Table 7.16   Journeys to the Midlands region, off-peak month

Area	Number of drop points	Journey times			Off-peak month					
		In area (min)	Journey frequency	Number of cases	8-ton loads		Time required			
					Drop frequency	Journey days	Number of van days			
							30-cwt	5-ton	8-ton	
B	24	910	1.6	1 520	3.8	6.1	1	–	6
BU	15	765	1.3	1 130	2.8	3.7	1	1	3
CV	20	885	1.5	1 250	3.1	4.7	1	1	4
WR	9	570	1.0	870	2.2	2.2	1	–	2
SH	8	545	1.0	830	2.1	2.1	1	–	2
WV	17	780	1.3	1 240	3.1	4.1	1	–	4
MW	6	480	0.8	210	0.5	0.4	2	–	–
ST	10	760	1.3	1 070	2.7	3.5	3	–	3
DE	11	745	1.3	1 210	3.0	3.9	2	1	3
LE	11	725	1.2	1 100	2.7	3.3	2	–	3
NN	13	805	1.4	1 320	3.3	4.6	–	1	4
PE	9	790	1.3	950	2.4	3.2	1	–	3
All	153	8 760	15.0	12 700	31.7	41.8	16	4	37

Monthly journey days by area

The journey days required for the whole region was the summation of the requirements for each area. The number of 8-ton vans required in the peak month was nearly three times as many as the number required for an off-peak month, but some of the smaller vans were redundant and they should be overhauled as necessary.

Table 7.17   Journeys to the Midlands region, peak month

				Peak month			
		8-ton loads			Time required		
	Number of drop points	Number of cases	Drop frequency	Journey days	Number of van days		
Area					30-cwt	5-ton	8-ton
B	24	5 030	12.5	20.0	–	–	20
BU	15	3 220	8.0	10.4	2	–	10
CV	20	4 270	10.7	16.0	–	–	16
WR	9	1 860	4.6	4.6	–	1	4
SH	8	1 680	4.2	4.2	1	–	4
WV	17	3 720	9.3	12.1	1	–	12
MW	6	750	1.8	1.4	2	–	1
ST	10	2 250	5.6	7.3	2	–	7
DE	11	2 460	6.1	8.0	–	–	8
LE	11	2 390	6.0	7.2	1	–	7
NN	13	2 610	6.5	9.1	1	–	9
PE	9	2 080	5.2	6.8	1	1	6
All	153	32 320	80.5	117.1	11	2	104

Vehicle requirements

The number of vehicles that was required for operating the regional distribution system was found by considering the number of journey days for each vehicle size divided by the number of working days in a month. A 22-day cycle was a condition for each month when the vehicle requirements were calculated; the journey days were obtained from Table 7.16.

Off-peak month requirements of vehicles

$$\text{For 30-cwt vans } \frac{Journey\ days}{Cycle\ days} = \frac{16}{22} = 0.73$$

$$\text{For 5-ton vans } \frac{Journey\ days}{Cycle\ days} = \frac{4}{22} = 0.18$$

$$\text{For 8-ton vans } \frac{Journey\ days}{Cycle\ days} = \frac{37}{22} = 1.70$$

Total vehicle requirements are shown in Table 7.18. The numbers had to be rounded up and combined so that the requirements were:

Off-peak period = one 30-cwt van and two 8-ton vans
Peak period = one 30-cwt van and five 8-ton vans

Table 7.18   Monthly vehicle requirements

Month	Vehicle requirements			Total capacity (8-ton loads)
	30-cwt	5-ton	8-ton	
Off-peak	0.73	0.18	1.70	1 963
Peak	0.50	0.09	4.75	4 909

It was decided to operate a basic vehicle fleet of one 30-cwt van and two 8-ton vans throughout the year, and to supplement them during November by hiring three 8-ton vans.

HANDLING HAZARDOUS MATERIALS

When hazardous materials are handled or moved, they must receive extra attention in order to prevent injuries to personnel and damage to property. It is always obligatory to abide by the transportation regulations described below for delivering hazardous materials, and the documents that accompany them must indicate the nature of the materials and precautions that have to be taken. Everybody must note these warnings when handling dangerous materials and see that the information is correctly displayed on all packages, containers and loads.

Warehouse hazards

Fires are a constant threat at warehouses and *no-smoking* is often a condition for employment in a warehouse. Most packing materials are highly inflammable and, once ignited, they can be very difficult to extinguish. High-rise warehouses are most vulnerable to fires, because the vertical spaces between stocks serve as chimneys to draw air through the stored materials. Remember that oxygen is essential for combustion! Cereal grain dust is also hazardous, both when breathed by operators and when ignited.

Warehouse cleanliness

Warehouse cleanliness should be a continuous concern for the manager, not only for fire hazards, but for health and sanitation reasons too. This is particularly important where organic materials are stored because they deteriorate quickly and attract pests (see the cartoon of Figure 6.2). The food and drugs authorities in most countries are concerned with sanitation; also, legislation supports the authorities to prosecute companies; for example, the president of a large US food chain was personally convicted in 1975 for the unsanitary condition of one of the company's warehouses. Similarly, an environmental protection group in Sweden brought a successful suit against a chemical concern that allowed toxic gases to escape into the atmosphere.

Transporting hazardous materials

Due to the ever-increasing public awareness of hazards to both themselves and the environment, the movement of dangerous substances has become a subject in its own right. Increased legislation has necessitated special training for the handling and transporting of hazardous goods. The subject is worthy of a book rather than a slim section of this chapter, and distributors in this field must study activities much more deeply.

The aim here is to give an overview of the problems, and to provide sufficient detail for managers to understand what steps need to be taken before tackling the handling of hazardous materials. It is often the case that a manufacturer, importer or distributor does not believe that the goods they are handling are dangerous. Sadly, because of this attitude or lack of appreciation of the hazards, many have ended up in court facing anything from a minor offence against the Road Traffic Act to manslaughter. Far more goods are classified as hazardous than is popularly believed, so the golden rule is to check out the items that you plan to handle.

Regulations governing the carriage of dangerous goods began as national laws which varied considerably from one country to the next. Shortly after the First World War, the League of Nations tried to weave a common thread through all these laws and introduce an international code of practice, or standards. As can be expected, there was considerable opposition to change from certain nations, and the bureaucratic process was extremely slow. It was not until the 1950s, after the formation of the United Nations, that things began to take shape. The result being the *Orange Book* which classifies dangerous goods into Hazard Divisions, like HD1 – Explosive Substances. It also included a list of materials and substances by common names and chemical names, allocated them to the hazard divisions, and ensured that national regulations were modified to include these divisions. However, the *Orange Book* does not stipulate laws for carrying those goods, only saying which ones must not be put together or handled at the same time.

The most important element of the *Orange Book* is that it allocates a serial number to each hazardous substance; these numbers are known universally as the UN numbers. Coupled with this element is the legal requirement of every producer to notify the UN of new substances and modifications to the existing ones that are dangerous.

A UN number has four digits that have no relationship to divisions or classes, although like substances are often grouped together with successive numbers, such as Bromomethylpropane 2342, Bromopentane 2343.

Hazardous materials

Bromopentane 2343, Bromopropane 2344, Bromopropyne 2345. The UN number is repeated in most sets of regulations and has to be displayed on *Tremcards* and vehicle placards so that distribution managers and vehicle operators soon memorize those that they commonly handle.

The natural progression from this point was to introduce detailed rules at an international level. The step was led by the International Maritime Organization with its IMDG (International Maritime Dangerous Goods) code, which has since become the general standard for the whole transportation industry. IMDG only weighs in at a slender five volumes, but it is by far the most comprehensive hazardous goods manual. The air transport industry followed through the recommendations of its two professional associations, the International Air Traffic Association (IATA) and the International Civil Aviation Organization (ICAO), both of whom developed their own regulations based around the IMDG code, but each produced in a single, closely typed volume. Needless to say, these two sets of rules are not compatible with one another, and it is necessary to know the code favoured by the airline that you plan to use. IATA was the leading authority until the mid-1970s, but the stricter ICAO regulations have gradually overtaken them, particularly in Europe.

The railways have always played a leading role in safety developments, thanks in Britain to the independent Railway Inspectorate. Every accident since the late 19th century has been investigated, and rules written to prevent a re-occurrence; this also applies to the carriage of dangerous goods. The British rule, which has gradually extended to the rest of Europe and most of the World, is included in the international regulations for the carriage of dangerous goods by rail (RID). The rule closely follows the UN *Orange Book* and the IMDG code, but is included in a single volume. Road safety was the last on the scene, although the European Agreement concerning the international carriage of Dangerous Goods by road (ADR) has been in force for several decades. The main problem with ADR is that it only applies to international cargo, and every country still enforces its own rules for internal traffic, causing confusion to road hauliers.

In Britain between 1985 and 1990, a series of new regulations has governed vehicle construction for carrying dangerous goods, as well as packaging, labelling and segregation of goods. The one saving grace with all these rules is that providing the cargo goes through a port, or on a seagoing or inland waterway vessel, the IMDG code takes precedence over all the other rules. Of course, this is dependent upon the load integrity being maintained and the packaging remaining intact according to the regulations.

Designating hazardous materials

As stated earlier, the UN designated nine hazardous divisions which have been accepted in all the other regulations, as have the symbols that go with them. Each of these divisions has sub-divisions which permit the segregation of non-compatible substances within a generic group.

Division 1

This contains potentially the most dangerous materials, and covers most explosive substances and mixtures ranging from Semtex to custard powder. It is by far the most complex, with compatibility groups within each sub-division; fortunately, a chart exists which allows users to see a simple relationship between all the groups and sub-divisions. The sub-divisions or classes indicate the level of hazard:

(1.1)   substances with a mass explosion hazard (Semtex);
(1.2)   substances with a projection hazard (bullets);

(1.3)   substances with a fire hazard and minor blast or projection hazard (photo flash bulbs);

(1.4)   substances which are explosive but present no significant hazard due largely to their size (primers and detonators);

(1.5)   substances which have a mass explosion hazard but are very unlikely to explode (custard powder).

These numbers have to be displayed on the standard orange exploding bomb label, as are the 11 compatibility groups, making a total of 55 labels of each size for this class alone.

The compatibility groups are exactly that, and specify the substances that may be transported together. It should be remembered that Class 1 cannot be transported with any other dangerous goods except in a few special circumstances.

Definitions of compatibility groups

Group A: Primary explosives.

Group B: Ammunition containing primary explosives and not containing two or more independent safety features.

Group C: Propellant explosives or other deflagrating explosives or ammunition containing such explosives.

Group D: Secondary detonating explosives or black powder or ammunition containing secondary detonating explosives; in each case, without its own means of initiation and without a propulsive charge. This also includes ammunition containing primary explosives and containing two or more independent safety features.

Group E: Ammunition containing secondary detonating explosives, without its own means of initiation, with a propulsive charge (other than one containing a flammable or hypergolic liquid).

Group F: Ammunition containing secondary detonating explosives, with its own means of initiation, with a propulsive charge (other than one containing a flammable or hypergolic liquid) or without a propulsive charge.

Group G: Ammunition containing a pyrotechnic substance, or containing an explosive with illuminating, incendiary, lachrymatory or smoke producing substance (other than a water activated device or one containing white phosphorus, phosphide, or a flammable liquid or gel).

Group J: Ammunition containing both an explosive and a flammable liquid or gel.

Group K: Ammunition containing both an explosive and a toxic chemical agent.

Group L: Explosives or ammunition presenting a special risk needing isolation of each type.

Group N: Articles which contain only extremely insensitive detonating substances and which demonstrate a negligible probability of accidental initiation or propagation.

Group S: Explosives or ammunition so packed or designed that any hazardous effect arising from accidental functioning is confined within the package, unless that package has been degraded by fire, in which case, all

blast or projection are limited to the extent that they do not significantly hinder or prohibit fire-fighting or other emergency response
efforts in the immediate vicinity of the package.

Division 2

Contains all gases to be transported in a compressed liquefied, dissolved or refriger-
ated state. Technically, this means any gas with a critical temperature of less than
50° Celsius, or which exerts a pressure of 3 bar at that temperature. The complica-
tion with this class is that the substances almost always have a secondary hazard,
such as being toxic.

Though potentially safe to transport this class of materials, it has been responsible
for some horrific accidents. Most notably, these have been in the United States,
where very large containers of butane and propane are moved by road and rail. The
resulting fires have caused the boiling liquid to expand and its vapours to explode or
BLEVEL, which can result in a 12 ton tank car being thrown through the air for up
to one mile. This effect can be easily demonstrated by placing an aerosol can of
butane in a fire, which is a sobering reminder to drivers who are involved with
transporting gas bottles.

Class 2 officially has no sub-divisions, but because three different labels are
associated with it, people commonly refer to:

(2.1)   Non-flammable compressed gases (green label).
(2.2)   Flammable gases (red label).
(2.3)   Poisonous gases (white label).

Due to these different labels, it is common for drivers, warehousemen and supervisors to misread the hazard. Labels for (2.1) are unique, but (2.2) is the same as for
Division 3, and Class (2.3) is almost identical to Class (6.1). Therefore, training in
identification is vital because the pressure in a gas bottle alone is a very real hazard
without the additional risk of fire or poison.

Division 3

Contains flammable liquids, including most paints and varnishes, but excluding
liquids covered under Division 2. The biggest problem here is that many substances,
like gasoline, are moved in bulk tankers which have their own regulations.

The description *flammable liquids* is misleading, because it is the vapour immediately above the liquid that burns to cause a growth fire, as the hotter the liquid
becomes the greater the vapour produced. Since the vapour is heavier than air, it
sinks and spreads outwards so that ignition can occur again, but at a distance from
the main fire.

Division 4

These are flammable solids, and they are divided into three sub-divisions, each with
a different hazard label:

(4.1)   Flammable solids (fire-lighters).

(4.2)   Substances liable to spontaneous combustion (white phosphorus).

(4.3)   Substances which are dangerous when wet or in contact with water (potassium and sodium).

(*Note*: dropping a 5 mm cube of sodium metal into a bowl of water produces a vigorous reaction culminating in a sudden loud explosion. Class (4.3) is rarely moved by sea and the regulations are particularly stringent compared with moving it by other means.)

Division 5

Includes the oxidizing agents, and it has a separate sub-division for Organic Peroxides (5.2). These substances are not particularly hazardous in themselves, though some are caustic or corrosive. The main problem is one of compatibility with the inflammable classes. It is particularly difficult to put out a fire if the source of oxygen is inside the flame area itself; even so, it continues to amaze us how many transport agencies can carry correctly packed and labelled substances under Divisions 3, 4 and 5 on the same pallets! Surprisingly, the airlines are the worst offenders in our experience.

Division 6

Contains toxic and poisonous materials, including a particularly complicated series of sub-divisions:

(6.1)   Group I: highly poisonous substances (cyanides) which are lethal.
         Group II: poisonous substances (pesticides).
         Group III: other harmful toxins.

(6.2)   Infectious substances including bacteria and biological material that may be harmful.

Division 7

Includes all radioactive materials that are not covered in these regulations; since only specially trained and qualified people can handle them, the amounts of these materials that can be transported are tightly controlled.

Division 8

Contains all corrosive materials which can cause severe damage when in contact with living tissue, or can damage or destroy other goods when they leak. The airlines dislike carrying goods in this category, and the International Air Traffic Association (ITA) and International Civil Aviation Organization (ICAO) regulations are very strict for Division 8 substances.

Division 9

This is the *catch 22* category, which covers anything that may pose a hazard but is not covered in the other divisions. The commonest material being asbestos – white, brown and blue.

TRANSPORTATION BY SEA OF HAZARDOUS MATERIALS

The 1929 conference on Safety of Life at Sea (SOLAS) recognized the need for regulating the carriage of dangerous goods at sea. However, the IMDG code did not come into being until 1960 in draft form, and until 1965 in full publication. Major revisions took place in 1972, 1977, 1981 and 1989, with continuous updates and consolidations in the intervening years.

Transporting hazardous materials

As mentioned earlier, the IMDG code is the leading set of regulations covering the carriage of dangerous goods; this fact is recognized by all other international safety organizations. Provided that a journey includes an international sea movement, then the whole journey is covered by IMDG codes with regard to the preparation, packaging and labelling of the goods. This is the only time when one set of regulations covers the whole shipment of a multimodal movement of hazardous material. It is for this reason that pressure is being applied on the Eurotunnel Consortium to announce their dangerous goods policy in advance of opening the Channel Tunnel. If trains in the tunnel operate under the railway regulations (RID), then road-hauled hazardous materials will have to comply with ADR and RID before starting a journey. The trucks using ferries only have to comply with the IMDG code and ADR, but the goods themselves need only be prepared in accordance with IMDG codes.

Hazardous loads

As a *rule of thumb*, if in doubt, prepare your hazardous goods in accordance with the IMDG code irrespective of the transport mode. The four volumes of dangerous substances cover a far more comprehensive list than any other set of regulations, and are easier to read. However, it is essential that the latest set of regulations are used, currently, inclusive of Amendment 25 that became effective in 1991 replacing all others, and it is in effect a completely new set of volumes. *Volume 1* contains the general articles of the code, indexes and definitions; *Volume 2* contains the first two divisions; *Volume 3* has Divisions 3, 4 and 5; *Volume 4* has Divisions 6 to 9; and *Volume 5* is a supplement containing emergency procedures, first aid and associated safety instructions.

TRANSPORTATION BY ROAD OF HAZARDOUS MATERIALS

In Britain, there is a complicated system of regulations, each under a separate cover, for controlling the movement of hazardous materials. For international journeys,

ADR covers Europe, and it was revised in 1990 to incorporate the carriage of explosives in Division 1 and radioactive materials in Division 7, which had had their own regulations previously.

The responsibilities are the same, regardless of which regulations are in force:

CONSIGNOR:
1 Label and package the goods correctly.
2 Provide *Tremcards* and other information about the goods.
3 Inform the haulier of any dangers.
4 Ensure that the loading, unloading and stowage of goods is safe.

OPERATOR
1 Ensure that vehicles are suitable to carry the goods, have the right safety equipment, labels and signs, and that they are clean.
2 Ensure that the drivers are properly trained.
3 Instruct the driver as to the hazards of the load being transported, including the provision of written information.
4 Ensure that loading, unloading and stowage of such goods is done safely.
5 Inform the *Enforcing Authority* of any fire or accident that could result from the release of the goods handled.

DRIVER:
1 Ensure that the vehicle and safety equipment are in good order.
2 Ensure that the written information, *Tremcards*, are available in the vehicle throughout the journey. These cards must only refer to the goods being carried at the time.
3 Ensure that the correct vehicle signs are being displayed for the load on board.
4 Ensure that all precautions are taken to prevent fire or explosion.
5 Ensure that the vehicle, cab and load are kept secure at all times.
6 Observe the regulations concerning the parking of the vehicle and its supervision.
7 Inform the Operator of any incident involving the load.

All three – consignors, operators and drivers – can be brought to court for offences; though in practice, only the drivers and operators are charged, because neither should have accepted dangerous loads that were faulty from the consignors. To date, no-one has been sent to prison, but fines of £1 000 in Britain and DM2000 in Germany are not uncommon for operators, and half these amounts for the drivers. However, if another explosion or chemical spillage causes fatal injuries, the penalties are likely to be increased. Two offences will probably cost the operator his licence, and the business may have to close down.

As general advice, a distribution operator should get some experience in allied areas before transporting hazardous materials. The driver should be professionally trained – the British Road Haulage Association runs training courses, as does Chemfreight Ltd of Runcorn, privately.

ADR regulations will be in force throughout Europe after 1992 for hazardous materials, except radioactive ones. Full details can be found in the ADR Manual, although it is not the easiest book to read! Therefore, the following summary should be a useful guideline:

1 *Identify* the goods to be carried – look up Appendix A in the division section, or check Appendix B5 and the supplementary list beforehand.
   The supplementary list also states whether the substance is covered by ADR or is prohibited for movement. In many cases, it also states those materials which are exempt under the regulations.
2 *Check* the packaging sizes and volume, and then look up the marginal numbers referred to in the Annex. The relevant numbers for packaging have an 'a' suffix. Different rules apply – depending on the packaging type and size, i.e. smaller quantities can be moved in breakable glass bottles than in boxed polythene drums.
3 *If in doubt*, follow the brief rules for packaging, labelling and documentation in Annex A, Appendix A.5 and in Appendix 9.
4 *Appendix B* deals with gross weights for whole consignments, and states whether the vehicle is exempted from any of the restrictions imposed in *Part 1*.
5 *Annex B* also deals with the carriage of dangerous packages on vehicles when they vary for different classes of hazard. *Part 2* is the primary area to read.
6 The movement of bulk fluids, liquids and powders in road tankers is covered in Appendix B1 for the materials and Part 1 for the vehicles: also, consult Annex B Part 2 for class restrictions.

British regulations

In the UK, the regulations are similar to those given above, but are made more complex by the following additions:

- CPL is the Classification, Packaging and Labelling of dangerous substances Regulations 1984 which covers all modes of transport, but is backed up by an Approved Code of Practice for packaging dangerous substances for conveyance by road (1987).
- PGR is the Road Traffic (carriage of dangerous substances in packages, etc.) Regulations 1986. There are a trio of back-up publications for making these regulations more easily understood:

  (1) *Authorized and Approval List* which is a modified version of CPL for packing and transporting specific substances.
  (2) *Approved Code of Practice* which has a legal standing in its own right.
  (3) *A Guide to the Regulations* which contains a simplified version of the original regulations, and is essential reading for all distributors in Britain. It costs £3 from the Government Stationery Office in London.

- RTC is the Dangerous Substances (Conveyance by road in tankers and containers) Regulations 1981. These are essentially the same as PGR, but cover bulk goods and are backed up by the 1928 Petroleum Act and regulations governing the construction of vehicles and tank containers.

- CER, The Carriage of Explosives Regulations 1989, which bring the civil regulations up to the same standard as the military rules.

The key area that traps most operators and drivers are the rules concerning the supervision of vehicles carrying dangerous goods, and where they may be parked. Though some checking of vehicles has been carried out on the road in conjunction with weight and load restraint checks, most detected offences occur at meal times. Police regularly patrol motorway service areas and transport cafes to check that vehicles are being left safely and do not present a hazard to the public.

TYPES OF HANDLING EQUIPMENT

The logistics of materials handling in the context of distribution refers to the movement of goods in and out of warehouses and transporting them; however, in this section, the types of handling equipment are restricted to those used for storage and loading – usually they will depend upon the goods themselves and the limitations of the equipment itself. Some equipment is specific for raw materials used in the production or construction industries, but the equipment for moving the materials stored in warehouses comprises mainly conveyors, hoists and trucks of one kind or another.

Conveyors

Moving materials from one point to another can be carried out with the following types of equipment:

1 *Gravity chutes* must have an incline between the inlet and the outlet that is steeper than the free flow angle of the bulk materials conveyed. Metal chutes are particularly suitable for liquids, for grains, for fertilizers, and for sand or aggregates.
2 *Roller conveyors* use gravity, or the materials in boxes are pushed along manually or by the force of others that are mechanically propelled onto the conveyor. The conveyor consists of tubular rollers that rotate freely in ball bearings without sudden changes in level; often, they are parts of a belt conveyor system.
3 *Belt conveyors* are mechanically driven; the endless belts of rubberized fibre material are moved by rotating rollers, and materials can be moved horizontally or up slight inclines.
4 *Slatted conveyors* consist of two parallel chains linked at regular intervals by cross slats or bars that drag the materials along a smooth trough. They can operate up steeper inclines, and the slats ensure that cartons or heavy products are delivered at regular times.
5 *Tow conveyors* have a chain or rope that is winched along a slot in the floor in order to tow wheeled trolleys in a straight line. They are suitable for assembling loads on different levels in a warehouse.
6 *Monorail conveyors* allow trays, buckets or platforms to be suspended from an overhead endless chain. The chain is driven by toothed wheels, and the containers can be adjusted to the correct height for filling.

7   *Hand-operated trucks* come in a range of types for a pedestrian operator, who controls the speed and direction of movement.
8   *Forklift trucks* are very flexible being able to lift, stack, lower, transport for short distances, or load other vehicles. The driver rides on the truck and controls its operations with dexterity. Power is supplied by an engine or electric motor, and attachments are available for special movements like loading and off-loading, side-shifting, grabbing, tilting or rolling over. The forks may be front, side or rear mounted.
9   *Pallet trucks* may be motorized or hand-operated for lifting goods in bulk on wooden pallets, standing them down or transporting them. The movements are performed hydraulically as a rule, and the maximum capacity is a weight of about 1 000 kg. The pallets may be single or double-decked slotted platforms, or boxes (fixed or collapsible), or expendable when made of cheap fibre or paper-board so that they are regarded as *non-returnable*.
10 *Stacking trucks* have telescopic arms which facilitate lifting and reaching in order to stack cartons in particular. They can only move short distances, and normally operate in one place at a time.
11 *Goods-vehicle loaders* are built into the vehicle to assist loading and unloading it. Examples are tailgate lifts which are an extension of the vehicle's floor, hoists for lifting loads in a cradle onto the vehicle, and floor conveyors which are handy for pushing loaded pallets into place on the vehicle.
12 *Automatic transfer equipment* is common on factory production lines, but it can have a place in the warehouse when there is a continuous throughput of mass-produced items.

Warehouse layout

The type of materials handling equipment will depend largely upon whether the warehouse is laid out for centralized or decentralized stock movements. Factors that affect the layout include the space available, characteristics of the items stored, the distances from receiving and despatching bays, and any special precautions that should be taken.

Good lighting is important, and the arrangement of goods should fit into the materials handling scheme . . . particularly, aisle widths, choice of racks, shelves or bins. Locations should be clearly marked, and the goods classified with a practicable method of coding, because the retrieval and handling of goods will be easier.

ANALYSIS OF MATERIALS HANDLING

Every analysis requires an objective, and plenty of data which will make it meaningful. Since materials handling is a service, to production and marketing mostly, its costs have to be kept to a minimum. When considering improvements to an existing system, it needs to be split up into cost components so that they can be used as standards for comparing alternatives. The basic costs will be:

*   operating costs, including fuel, power, labour and other consumables;
*   maintenance costs of the equipment, machinery and vehicles;
*   capital costs and depreciation of the equipment and buildings.

Collecting data

Preparing a checklist in advance is the most convenient way of collecting data for any analysis, and the main headings for a materials handling checklist are:

1 *Goods data*: sizes, quantities, frequencies, shapes, weights, pallet loads, storage locations and physical characteristics.
2 *Equipment data*: types, capacities, utilization, breakdowns and safety regulations.
3 *Warehouse data*: storage areas, floor layout, aisle widths and heights, clearances and special situations.
4 *Work study data*: flow diagrams, time studies, dimensions and activity sampling.
5 *Movements data*: routes, loads, bottlenecks, distances and special provisions.
6 *Structural data*: floor construction, storage racks, shelves or bins, equipment requirements and layouts.
7 *Administrative data*: clerical control paperwork, computer programs and print-outs.

Benefits of analysing materials handling operations

Improving materials handling for distribution will reduce costs, increase throughputs and customer service, as well as reduce breakages, accidents, congestions and demurrage charges. Consequently, safety records will be better, turn-rounds will be quicker and the overall efficiency will be greater. Analysing operations and costs will lead to standards for workmanship and levels of service that attract more business. However, the amount of data collected must produce benefits that outweigh the costs involved.

8 Routing delivery service

After the best supply sites for a distribution system have been decided, the next stage of planning and controlling is to develop the routes for supplying goods to customers. There are many different methods available for delivering goods: by mail, by public carriers, by air, by water, by rail or by road. Only the last method is within the direct control of suppliers, when their own vehicles are used; therefore, delivering goods by road is the most important from their viewpoint when planning a distribution system.

When planning, each of the different methods available for delivering goods must be considered, and public transport should come first. If public transport has been proved unsuitable, hiring or owning the vehicles can be considered. The main drawback to using public transport is the reduced control, particularly of the delivery times to customers, which may affect the service level that can be provided. Despite this disadvantage, the merits of public transport often include cost savings, and they should be investigated fully before a company acquires its own vehicles. The most successful decisions result from analysing every alternative.

Routing vehicles for delivering goods can start as soon as the best supply sites have been decided and established. Initially, it is advisable to prepare a map of the distribution system in order to show the supply points and customer locations. The first routes to be examined will be straight lines between points, because they will give an overall impression of the complete network.

Starting diagrammatically and proceeding step-by-step is the surest way of discovering the best routes for vehicles. Many years of experience can provide good solutions more quickly, but there will be a certain amount of luck involved in most cases. The future of a company may depend upon a good distribution network, and it is too big a risk to gamble on guesswork. However, good guesswork is enhanced by systematic planning, which can turn an experienced person into an expert.

A scientific approach is essential for reducing the considerable effort that is involved when planning vehicle routes. Science has three successive stages; first, getting the facts related to a particular objective; second, examining the factual information and developing theories that can explain causes and effects; third, testing and developing the theories in order to see if they are acceptable in practice.

The value of the scientific approach for routing vehicles is illustrated by the simple example of delivering goods to three locations A, B and C. The first route investigated could be delivering to A, then to B, and finally to C. Writing down all the combinations that are possible for routing vehicles to these three points produces six altogether.

The total number of combinations is a factorial of the locations involved. A factorial is the product of all the whole numbers involved. For example, the factorial number of routes for delivering to three locations is $3 \times 2 \times 1 = 6$. For four locations, it is $4 \times 3 \times 2 \times 1 = 24$, and so on.

It needs very little thought to realize that the number of alternative routes that can be developed for large distribution systems is colossal. Reducing this number is where logic or the scientific use of commonsense is valuable. For instance, if there is a big mountain between points A and B in the three locations example given earlier, the route combinations ABC, BAC, CAB and CBA can be ignored because they are impractical. This is logical thinking, and it has eliminated four of the six possible routes straight away. Routing problems are never as simple as this, but a scientific approach is certain to reduce the effort of considering every possible route.

SCIENTIFIC ROUTING

Scientific procedures start with getting the facts, and the facts for scientific routing include details of the supply sites, customer locations, delivery vehicles and operating conditions.

Getting routing facts

The source of supply may be a warehouse, a railway truck, a sand pit, or any one of a number of alternatives. Details of the supply site will be the first facts to be collected when routing vehicles scientifically.

Facts about customer locations include the map references for drop points, details of the goods ordered, order frequencies and lead times, accessibility at drop points, working hours, and other relevant information. Collecting facts about supply sites and customer locations will reduce the number of possibilities that need to be considered when selecting the vehicles and routes.

The goods ordered will determine the type and size of vehicles that are suitable for different routes. The accessibility at drop points will limit the wheelbase or height of vehicles that can be used. It has already been stated that large vehicles are the most economic to operate when fully laden; therefore, the largest size of vehicle that can be fully loaded should be considered first when routing delivery vehicles. Often, this restricts the number of routes that can be used and the speeds of travel.

The capacity of a vehicle may be limited by its laden weight or volume, the financial value of its load, or by the time needed to deliver a load. Delivery times are affected by average speeds, road conditions and unloading times.

Operating conditions vary with different distribution systems, but some conditions that must be considered include the capacity limits, the road restrictions, gradients and obstacles, the human element, the types of road and the working hours.

Examining the facts

Every examination must have a standard for exercising judgement, since decisions are based upon choosing between alternatives for achieving objectives. It follows that examining routes involves inspecting the facts and judging them against the objectives. When planning delivery routes logically, the facts collected must be examined in relation to the objectives for routing the vehicles between supply sites and customer locations.

The standard for judging the alternatives may be just a mental picture, or it may be a complex mathematical equation. The former is suitable for judging a beauty competition, but the latter will be more suitable for designing a torsional suspension unit for a truck. Routing standards are rarely as specific as these examples, because they have to be flexible or adaptable.

The first feasible route developed for a delivery journey will provide the standard for judging the best of several alternatives. Every route that is developed must be first compared with the objectives in order to see if it is feasible. At this stage, the best route will be hypothetical, although it may appear to be quite feasible.

Testing the theories

Any feasible route that has been developed in the mind, on a piece of paper, or as a working model, must be tested in practice before it can be incorporated in a practical distribution system. In practice, vehicle routes must ensure that the greatest customer service and the most economical vehicle operations are provided.

Optimal routes

The operating conditions for success when routing vehicles are the least operating costs and the quickest delivery times. The least cost is essential from the company's point of view, and the quickest time is an appropriate measure for the customer's service level.

Costs can be reduced by investing money in only the bare essentials that are necessary for providing the service desired. Delivery times can be reduced by planning for the fastest vehicle speeds. Delivery speeds are increased by selecting the shortest routes, the fastest vehicles and the quickest turnarounds.

Fundamentally, the efficient routing of vehicles for distributing goods depends upon selecting optimal depot sites. Conversely, an optimal depot site depends upon efficient routing. This is paradoxical, because there is no such thing as an ideal route when many alternative vehicles are involved.

FACTORS AFFECTING VEHICLE ROUTING

In some cases, the theoretical solution to a routing problem will be illogical because it may recommend an inexact number of vehicles. Consequently, it will be necessary to round up the number of vehicles to the next whole number and reduce the overall efficiency slightly; however, minor adjustments between adjacent delivery areas can produce some cost savings. In general, it may be possible to save up to half the number of theoretical vehicles required for several delivery areas when small adjustments are made to the vehicle routes and schedules.

The best solution results from analysing the whole distribution system before allocating vehicles to specific delivery areas and routes.

Effect of area boundaries

Looking at the broad picture of a distribution system helps to determine the boundaries for delivery areas, because the routes and depot sites are considered together. A change in one area may start a wave of changes throughout the whole system: on the other hand, an extra vehicle in another area may have an insignificant effect on the whole system.

Reviewing vehicle routes

Distribution systems are continually changing; therefore, the best system applies for a short time only. Each system needs reviewing regularly, but the frequency of re-routing vehicles will vary according to the nature of the products distributed and their markets.

It is advisable to allow a little slack time when routing vehicles, but each vehicle must start on its journey fully laden for greatest economy. Regular delivery times and frequencies are a measure of good customer service, but they do restrict the optimization of vehicle routes.

Variable routing factors

When routing delivery vehicles, there are four basic conditions that affect vehicle operating costs and times; if the vehicles are operated economically, they will be:

1   *Fully loaded*: up to the first call.
2   *Partly loaded*: between calls.
3   *Unloading*: at the drop points.
4   *Empty*: when returning to the depot.

Speed restrictions

The speed of a vehicle varies with its load, with the congestion of the roads, and with other minor restrictions. According to British law, heavy goods vehicles are restricted to 40 mph (65 km/h) on open roads; 80 km/hr elsewhere in Europe, and eventually 70 km/h in the USA. Trade Union agreements set the upper speed limits in Britain for the vehicles weighing under 5 tons; these limits are averages of 22 mph (35 km/h) in restricted zones and 28 mph (45 km/h) in de-restricted zones. Also, the length of time that one driver may drive in any day is ten hours maximum, but not continuously.

Distance restrictions

The speed restrictions make it unlawful in Britain to exceed 280 miles or 450 km a day on open roads with one driver, or 220 miles or 350 km per day in restricted zones. It follows that the overall length of a delivery route for any one day must be less than these legal distances.

Time restrictions

Other restrictions will arise from such factors as the time spent at drop points, the length of time spent loading and unloading, and the delays that occur on the journey or at drop points. In order to allow for these restrictions, certain contingency time allowances must be included in the delivery schedules.

Capacity restrictions

Restrictions in the load capacities of vehicles are caused by variations to the permissible size or type of vehicle. Normally, large deliveries will incur the smallest handling charges, but compromises will have to be made between order sizes, vehicle capacities and similar scheduling factors before it is possible to determine optimal routes.

The capacity of a vehicle affects the number and type of calls that it can make on any particular route. Also, it restricts the size of orders, the nature of routes and calls, the distances between drop points and the times for unloading.

DEVELOPING VEHICLE ROUTES

Efficient routing means finding the shortest distance and time between a number of points in combination. The least number of vehicles that will provide customers with a desirable level of service will keep down operating costs. Transport costs are related directly to services, in most cases.

The number of vehicles for delivering to a network of customers depends upon the restrictions outlined already, but this number has to be decided before it is possible to develop the routes. Then, the next step is to check the feasibility of a predetermined minimum number of vehicles. That number of vehicles will probably have to change because of inter-relationships with other variables in the system. Complex systems will contain many alternatives which have to be compared before it is possible to develop the best combinations. The use of a computer is recommended when developing routing networks; however, it is possible to develop a network by *rule of thumb*, but some of the restrictions will be uncertain until after the system has been tested. The least disastrous tests are made with computer models.

Pin and string method

Basically, this method is a practical model that comprises a map of the area mounted in a board, with a pin inserted at each customer drop point. A length of thin string is then cut for the time available for each vehicle, namely, the driving time per day per vehicle. A feasible route will be found by pinning one end of the string to the depot and passing it around a set of pins representing the drop points and back to the depot. Any surplus string after returning to the depot indicates the time that is available for other work with a vehicle. The expected unloading time at a drop point can be represented by winding the string around the pin until an equivalent length has been used. Iteration, or *trial and error*, will be necessary in order to find the best routes for each vehicle. Although trial and error can be time-consuming, this method is easily understood by operators and it produces satisfactory personal routes.

The pin and string method is suitable for developing long-term trunking routes, but a different method should be used for routing short-term deliveries.

Sub-area group method

This is a simple model that is suitable for planning daily routes and local deliveries. The local delivery area which can be served from a depot is divided into a number of sub-areas. Map coordinates can be used for this, but it has been found that Post Office postcode areas are very good, particularly when orders are received or invoices despatched by mail. It is advisable to equate the orders and the vehicle loads as units of the goods to be delivered; for example, as cases, drums or pallet-loads. The order units are totalled and divided by the capacity of one vehicle in order to calculate the number of vehicles that will be required for each sub-area.

In this routing method, the number of vehicle loads for each sub-area are allocated to clusters of customers, starting at the outer edge of the sub-area and working inwards towards the depot. It is assumed that the vehicles assigned to the outer clusters will set out first, and a route is planned for dropping each load. Delivery times can then be calculated, and adjustments made by iteration until the best routes are found. A combination of the sub-area group method and the string and pin method will solve most routing problems.

It should be appreciated that these methods can be somewhat long-winded, but computers are more suitable for iterations. Computers do not get bored going round the same routine time and time again in order to refine solutions. Although, in practice, a computer model takes the tedium out of routing, it is no bad thing for the manual methods to be used to find out what it is like to drive along the routes!

When there is little demand for deliveries in an area, it may be advisable to extend the routes over two or more days rather than operate with under-extended vehicles and returning to the depot each day. If the distance is too great for a round trip to be completed in one day with one driver, there are a number of alternatives that can be investigated.

Staging points

Two or more drivers can be assigned to each vehicle; the first drives to a staging point where the second takes over. The second driver makes the drops whilst the first is taking the compulsory rest. For very long journeys, sleeper cabs on vehicles should be considered so that each driver can rest whilst the other drives. Due to the advent of recording tachometers, it is not wise to permit drivers to exceed the legal maximum number of hours at the wheel.

Overnight stops

Many distribution companies have purchased small houses along their main trunking routes, so that their drivers can sleep overnight before starting again early the following morning. This option is cheaper in some circumstances than building another depot, particularly if there are insufficient customers to justify a local service. These houses could also be a good investment, as often they can be sold at a profit when the system changes.

Transfer depots

It is often worth setting up a depot if goods can be delivered locally by smaller vans. For a national network, consideration should be given to siting depots near to the main trunk routes, not only to allow easy access to the depot, but also to allow longer distance trunking vehicles to stage through them.

Multi-modal transport

For journeys in excess of 300 km (200 miles), it is generally cheaper to send loads by rail or air and to operate a local distributon depot at the far end. The major problem is the double handling of goods at each end of the rail or air link. Do not discount this option without investigating it; many distribution managers have been surprised by the financial and time savings that can be made, particularly on international routes.

COMPUTERIZED ROUTING

When the objectives of a distribution system can be expressed in numerical terms, equations can be developed for describing the operations; it is then possible to perform iteration with a computer to obtain an optimal routing solution. Computers perform repetitive calculations rapidly and accurately provided that they are programmed correctly. Remember the adage *Garbage in equals garbage out.* A program can be an equation for the routing objective, and that will have to be fed into the computer along with relevant data. The computer compares the data with the objective electronically, and discovers the combination of facts that best complies with the requirements.

Developing a program which tells the computer how to arrive at an optimal solution by trial and error may be the limiting factor. Programs for standard distribution problems are available, and some are suitable for including different restrictions or variables. A fuller description of some available programs on the market will be found elsewhere in this book.

Savings theory

A useful program for computerized routing is the savings theory, which compares the costs of alternative routes from a supply source by iteration. The first feasible solution accumulates the total costs of delivering to each customer separately. Combining the customer deliveries together reduces the total number of journeys required so that savings will be obtained. The more customer drops that can be combined to form a single vehicle journey, the less costly the total distribution will be.

An optimal route will be one with the least delivery cost or distance, and will occur when no further savings can be made by combining the customer drops. Several computer programs are based upon this concept, but it is important to use one that is appropriate to the system under consideration.

Measuring delivery costs

Records of delivery operations provide the facts for determining operating costs. These costs must be expressed in terms of route distances or volumes in order to make them meaningful for the purpose of measuring delivery costs. The most appropriate measure is cost per unit of distance; for example, pence per mile or cents per kilometre. Subsequently, route costs can be compared in terms of route distance multiplied by the cost per distance unit.

Computers can be programmed to measure distances between distribution points and to calculate route costs. Distances are measured relatively on a digitized map of the type produced by the UK's Ordnance Survey. Each road junction is given a unique reference number, and the road between reference points is given a speed factor. By specifying a series of likes and dislikes, i.e. maximum use of motorways or quickest route, the computer can determine which exit to take at each junction.

ESTIMATING ROUTE DISTANCES

When comparing routes, the delivery costs can be estimated by calculating route distances. Naturally, the most accurate method of measuring distance is to travel the route with a vehicle and observe the odometer readings. However, this can be involved and time-consuming; it is also quite expensive unless goods are delivered on the way. If the vehicles are hired during this initial planning phase, higher charges would also be involved. Therefore, approximations are more acceptable in practice.

Distances can be estimated readily with the aid of scale maps and grid coordinates. The use of coordinates and simple geometry produces route distances quickly, and they are sufficiently accurate for vehicle route planning. This is particularly true on the continent, but as the distances are 'as the crow flies' they can be as much as 25% out for twisting British roads! The alternatives are to add up the distances on each section of road shown on the map, or measure the route with a piece of twine, or consult a computer mapping program such as AUTOROUTE.

The use of coordinates will be illustrated by estimating the alternative distances between distribution points so as to optimize the costs of routing newspaper delivery vehicles.

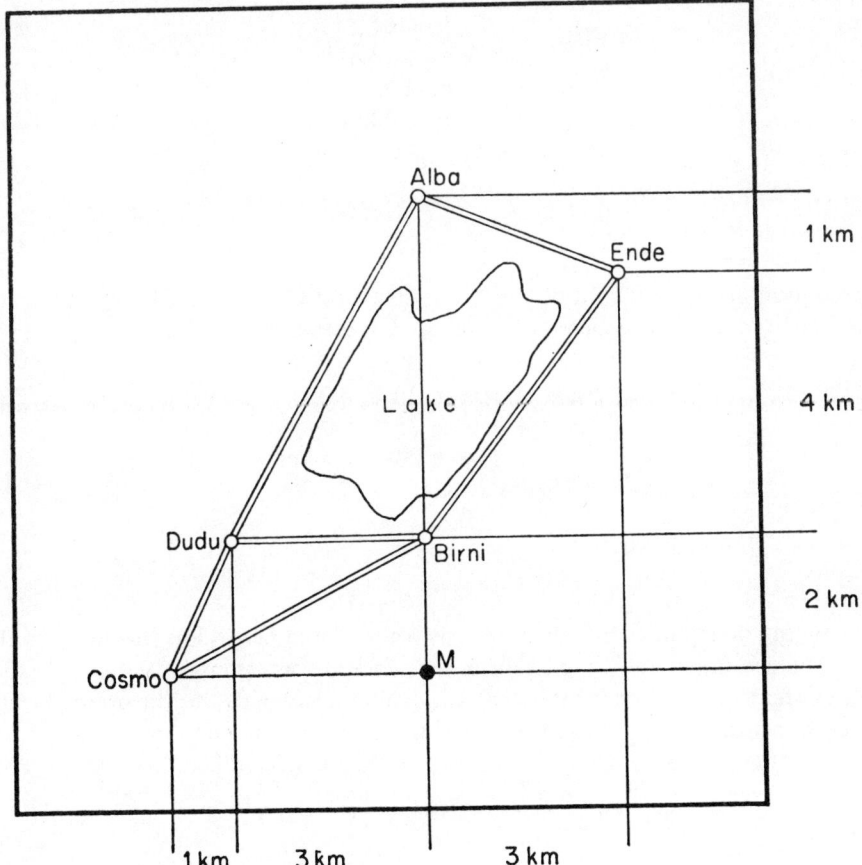

Figure 8.1 Route optimization with coordinates

Route optimization example

A local distributor of newspapers wished to optimize the delivery route from Alba to Birni and Cosmo, as shown in Figure 8.1. Two alternative routes could be used to avoid the lake: the direct route that involved travelling from Alba to Cosmo and supplying Birni from Dudu; or the circuitous route via Ende.

Coordinates for the locations were drawn on a map to obtain horizontal and vertical distances between locations (see Figure 8.1). Distances could be estimated with the aid of Pythagoras' Theorem.

Direct route

In the triangle ACM, the distance AC is the square root of CM squared plus AM squared and the distance for supplying B, which is twice DB:

$$AC = \sqrt{4^2 + 7^2}$$
$$= \sqrt{65}$$
$$= 8.1 \text{ km}$$
$$2DB = 2 \times 3$$
$$= 6.0 \text{ km}$$
$$\text{Total distance} = 14.1 \text{ km}$$

Circuitous route

The continuous route for supplying Alba, Birni and Cosmo is AEBC. Once again, coordinates and simple geometry can be used to estimate the total distance:

$$AE = 1 + 3 = 10 = 3.2 \text{ km}$$
$$EB = 4 + 3 = 25 = 5.0 \text{ km}$$
$$BC = 2 + 4 = 20 = \underline{4.5 \text{ km}}$$
$$\text{Total distance} = 12.7 \text{ km}$$

Solution

Distributing newspapers by the circuitous route would be 1.4 km shorter than the direct route with backtracking to Birni; therefore, it was optimal.

The contingency factor for this example can be calculated after the optimal route has been measured in practice. It is found to be 13.9 km, in fact:

$$Contingency\ factor = \frac{13.9}{12.7} = 1.1$$

In future, estimates for this distribution area can be made more realistic by multiplying the estimated distances by 1.1 in order to produce acceptable delivery distances.

JOURNEY PLANNING

Journey planning can be described as a technique for breaking down distribution areas into routes which ensure that the largest possible vehicles are operated, the route distances are minimal and the service provided is maximal for the least total operating costs.

Distribution areas

The size of a distribution area affects the length and duration of the delivery journeys. The shorter a journey, the quicker the goods can be delivered to customers, but long journeys have the ability of absorbing delays along the route. Effective vehicle utilization depends upon the loading and unloading times with short journeys, and upon the loadability with long journeys.

Service level

Journey planning has the objective of optimizing routes in terms of delivery times which determine the customer service level that can be provided. The length of a journey affects the delivery times to customers, but return journeys must also be taken into account. Other factors that affect the journey times include loading and unloading; good load organization will save time.

Journey effectiveness

When an effective journey has been developed, all the ineffective times such as delays, slow driving, faulty loading and stoppages will have been minimized. Delivery operations must be speeded up whenever possible; for example, mechanical handling can cut the time for loading goods to one-fifth of the time required for manual loading. The value of this reduction can be appreciated when it is realized that the shorter the time spent loading a vehicle, the longer the time it can be on the road, where it will be more effective.

Increasing journeys

When the average distance for delivering a load of goods is 30 miles (50 km), a vehicle can be expected to deliver ten loads in a week if it is loaded manually. Under similar conditions, mechanized loading can increase the number of journeys to eighteen.

The value of mechanical handling can be determined by estimating the savings that it affords and comparing them with the costs of buying the equipment. In the above example, the vehicle fleet required would be halved with mechanized loading, which could cover the extra cost of buying forklift trucks and conveyors.

Mechanical loading

The main objectives of using mechanical handling equipment at warehouses are to reduce time and effort, giving faster throughputs and less storage space required for holding goods. From the production point of view, a move to just-in-time delivery could cause problems, as the distribution department will no longer be holding enough stock to cover any equipment down times.

Handling individual items can be eliminated by using bulk vehicles, pallets, containers, or vehicles with removable bodies. Time is reduced when loads can be assembled in quantity, on pallets, for example; also, loading and unloading will be made easier. Operational times can be controlled more accurately with mechanized equipment, because work durations are more predictable.

Analysing routes

The analytical methods for routing delivery vehicles that have been described in this chapter are suitable for solving most static routing problems. Difficulties arise when trying to plan a number of different routes with a variety of vehicles that have different delivery times.

Complex problems are the result of conflicts between variables, and they can be solved satisfactorily only after defining each objective clearly. Then, restrictions to the achievement of each objective can be determined, and steps taken to overcome them. In practice, changes always occur with the passage of time and new problems will arise continually; therefore, routes must be reviewed and revised regularly.

ASSIGNING VEHICLES TO ROUTES

Distribution systems are rarely consistent: routes differ, loads differ and vehicles differ. Practical problems of assigning different vehicles to different routes can be solved with linear programming by intelligent distribution managers. An appropriate technique that uses iteration can be performed on pieces of squared paper with simple arithmetic, step-by-step systematically.

The problem that confronted the distribution supervisor of a bakery will be used to illustrate the technique of linear programming related to the assignment of vehicles to routes.

Assignment problem

A bakery with a small fleet of delivery vehicles wanted to provide an efficient service to customers in its locality without hiring additional vehicles. The distribution supervisor obtained a list of the retail outlets and their daily requirements of bread which was needed before 12 o'clock. The delivery vans started out at six each morning. This information was related to the capacities of available vans and the daily delivery routes so that a table could be produced for showing the work times involved.

The assignment method of linear programming was used to find the best solution for assigning the bread delivery vans to routes. It was an appropriate method that was quick and easy to use manually.

Basically, the method uses a matrix (or table) of the variables, and manipulates them mathematically without altering the overall objective. In this case, the variables were different delivery vans and different customer locations, while the objective was to deliver all the orders before noon. The units to be compared were delivery times, which varied with the van capacities, and the route distances.

Each van has been given a letter for identification, and each delivery route is defined by its town. The delivery time for each combination of van and town has been expressed in hours in the time matrix. Iteration proceeded according to the five recognized steps, starting with the preparation of a square matrix for the times, which is shown in Figure 8.2.

Step 1   Prepare a time matrix of the times required for delivery bread to the different towns with the different vans. Delivery time is really a measure of cost, and the first matrix is therefore normally called a *cost matrix*.

Step 2   Perform zero computation along the rows of the matrix. This means finding the optimal van for each route and making its delivery time equal to zero. In

Routes \ Vans	A	B	C	D	E	F
Kington	4	2	8	4	5	4
Lenham	6	8	7	5	7	5
Milton	3	6	3	5	5	3
Norton	3	6	2	3	7	8
Otford	7	6	3	8	4	3
Purley	7	4	5	4	5	3

Figure 8.2   Time matrix

Routes \ Vans	A	B	C	D	E	F
Kington	2	0	6	2	3	2
Lenham	1	3	2	0	2	0
Milton	0	3	0	2	2	0
Norton	1	4	0	1	5	6
Otford	4	3	0	5	1	0
Purley	4	1	2	1	2	0

Figure 8.3   First revised time matrix

the case of Kington, delivering with van B requires the least time of two hours, and it has been made zero by subtracting two hours from every delivery time in the row.

The *time matrix* is revised (see Figure 8.3) to find the optimal van for each route – that is, the least time for delivering to each town. The solution may be impractical at this stage, because more than one route may require the same van, while in this case, there is no work at all for van E because there is no zero in its column.

Step 3   Repeat zero computation down the columns. This means finding the optimal route for each van and making its delivery time equal to zero in the same way as for the previous step. It is perfectly legitimate to perform zero computation, because the overall relationships between the times are not altered.

The second revised *time matrix* is shown in Figure 8.4. It can be seen that the same route can be delivered optimally by more than one van in three instances, to Lenham, Milton and Otford. However, there are optimal options for each row and column.

Step 4   Examine each row systematically in order to have only one option in each row. When there is only one zero in a route row, that van is optimal and it should not be assigned to any other route. Consequently, any other zero options in the same column and row as the single zero can be crossed out. The optimal van for each route has been denoted by putting a square around the zero options in Figure 8.5.

In this step, Kington, Norton and Purley have been accounted for, and vans B, C and F allocated to them.

Step 5   Examine each column systematically in order to make one route optimal for each van. The same procedure for marking zero options and crossing out others in the same rows is used as in the fourth step.

The *final matrix*, which is presented in Figure 8.6, shows an optimal combination

Routes \ Vans	A	B	C	D	E	F
Kington	2	0	6	2	2	2
Lenham	1	3	2	0	1	0
Milton	0	3	0	2	1	0
Norton	1	4	0	1	4	6
Otford	4	3	0	5	0	0
Purley	4	1	2	1	1	0

Routes \ Vans	A	B	C	D	E	F
Kington	2	[0]	6	2	2	2
Lenham	1	3	2	0	1	⊠
Milton	0	3	⊠	2	1	⊠
Norton	1	4	[0]	1	4	6
Otford	4	3	⊠	5	0	⊠
Purley	4	1	2	1	1	[0]

Figure 8.4 Second revised time matrix   **Figure 8.5 Third revised time matrix**

Routes \ Vans	A	B	C	D	E	F
Kington	2	[0]	6	2	2	2
Lenham	1	3	2	[0]	1	⊠
Milton	[0]	3	⊠	2	1	⊠
Norton	1	4	[0]	1	4	6
Otford	4	3	⊠	5	[0]	⊠
Purley	4	1	2	1	1	[0]

Figure 8.6 Final time matrix

for each row and column. Therefore, it is an optimal solution for this assignment problem; it can be resolved easily because only one zero has been left in each row and column after *Step 4*. Many problems will not produce such a tidy solution, and columns or rows will be left with two or more zero options, or none at all. *Steps 4 and 5* must be repeated continually until an optimal solution is reached. This matrix iteration principle is used by most computer programs designed to sort out fleet operations and scheduling.

In summary, the final solution to the bakery problem is:

1 Assign van A to Milton for 3 hours work.
2 Assign van B to Kingston for 2 hours work.
3 Assign can C to Norton for 2 hours work.
4 Assign van D to Lenham for 5 hours work.
5 Assign van E to Otford for 4 hours work.
6 Assign van F to Purley for 3 hours work.

In five simple steps, a complete assignment solution had been obtained in which all the delivery work involves less than five hours duration, i.e. completed by noon. The same solution could have been obtained with pure mathematics, but it would have required $6 \times 6 = 36$ calculations and comparing all the results in order to find the least times.

This example shows that the use of logic in conjunction with scientific procedure can solve routing problems with logistics without resorting to the expense of a computer.

Delivery schedules

It has been shown that time taken for delivering goods to customers affects the cost of deliveries and the service level provided. Routes are static, but they become dynamic when delivery times are incorporated; they are then known as *schedules*. Routing and scheduling have to be considered together in order to make them compatible.

A schedule gives the time sequence for making deliveries to customers, and the process of scheduling cannot commence until the vehicles have been routed.

OPERATIONAL SCHEDULING

Optimal scheduling implies performing various operations in a sequence that maximizes effectiveness or minimizes cost. Mathematically, an optimal solution is obtained by calculating the outcome of every possible combination of events in the correct sequence. Operationally, logic can be employed usefully for programming sequences; feasible sequences must be produced and examined on a time basis, step-by-step.

An optimal schedule is the combination of events that complies with requirements for the least time or cost. A chart can be used for examining the feasible sequences on a *time scale*, while the sequence that is required for feasibility can be shown in a table that allows comparisons to be made. The procedure for using logical iteration will be demonstrated with the aid of a problem that concerned the scheduling of journey load assembly at a textile warehouse.

Customers	Sequence of items			
Green	A	B	C	D
Black	A	C	B	D
Brown	B	C	D	A
Grey	B	C	D	A

Figure 8.7   Sequence matrix

Operational scheduling problem

Orders for wool and cotton cloths were processed by the despatch office of a textile warehouse, and this problem concerned the best sequence for assembling cloth into four orders. The cloth was used for clothing manufacture, and it was essential for the vehicles to be loaded in sequences that complied with customers' factory requirements. In order to obtain the best utilization of the materials handling time, it was necessary to prepare an operational schedule for assembling the orders.

The four orders were from four customers, called Green, Black, Brown and Grey; although each customer required all four types of cloth, called A, B, C and D, the sequences for loading them differed. For convenience, a standard time of 10 minutes was taken for assembling each item of cloth ordered. Each order represented a full vehicle load, and each type of cloth in rolls was removed from the warehouse by its own forklift truck operator. The sequences for assembling the items into loads according to the order requirements were compiled into a sequence matrix (see Figure 8.7).

Each item had to be assembled individually, and it could be seen from the sequence matrix that, initially, two orders required item A to be assembled first and two required item B first. This meant that the assembly of two orders could commence immediately, and the operators who handled items C and D would be idle for the first ten-minute period. In order to reduce the total idle time, an operational schedule was prepared for showing successive steps.

Step 1   A basic chart was prepared for the process of developing the operational time sequences for assembling customer orders. The basic time chart that was employed is shown in Figure 8.8. Customer orders, by name, were extended vertically on the left and the available time (80 minutes) was shown horizontally at ten-minute intervals.

Step 2   The objective for the optimal sequence was defined as the assembly of as many items at one time as possible in order to reduce the idle time to a minimum.

Initially, only items A and B could be assembled in the first ten-minute period of time, and they were entered on the time chart against the orders for Green and Brown (see Figure 8.8).

Customer orders	Operational time available (Minutes)							
	10	20	30	40	50	60	70	80
Green	A							
Black								
Brown	B							
Grey								

Figure 8.8 Basic time chart

Step 3 The assembly of items for the orders continued, gathering as many items at a time as possible. The sequence matrix was consulted (see Figure 8.7) to find that three items could be assembled in the second time period.

Item B was assembled with the Green order, item A with the Black order, and item C with the Brown order. The Grey order was still waiting to commence assembly.

Step 4 In the third period of time, three more items could be assembled in order to comply with the sequence matrix (see Figure 8.7). The operator who handled item A would be idle this time.

Item C was required for both the Green order and the Black order, and the choice was made in favour of Green because this order was the more urgent of the two. In this period, the assembly of the Grey order could commence with the availability of item B.

Step 5 The orders for Green and Brown were completed in the fourth period of time, and the Grey had to wait again.

The state of affairs after assembling loads for 40 minutes is shown in Figure 8.9, when the first two completed orders were ready for loading into vehicles.

Step 6 Only the orders for Black and Grey remained to be assembled, and items B and C were gathered in the fifth time period.

Step 7 In the sixth time period, item D was required for both of the remaining orders. It could be assembled with the Black order so as to complete it, but this would mean that the Grey order could not be completed until the last available period. However, assembling item D with the Grey order would reduce the overall time required by ten minutes, and this was done.

Step 8 The remaining two orders for Black and Grey were completed by gathering items A and D. The final schedule was checked with the sequence matrix in order to confirm sequences. Figure 8.10 shows the final time chart.

Customer orders	Operational time available (Minutes)							
	10	20	30	40	50	60	70	80
Green	A	B	C	D				
Black		A		C				
Brown	B	C	D	A				
Grey			B					

Figure 8.9   Partially completed time chart

Customer orders	Operational time available (Minutes)							
	10	20	30	40	50	60	70	80
Green	A	B	C	D				
Black		A		C	B		D	
Brown	B	C	D	A				
Grey			B		C	D	A	

Figure 8.10   Final time chart

Solution

An optimal sequence of operations was achieved in this example after eight steps using logical iteration. The total elapsed time was 70 minutes, which was within the objective time limit, and each operator was only idle for 30 minutes. In specific cases, the idle times can be utilized by performing other work, but this example has been used to illustrate a method of scheduling operations that others can put into practice according to their individual needs.

International scheduling

Modern distribution systems often require the development of international delivery schedules, when the sequence of delivery operations may be determined by different factors. The scheduling of deliveries from the Netherlands to Iran is a typical example. Originally, electrical equipment from Eindhoven was sent by rail across Europe and the Middle East directly to Tehran, but increases in the transit taxes charged by certain countries on the way made this method uneconomical. Other forms of delivery were considered, but transport by air was too expensive, by sea it took too long, and by road suffered from similar transit taxes. When it was realized that this distribution problem could be solved by reviewing the scheduling objectives, an economical solution was developed. Deliveries need not be confined to one form of transport, because different forms are best for different circumstances, and *multi-modal* distribution was a possible solution. Different modes of transport can be used to reduce delivery times or costs, but control is more difficult; however, the establishment of additional *multi-modal interchanges* throughout the world will assist managers to take better advantage of them. The Dutch distribution manager investigated seven different modes of transport before he arrived at the present schedule for delivering the electrical equipment, and its description would not be out of place in a travel guide!

International deliveries require continual monitoring in order to control costs, and the service provided to customers: the schedules often have to be changed from time to time. *Containerization* is advisable in many instances today, and such was the case in this example. In fact, a container load of electrical equipment can leave the factory by road or canal barge for Europoort, where it will be transferred to a ship which takes it to Finland. From Helsinki, the container joins the rail network to cross Russia to the Iranian border; here it is lifted on to a road vehicle which transports it to Tehran. This roundabout route has some disadvantages and many advantages, but it meets a delivery schedule for the least cost and delay.

Planning efficient delivery schedules requires flexibility and the ability to decide which is the best procedure for the circumstances; consequently, it needs a good understanding of scientific scheduling methods and, above all, a first hand experience of the operating conditions. The best plans are based upon facts.

9 Choosing transportation

The type of transportation chosen very much depends on the goods to be moved. A single product type makes the choice easy because specialized transport can be used, though it means that the product cannot be changed in the future without also changing the transport. With transport costing anything from a few thousand pounds for a light van to several million for an aircraft or ship, it is vital that this part of the distribution plan is perfect from the very beginning. The risks can be minimized, however, by hiring the transport from a specialist distribution company.

CHOOSING ROAD VEHICLES

Choosing the right road vehicle for the job is generally quite easy, as most manufacturers or specialist vehicle suppliers will readily give advice on the options available using their own experience. However, before approaching such a company, a distributor must have a very clear understanding of what is wanted. The objective may be as simple as delivering coal from a yard near a housing estate, or as complex as distributing a wide range of products from a central warehouse in one country to several depots and retail chains throughout Europe. The former requires just one small flat platform truck, but the latter may involve several modes of transport, both large articulated vehicles and smaller delivery vans.

Starting with the design of a system, the first task is to gather background data on the appropriate means of transport, and to look at the advantages and disadvantages of each. Some examples of the characteristics that should be taken into consideration when choosing vehicles for a road distribution system are shown in Table 9.1; however, there are other special considerations. Table 9.2 includes some factors affecting different modes of transportation that should be considered in international or long haul operations.

Table 9.2 gives a few of the obvious and more common advantages and disadvantages of different forms of transportation, each of which is a subject on its own.

Table 9.1   Road vehicle characteristics

Vehicles	Factors	Advantages	Disadvantages
Light van	Small load	Fast Door-to-door Turn round time Secure	Man-intensive Load size/weight Vehicles' life short Short distances only
Pick-up truck	Small load	Fast Door-to-door Turn round time Load height	Load limited Vehicle life Insecure Short distances only
Large van	Medium load	Fast Door-to-door Secure Medium distances	Special driving licence needed Mechanical loaders needed
Heavy truck	Bulk load	Speed Open back Good load size	Special driving licence needed Loose loads Mechanical loading Insecure Short distances
Articulated tractor and trailer	Large load	Swap body Speed Load size Long distances	Security High insurance Expensive loading equipment Special driving licence needed

However, it is worth expanding on a couple of areas in the road transport field as they are most commonly used for physical distribution. Load conditions are peculiar to products, and only the transport manager can decide which type and sizes of cargo can be handled. The main area for consideration is financial, both capital investments and general running costs.

Transport operations

Having decided on the locations for depots, it is worth looking at gaps in the network that can be filled by transport vehicles: in some cases this may be solved by direct delivery from factory to customer; in others it may need a more complex, hub-based system. In the former case, each vehicle required has to be large enough to carry the average load required by customers. Larger loads will require two or more vehicles, which is preferable to having a large vehicle under-utilized for much of the time. Controversies often involve transport priorities, because either the production

Table 9.2   Comparison of transportation modes

Mode	Advantages	Disadvantages
Road	Flexibility Door-to-door deliveries Speed Links to all transportation modes Delivery times Intermediate stops	Environmental pollution Congested at peak times Fuel costs Tax/insurance Load size limit = 40 tons Dangerous goods restrictions Manpower intensive Load security
Rail	Large load weights Speed Environmental friendly Long hauls No road tax	Double handling Expensire for short haul Manpower intensive Load size (except length)
Air	Very fast Security Long distance	High cost Double handling Restricted load sizes
Sea	Very large load size Security Loose or bulk loads Long distance	Double handling Water damage Insurance Speed
Inland water ways	Large and heavy loads Low cost Long distances Load integrity Low cost	Speed Route limitations Double handling

manager wants to control the transport, so as to clear factory stocks, or the marketing manager wants control in order to meet customer needs. Generally speaking, both sides should have a say in controlling transport, but the only way that the transport manager can keep them both happy is to have a warehouse close to the factory so that the production lines can be cleared quickly with just a few vehicles and then the customer deliveries can be handled separately. For environmental reasons, the customers often can only accept loads at particular times. For example, town centres are often closed to heavy traffic from 08.30 until 17.00 hours daily, or a large retail warehouse cannot afford to have too many deliveries at the same time otherwise the arrival bays will be clogged with goods. Also, on the environmental front, some country routes pass through villages which have bye-laws that restrict access to heavy vehicles at various times, particularly at night. These are just some of the problems that affect road deliveries.

Delivery distances

The next consideration affecting the choice of road vehicles relates to distances and, indirectly, operating costs. The longer the distance to be covered, the longer the time needed for deliveries which means higher costs. A long haul involves double-manning and a sleeper cab on the vehicle, due to restrictions on driving hours. One way to offset the higher cost of manning and vehicle operation is to increase the vehicle size and spread the cost over bigger loads. Marketing people then have the problem of disposing of the surplus goods, so transport control has turned in favour of marketing rather than production. The reader will by now appreciate that no element of a company can be looked at in isolation, but the distribution manager has the difficult task of keeping the balance between production output and sales.

Centralized control

Moving to the hub-system of distributing goods, the transport fleet is divided into several small parts, but *command and control* has to be at the highest level, otherwise perspective will be lost. The transport control hub should therefore be at the factory or central warehouse, from where the bulk or trunking vehicles operate, leaving control of smaller delivery vehicles to the depot managers. This avoids having too many links in the chain which increase operating costs as well as introduce commu-nication difficulties. The main problem with the hub type of transport system is the need to have at least two types of vehicle, but usually as many as 20 when company cars, two truck types and other support vehicles are added. This is further com-pounded by having to modernize a large fleet only a few vehicles at a time, due to the high capital cost involved.

Transport fleet renewal

Penny packet fleet renewal looks good in the company accounts and appears to give value for money, but it brings with it many headaches. A company may start with a fleet of ten articulated tractors and trailers, plus 20 small vans; the estimated life expectancy of the former being 10 years, and the latter five years. However, after two years, a major market breakthrough may require a production expansion to match it, so that distribution has to increase its capacity by 50%. In any system there must be some slack. With improved operating procedures, in this example, it has been estimated that three articulated trucks and five more vans will be required. Fortuna-tely, the van manufacturers still makes the same model, so the running costs will be kept down by buying more of the same model! The truck manufacturer, however, has been taken over and now produces another model under licence. Luckily, a discount can be offered to favoured customers, and the new truck has the same specifications as before, although most of its components are different. Therefore, the in-house maintenance workshop will have to expand to deal with the additional vehicles, and the stores will have to hold a wider range of new spares. The next crisis will come three years later when the original 20 vans are fully depreciated; ten can be sold and the five best vans can be operated for another couple of years, the remaining five will be cannibalized to provide spares for the five still being run.

Needless to say, the van maker offers to sell a fleet of the new Mark 2 vans which use only 20% of the Mark 1 components, and the running costs will escalate as the workshop adapts to the new model.

This example may seem a little gloomy, but it is quite typical of the problems that occur in large fleet operations. The choice of vehicle from the outset is a crucial factor in the overall running costs and, therefore, it will affect final distribution costs. In very few companies operating their own transport for distribution is it possible to be self-sufficient without relying on a financial handout from the sale of company products and, therefore, they are in competition with all the other company departments when it comes to seeking money for expansion and modernization, which must be paid out of increased profits.

To recap, the choice of vehicles is vitally important, and the following questions should be answered:

1 What job must the vehicle do?
2 Is it cheap to run?
3 What is its life expectancy?
4 What is the company's forecast growth rate?
5 How much redundancy and depreciation has to be included for servicing and repairs?

VEHICLES FOR SPECIALIZED DISTRIBUTION

This section deals with choosing vehicles for a specialist distribution system. Many specialized distributors started with just one or two general cargo vehicles hauling whatever they could; however, at some time they struck up a good relationship with a big customer, and were invited to tender for a contract to distribute larger quantities of a single item. This would prompt a change in the shape of the vehicle fleet, and more vehicles would have to be bought in order to meet the increased work, so that the old cargo vehicles had to be sold or kept on as a subsidiary business.

When developing a specialist distribution business, the first task is to sit down with the customer and plan the level of service that is required, and how the products will be presented for distribution. Next, the destinations, quantities and delivery schedules have to be decided upon. That is the time to begin thinking about the size of the operation and the number of vehicles required, but first there is one more essential process to go through, and that is to make a thorough reconnaissance. Visit each depot and delivery point to look at the access for loading and unloading, the bays and the route restrictions between the pick-up and delivery points. Having identified the worst restrictions, revisit them and determine the reasons. During this phase, think laterally in order to remove the restrictions; they may be:

1 Height limits.
2 Width limits.
3 Length of loading bays.
4 Turning circles.
5 Parking restrictions.
6 Side or end loading only.

7   Weight restrictions on bridges, either axle or gross loadings.
8   Ferries and toll bridge charges based on vehicle sizes.
9   Long distances that affect driving times and rest periods.
10 Vehicle body design features.

Now a picture of the type of vehicle needed can be built up: it must be able to deliver the quantities involved each time, which may mean double stacking of pallets that could make the vehicle too high either legally or for low bridges. On the other hand, small wheels or a low level fifth wheel will have to be considered. High vehicles suffer from high wind resistance and, therefore, poor fuel economy unless spoilers or aerodynamic devices are fitted; then perhaps a crew cab will be needed, which increases the cost and weight of the vehicle, as well as increasing its overall length. So many of these factors are inter-related that they cannot be resolved in isolation without damaging the complete system.

No formula exists for making these decisions, but lots of small calculations have to be made so that a framework for the design and size of vehicle is reached. The subsequent stage is the most fun, but can be the most harrowing. It involves discussing the requirements with dealers or manufacturers in order to discover which vehicles will fit the specifications. After that, costs have to be considered in depth, and you must remember that selecting the cheapest vehicle is rarely the right answer; aspects like the following are more important:

1   Reliability, spares availability and back-up facilities are vital because a missed delivery may lose the contract.
2   Fuel economy is crucial because wasting one kilometre (half a mile) per 5 litres (one gallon) of fuel can add up to the initial cost of the vehicle over two years.
3   Type of gearbox affects fuel consumption and wear on the vehicle. Diesel engines and automatic gearboxes cost much more initially, but they are more reliable and not damaged so much by poor driving. This is important when drivers change frequently; this is a problem experienced if you have a variable work force like bus operators. Almost all buses are now automatic or at least semi-automatic. This is a reminder that constant stopping and starting is a further consideration.
4   Rigid-sided vehicles provide advertising space for the customers, so they may well offset the extra cost of buying vehicle reliability and economy.

Having considered all these factors, you may decide to opt for a different mode of transportation. Ever escalating fuel prices and other operating costs could be overcome by letting 'the train take the strain'.

RAIL DISTRIBUTION

The Union Internationale des Chemins de Fer (UIC) unites the railway administrations of the whole of Europe into one international organization which regulates international rail freight operations. The International Convention on the carriage of goods by rail (CIM) governs international goods traffic; the International Regulations for Vehicle exchanges (RIV) contains the regulations for the exchange of freight between railways, both in privately owned wagons and those owned by the national railways; the International Regulations for Dangerous goods (RID) governs the transport of dangerous goods by rail, and is very similar to the European Agreement for the conveyance of Dangerous Goods (ADR) for road transport. With the correct regulatory documents, it is possible to send a wagon across the continent knowing that it will meet the requirements laid down by each country, and one consignment note contains the instructions to take the wagon to its destination.

Rolling stock

Approximately 600 000 wagons are operated by the national railways of the European Economic Community, and around one third of them are owned privately. Private ownership is expanding, and the number of private wagons increases each year; in some countries, the national railways even allow the private ownership of main line locomotives. Foster Yeoman have some six large General Electric diesels for hauling stone around Britain.

In each country, the national railway cooperates with private owners, who generally form themselves into an association or federation. In the UK, the body is the Private Wagon Federation (PWF); it liaises with the UIC on behalf of the private owners. Annually, at a week long conference, private owners discuss and agree on the trading policies and technical details for the use of private wagons on international railway lines. The results are published in the form of UIC leaflets and a Private Owners' *Aide Memoir*, although a manual would be a more accurate description.

The UIC Council represent the private railways in ten European countries – Ireland, Denmark and Greece was not included yet, though the latter two are expected to join by 1992. Private wagon owners include many of the top multinational industrial companies; most notable are the major oil, chemical and cement companies. Less wealthy companies can lease or hire rolling stock from the manufacturing companies based in various countries. Actually, three European private organizations have over 80 000 wagons between them, they are:

- *Group CAIB*, a division of the Australian company, Brambles Europe, with its headquarters in Brussels. It manages a fleet of 40 000 wagons through companies in nine countries, including CAIB (UK) Ltd. The group has a history stretching back to the 1870s, which was the peak period of railway growth in Europe.
- *VTG*, a German subsidiary of Preussag which owns some 25 000 wagons and operates in seven countries, including Britain. Its headquarters are in Hamburg, and it controls its operations from there.
- *ERMEWA*, a Swiss company which has expanded considerably in recent years to around 17 000 wagons. Its rolling stock can be found in most mainland European countries, and currently their new wagons match the British loading gauge.

All three organizations will soon be operating wagons capable of using the Channel Tunnel link between Britain and the continent of Europe.

Private owners dominate the specialized freight wagon scene, including the following rolling stocks:

- Wagons for LPG, gasoline, fuel oil and bitumen.
- Chemical tankers made of stainless steel, insulated wagons for compressed gases, as well as bulk powder wagons and pallet vans for fertilizers or food-stuffs.
- Automobile transport wagons, container flats and the new types of wagon for trailer transfers.

Rail restrictions

The limiting factors for rail operations are weight and size, although to a lesser extent than for road transport. British Rail has a smaller loading gauge than other countries – the envelope through which loaded wagons must pass. Wagons for European rail freight have to comply with both sets of loading measures. The track gauge, however, is the same throughout Europe for main line traffic, though to get to some of the more remote areas, narrow or metre gauge tracks have to be used. Britain can, however, accept heavier wagons on the national railway system – up to 25 tons per axle, or 102 metric tonnes for a 4-axle bogey wagon. The gauge differences have been a constant source of concern since the Channel Tunnel was given the go-ahead.

The new generation of low platform wagons is being developed in Britain to cater for containers up to 9 ft (2.75 m) high and, in certain circumstances, three metres, but the standard deck height will only accommodate low containers. Freightliner wagons are now designed for 8 ft 6 in (2.6 m) high containers in Britain.

Prior to the Channel Tunnel, all of Britain's international rail traffic crossed the Channel on a train ferry. One new vessel, the *Nord Pas de Calais*, sails on the Dover to Dunkirk crossing three times a day, and has the capability of making a fourth trip. This currently equates to two million tonnes of freight per year, which is expected to increase to over six million once the tunnel is in full operation. The usual train ferry boats will continue to run after 1993, as the tunnel will not accept certain categories of hazardous materials and they will still have to travel by sea.

Road/rail distribution

Road transport accounts for 80% of freight tonnage in Britain, and this means a substantial dependence by British industry on the efficient use of road vehicles and on the overloaded road network. Without the efficiency and flexibility provided by this mode of transport, industrial Britain would grind to a halt. Over recent years, despite major road improvements and the construction of new motorways (presently around 3 000 kilometres), the trend has unfortunately been towards increased traffic congestion on the roads.

The juggling act needed to meet customers' delivery requirements is still to move the right goods to the right place, at the right time, for the right price and in the right condition. The solution in the present climate could rest on a suitable interface between the road and rail transport systems for long distances. As explained earlier, the current economic break-even point is distances of about 300 km, though it is anticipated that this will reduce to between 200 and 250 km for international traffic

once the Channel Tunnel is open, the reduction being brought about by the following three factors:

1 *Toll charges for freight trains* through the tunnel will be less per tonne than the
toll charges for vehicles utilizing the ferry shuttle trains.
2 *Loading times* for transfers between road and rail will remain largely unchanged,
but *road only* traffic will be subjected to an additional cross-loading time penalty.
This penalty will not be as long as for a road/rail transfer, but the extra time will
cost extra money, as the saying goes!
3 *Rail traffic* speeds are steadily increasing, with freight trains now running at the
speed of the passenger trains of only a few years ago. This trend is set to
continue, and 150 kph freight trains are a practical proposition. Road traffic can
at best manage 120 kph on motorways and normally only half that elsewhere,
while congestion tends to produce even slower speeds. Fuel is expensive and
slower road journeys are tipping the transport balance in favour of the railways.

It has long been recognized that a distribution service capable of combining the
best features of rail freight and road haulage would benefit both the hard-pressed
transport manager and the environment. Nothing can compete with rail traffic for
speed and efficiency when delivering over long distances, whilst road vehicles cannot
match its environmental advantages in terms of noise and pollution. Rail traffic
moves mainly at night, safely and securely at speeds currently up to 120 kph. Each
load by rail means fewer trucks to cause pollution and congestion on the roads.

The use of local road distribution vehicles for transit to and from rail terminals,
and overnight rail transit over long distances, offers better economy, warehouse
terminals and cost effectiveness for *door-to-door* deliveries.

Recent developments in rail freight wagons include the TrailerTrain, the Tiphook
Piggyback and the Powell Duffryn; they also serve to improve the cost effectiveness,
efficiency and flexibility of rail traffic.

TrailerTrain

This British invention allows specially adapted road semi-trailers to be carried on
railway wagons. The current size limit is 24 tonnes gross load weight for the trailer,
which is hauled by any conventional fifth wheel tractor unit. Transfer from road to
rail can take place at any railway siding which has a concrete hardstanding adjacent
to it, or at Freight Liner terminals, sea harbours and even level crossings. The
trailers are transferred to a rail wagon by means of a special integral ramp on the
wagon, with power being provided by the road tractor unit, and loading is
controlled by its driver.

Tiphook piggyback

The wagons of this system are a variation on the TrailerTrain wagon's, but conventional trailers can be used with them. Again, the road vehicle driver carries out the
loading with power coming from the vehicle's engine.

Powell Duffryn

This approach to the transfer problem is highly technical and innovative. It comprises small-wheeled wagons capable of carrying trailers with containers weighing up to 40 tonnes; they can travel on British Rail tracks at speeds of 120 km/h. This idea may seem simplistic, but the small wheels having a diameter of 500 mm have to rotate at speeds around 1 250 rpm. This poses major problems to bearings carrying an axle load of 13 tonnes, which is a force rarely encountered in diesel engines at those speeds.

In conclusion, it would be wrong for transport and distribution managers to write off the rail option, the national railways are beginning to fight back with a vengeance; rail must therefore be included among the choices for long haul transportation after 1993.

AIR FREIGHT

The aviation industry is well known for its use of mainframe computers, especially for booking passengers on flights; however, it is turning more to microcomputers for controlling air freight. There are very few software programs written for air freighting, but there is a whole host of off-the-shelf transportation programs that are suitable for all modes of transporting goods. They include databases, spreadsheets, word processing and graphics which can be used for controlling administrative, handling, despatching and maintenance operations. Another area for PC application is communications, where the transmission of electronic data is so important; a PC can be anything from a dumb terminal for providing information to an active Remote Job Entry station.

Most air freight distributors are transportation agents rather than operators, and their main function is to buy space on aircraft operated by the airlines. The International Air Transport Association (IATA) sets the tariffs for member airlines who sell space to the freight-forwarding agents; unfortunately today, these tariffs are ignored because they are under-cut by the 'cowboy' airlines in the same way as 'flags of convenience' are used by maritime operators. The European market economy promotes this kind of competition, although India and Pakistan abide by the rules. An example that shows the wide range of rates for air freight is the cost of freighting goods from Amsterdam to New York by air: the IATA tariff is f10.20 per kg; a reputable shipper like Wassing International charges f3.50, but opportunist airlines only charge f2.00!

It is not surprising that most shippers offer two rates, depending upon the airline that they will use, and it pays to 'shop around', although there is no guarantee of efficiency or safety.

Air freighting operations

The procedure for sending goods by air is very similar to sending them by sea, and a general flow chart is shown in Figure 9.3 for the main activities.

A brief description of each operator in Figure 9.3 follows; the information was kindly provided by Wassing International of Tilburg in the Netherlands:

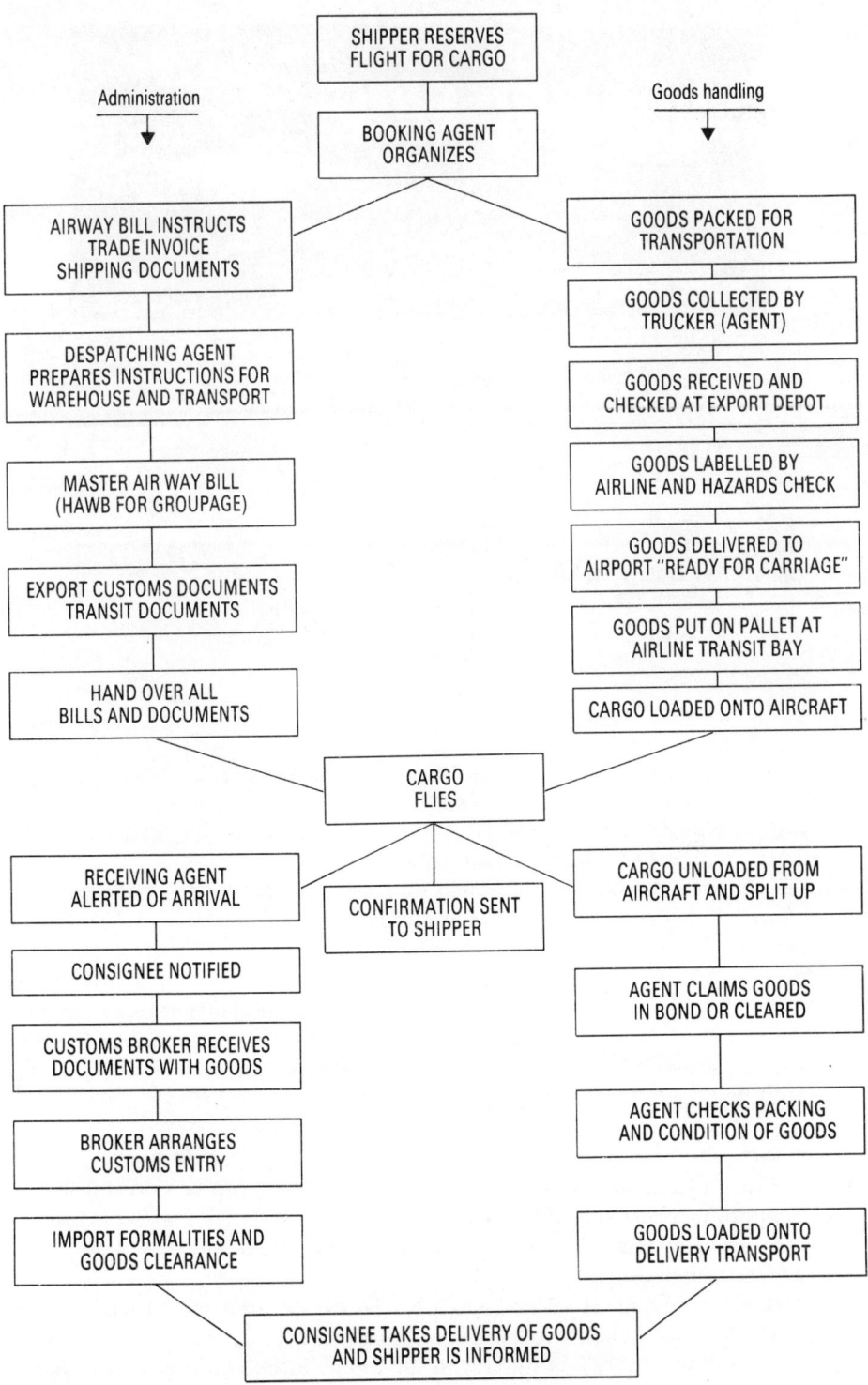

Figure 9.3 Flow chart of air freight operations

Figure 9.4   House Airway label

1   *Booking Agent* – this can be an airline or an appointed agent that sells space on aircraft for shipping cargo for a distributor or freight forwarder.
2   *Airline* – either a member of IATA or not, and most airlines are prepared to deal directly with the shipper/distributor/manufacturer.
3   *Integrator* – a combination of freight forwarder and airline that offers specialist door-to-door services using owned trucks and aircraft (e.g. UPS, Federal Express).
4   *Freight forwarder* – performs the same function as the counterpart sea or road freight distributors. The objective is to sell space to shippers using the most suitable means under the circumstances (e.g. Wassing International). Selling space on scheduled airlines and charter aircraft differ; the former allows 28 days credit, but the latter requires cash before take-off.

The forwarder takes over the shipment and stores it temporarily or transports it to the airport. Each shipment is accompanied by the appropriate documents, the most important being the Master Airwaybill (MAWB), which is the instruction from the agent to the airline giving details of what to do with the cargo, and it displays the freight charges that apply.

A House Airwaybill (HAWB) is used by the freight forwarder when exporting goods which are collected together in groups in order to fly them economically to different countries. It is of no interest to the carrier airline, as it gives instructions from the agent to the destination airport and receiving office. The HAWB describes the cargo and the agreed freight rate (see Figure 9.4).

The receiving office is notified by the airline when a cargo arrives and, in turn, it informs the consignee. Whereas the freight forwarder submits the export documents to the customs office, a broker is engaged in order to obtain important clearance. It is usual for the larger forwarding companies to have offices at all major airports so that they can deal with both export and import formalities; however, in the USA by tradition, forwarding and customs broking are kept separate.

TRANSPORTATION TRENDS

Developments in modern transportation for delivering goods have to keep pace with developments in the markets, and the biggest change in Europe recently is the formation of a common market. Consequently, deliveries are no longer national, let alone local, but international. Some of the consequences are longer distances, different languages of communication, enlarged distribution networks and the need for international warehouses. Above all, the scope of distribution logistics has become much wider.

General trends

The general trends that affect developments in the field of distribution logistics are:

- the change from a sellers market to a buyers market;
- the reduction of product life cycles and a wider range of products;
- the shift from production cost control to logistics cost control;
- the move towards international trade and wider markets.

The outcome has been an improvement in international relations and a greater demand for distribution companies to offer better service to customers. These general trends have a big influence on the transport sector, and the quality of the service it provides must be upgraded in the light of recent changes. For instance, the greater need to find an optimum within the boundaries of improved competitiveness and management control. Centralized distribution is replacing decentralized distribution in Europe as competition moves to the multi-national level. To remain in the wider European market, distributors have to be more efficient, trustworthy, flexible, better organized and fast, in order to offer the best services.

Some countries have a head start on the others – the Netherlands, for example, has been trading internationally for many centuries. Distribution is replacing agriculture as the primary source of that country's GNP. A quarter of a million Dutch people work in the distribution sector, and the incomes of four million people depend upon it. Fortunately, the Netherlands is strategically placed for delivering to the rest of Europe, and today it helps itself to a 30% slice of the European distribution pie. The country benefits from an effective development of all forms of transportation; Rotterdam is the busiest seaport in Europe, and Schiphol handles most of the air freight; whilst inland there are good road, rail and canal networks that ensure that goods move continually.

It must be remembered that static goods earn no money, and 25% of their prices in the shops is contributed by distribution costs.

The Netherlands has an ideal infrastructure for distribution, not only for transporting goods but for controlling their movements too. Modern logistics control requires computers and software for which the Dutch have coined a new name – telematics. This subject integrates automation with international transport, and it has developed software for controlling the transportation hardware, for automating customs formalities, for coordinating transport data processing and for removing language barriers. It is no wonder that the country promotes itself under the banner of 'The Distribution Land'.

The transport link

Distribution comprises a static part – the warehousing sector – and a dynamic part – the transport sector. Both are essential for providing customers with the right goods in the right places and at the right times, but paradoxically, the best service costs the most money. A compromise is always then required. When balancing distribution costs against customer service, the aim is to link production outputs to retail outlets as efficiently as possible for the least overall cost and still make a reasonable profit.

The transport link is probably the most important connection in the distribution chain, because it controls each of those requirements that comprise the level of customer service. Admittedly, the warehouse staff are responsible for assembling the right products for customer orders, but the transport driver accepts the load and must check it is right when loading the goods. Then, the driver is responsible for delivering the right goods to the right place and at the right time. It follows that the transport link between factory and customer is a key that turns on the service that it provides.

10 Servicing customers

In addition to reducing costs, the other prime objective of a distribution system is to provide the customers with the best service possible. The best service depends upon the terms of reference for the service to be provided, and the best is the alternative that meets the terms of reference most closely. The obvious best measure of customer service is the satisfaction of demand.

The service provided to customers rests directly on who they are and where they are located; what kind of goods they require and in what quantities; what ordering patterns they follow, and how their goods should be delivered. There are surprising similarities between the services required in different industries, and a knowledge of the activity patterns helps to plan and control a distribution system.

DISTRIBUTION SERVICE PATTERNS

Important patterns for distribution services include the location and size of suppliers, the location and size of customers, ordering methods for goods, and the degrees of predictability. Usually, customers show a greater similarity in these patterns than suppliers; therefore, it pays to look mostly at market patterns when planning the level of service.

Customer locations

Markets are not uniformly distributed around a country, even less around the world, because they follow certain indicators:

1 Economic indicators include the distribution of wealth, centres of population and cultural characteristics of the people.
2 Geographic indicators show where the markets are most likely to be situated.
3 Demand indicators suggest both purchasing and selling characteristics.

An analysis of the market for a particular product will indicate the level of service that distribution has to provide. Markets develop because potential users are made aware of the products either, by sales promotion, or from satisfied customers. For example, specific local fashions spread and demand becomes wider than originally. Leisure clothing and pharmaceuticals often have this kind of market distribution, and past trends or experienced judgement are useful for gauging changes in demand patterns.

Historical patterns of demand

Trends for particular products vary with time and events; therefore, it pays to keep historical records that associate demand changes with particular happenings. The usual procedure for forecasting demand is to look at trends and to try and spot specific relationships with historical events or other factors.

Seasonal patterns of demand

Over periods of time, variations in demand can be analysed statistically to discover whether they relate to different times of the year. Most seasonal trends appear to be caused by traditional purchasing patterns, including public holidays and climate. For example, demand for air conditioners is highly seasonal, not only the advent of hot weather but during previous holiday periods when householders have more time to consider expensive things needed in the home. Other seasons are important to particular tasks. Greetings card manufacturers have worked hard to promote commemorations other than Christmas or Easter in order to smoothe out their peaks during the year.

Seasonal demand patterns can be observed in many industries, and some indicators have been published in the USA as aids to forecasting. Table 10.1 shows the indicators calculated for automobiles, refrigerators and television sets in the late 1980s.

Many climate-dependent seasonal patterns are being removed due to modern refrigeration techniques and distribution by air freight. Spring flowers grown in the southern hemisphere are available in the autumn in northern markets; while fresh fruit and vegetables can be purchased all the year round anywhere in the world.

Demand for individual items

The demand for individual items in a range of products is never uniform across the spectrum; generally, the distribution of demand is skewed – a large number of dear items have a relatively low throughput, and a few cheap items account for most of the demand. A typical graph for such a demand looks rather like Figure 10.2, which is called a normal graph, because plotting the values of items against demand gives a uniform bell-shaped distribution. The graph is skewed when its peak is not in the centre of the range of the distribution.

A log-normal graph is a straight line version of the bell-shaped normal graph, because the demand and cumulative percentage of items are plotted on logarithmic scales.

Table 1   *Seasonal indicators in the USA*

	Percentage of sales		
	Automobiles	*Refrigerators*	*Television sets*
January	7.6	4.9	8.2
February	8.6	6.3	7.9
March	11.5	7.5	7.8
April	8.8	8.4	6.8
May	8.4	10.2	10.9
June	8.3	12.4	7.7
July	8.0	10.0	7.2
August	9.8	9.5	8.6
September	8.5	9.4	9.1
October	7.9	8.8	9.0
November	6.7	7.5	9.0
December	5.9	5.1	7.8
	100.0	100.0	100.0

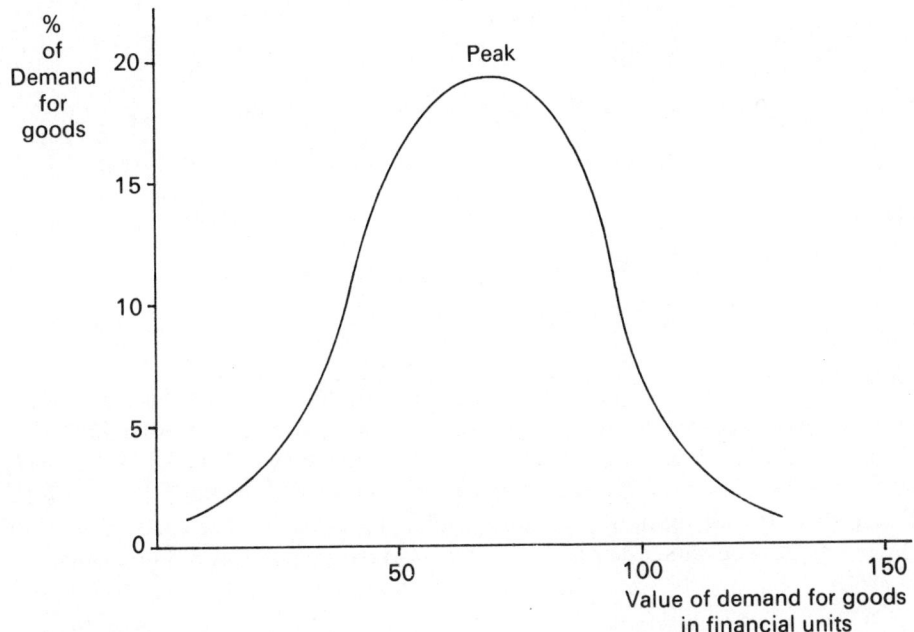

Figure 10.2   Normal demand graph

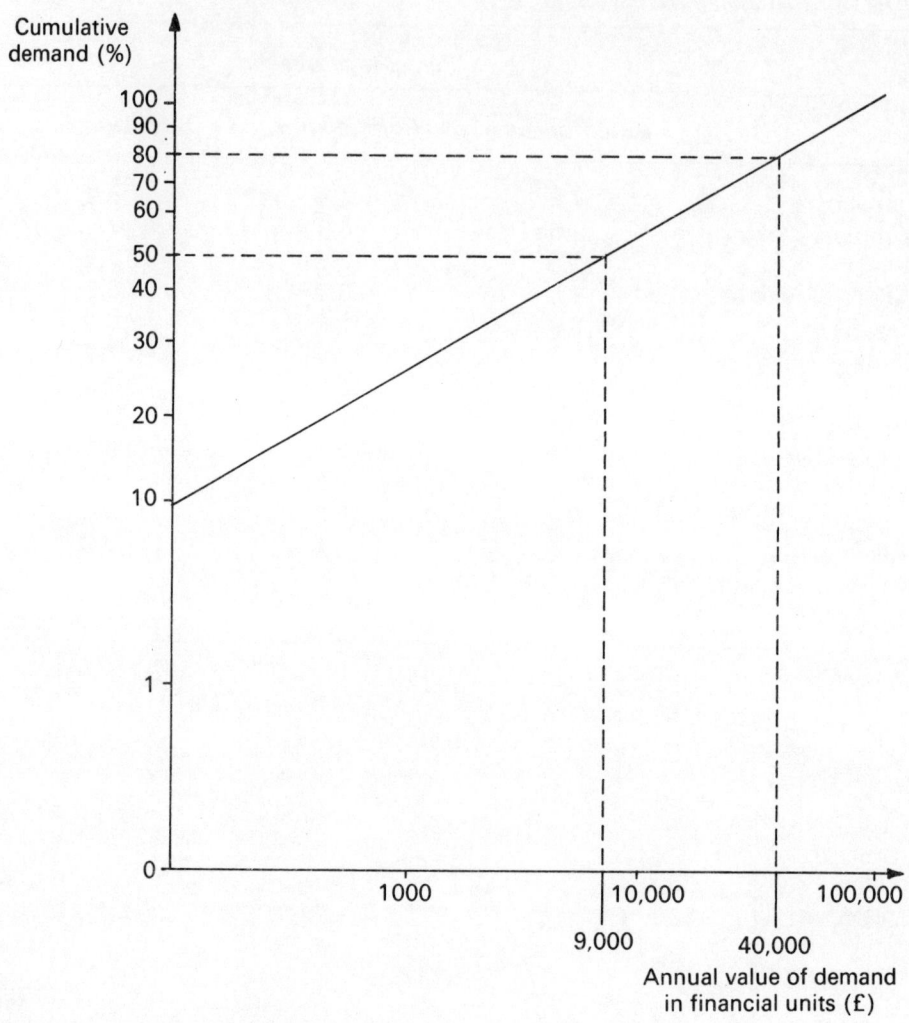

Figure 10.3   Log-normal demand distribution graph

Figures 10.2 and 10.3 represent the same data in different ways; the slope of the second graph indicates the *item-demand* rates, showing, for example, that 50% of all items account for £9 000 p.a. of demand, yet 80% account for £40 000 p.a. A more detailed explanation of item-demand can be found in any book on statistical forecasting. In distribution, it is quite useful for analysing the costs of meeting orders, making customer deliveries and forecasting other service requirements.

Forecasting demand

Here is a general procedure for forecasting aggregate demands:

1 *Develop* a model for the demand.
2 *Update* the model regularly to smoothe out variations.
3 *Adjust* for seasonal factors.
4 *Review* the forecast and compare it with previous years.

PLANNING FOR BETTER CUSTOMER SERVICE

In a distribution system, logistics tries to answer questions in order to stabilize operations so that customers can be assured of receiving recognized standards of service. Mathematical methods can be used for controlling physical operations, but everyday situations are not predictable with mathematical accuracy; therefore, modifications and compromises have to be made. When a system is subject to natural elements in the form of the weather and the frailties of human beings, it requires a weather prophet or a personnel expert to forecast it effectively. Unfortunately, both are very rare and substitutes need to be found. Knowledge-based techniques have arrived for this purpose, and they can be used to prepare data for computer processing by taking uncontrollable variations into account such as the weather, road conditions, accidents, breakdowns and faulty decisions.

Knowledge-based and learning techniques are known collectively as *expert systems*, because they require knowledge about the way that an experienced person learns and makes decisions in special circumstances. They are able to 'tune' mathematical programs so that they can analyse the data collected in the light of past experiences as a basis for tactical planning.

'Fuzziness' is logistics jargon for uncertainty, and it applies when decisions are not mathematically perfect, but are the best under certain circumstances. Variables make decisions 'fuzzy', and the greater the experience of a decision-maker, the less 'fuzzy' are the decisions. Obviously, the least 'fuzzy' solutions to distribution problems will give the best service; so expert systems have a role to play in planning for better customer service.

Expert systems

Learning from practical experience comprises a logical sequence of steps, which are called learning and knowledge-based modules in an expert system. A module gives advice to decision-makers whenever there is a choice of alternatives. Figure 10.4 expresses a delivery system in terms of modules; there are four kinds:

1 Input modules contain available information.
2 Processing modules suggest alternative actions.
3 Decision modules make a choice of the alternatives.
4 Output modules display the operational plans.

There are a number of advantages of expert systems for fuzzy situations:

1 They can use qualitative information.
2 They can possess incomplete and uncertain information.
3 They show where decisions have to be made.
4 They suggest the outcomes of alternative actions.

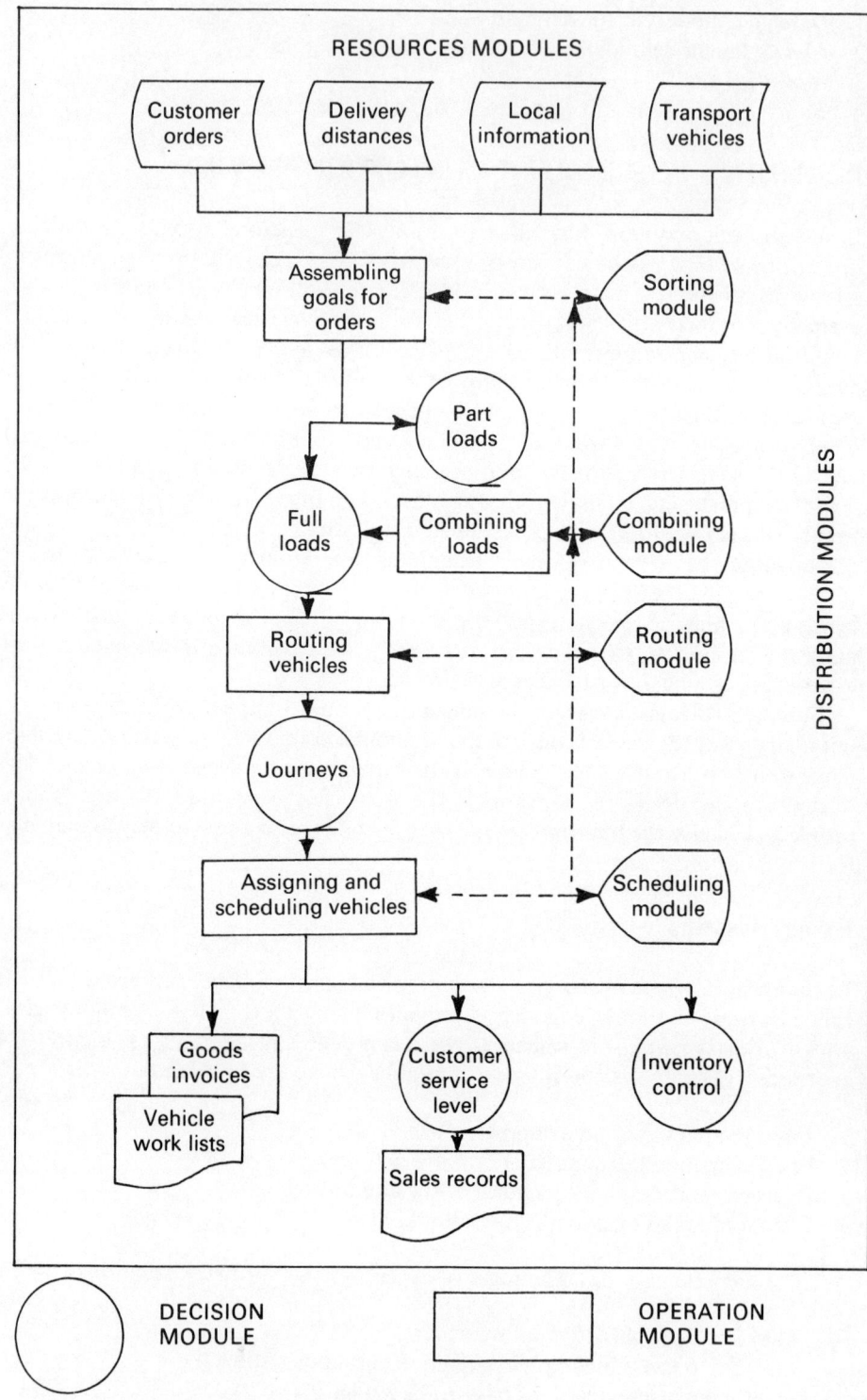

Figure 10.4   Modular system for delivery planning

5   They are comprised of modules that can be rearranged into new systems.
6   They provide outputs of documented information.
7   They can be developed for strategic, tactical, or operational levels.
8   They identify where improvements can be made.
9   They encourage logical thinking.
10 They improve the usefulness of databases for the logistics process.
11 They can simplify complex problems so that they are programmable for a computer.
12 They model the outcomes of decisions when personal experience is unavailable.

Applications of expert systems

Knowledge-based systems can monitor and control logistics functions to provide a method for evaluating performances; for example, inventory coordination or customer service. They can then give advice in the form of a 'prescription' for what should be done to improve the effectiveness of a system.

A second area concerns the rules for logical actions which can interpret the data collected into a database in order to show up exceptions in customer orders or delivery routes. Next, applications in a third area concern *on-line*, or routine on-the-job decisions, such as with order processing, locating items in a warehouse, vehicle routing, or loading delivery vehicles.

Fourthly, an expert system can diagnose faults, which helps to prevent downtime when a plan is put into action. This is important in the development of a decision support system which asks questions like: 'If this is done, what will happen?' Finding the answers helps considerably when trying to make the right decisions.

Data on its own is meaningless. It is only when data is coordinated into information that it can be used practically for drawing conclusions. For example, when delivering goods, observations of road signs, buildings, time, weather conditions and speeds enable the driver to decide where he is, how far it is to the next drop, what time is available and which way to drive. That sounds too simple, doesn't it? But people are easily distracted, and the obvious may be overlooked; however, a computer that is programmed to think like that will be completely reliable.

Example of an expert system for delivering goods

The modular delivery system shown in Figure 10.4 has been modified into Figure 10.5, which includes knowledge-based and learning modules in order to provide advice, or to schedule the program so that it is more suitable for the circumstances. The reasons for adding the new modules will be explained below.

Special loads advisory module

This knowledge-based module contains the rules governing special loads which may be large numbers of items, large in size, heavy in weight, hazardous to handle, or not

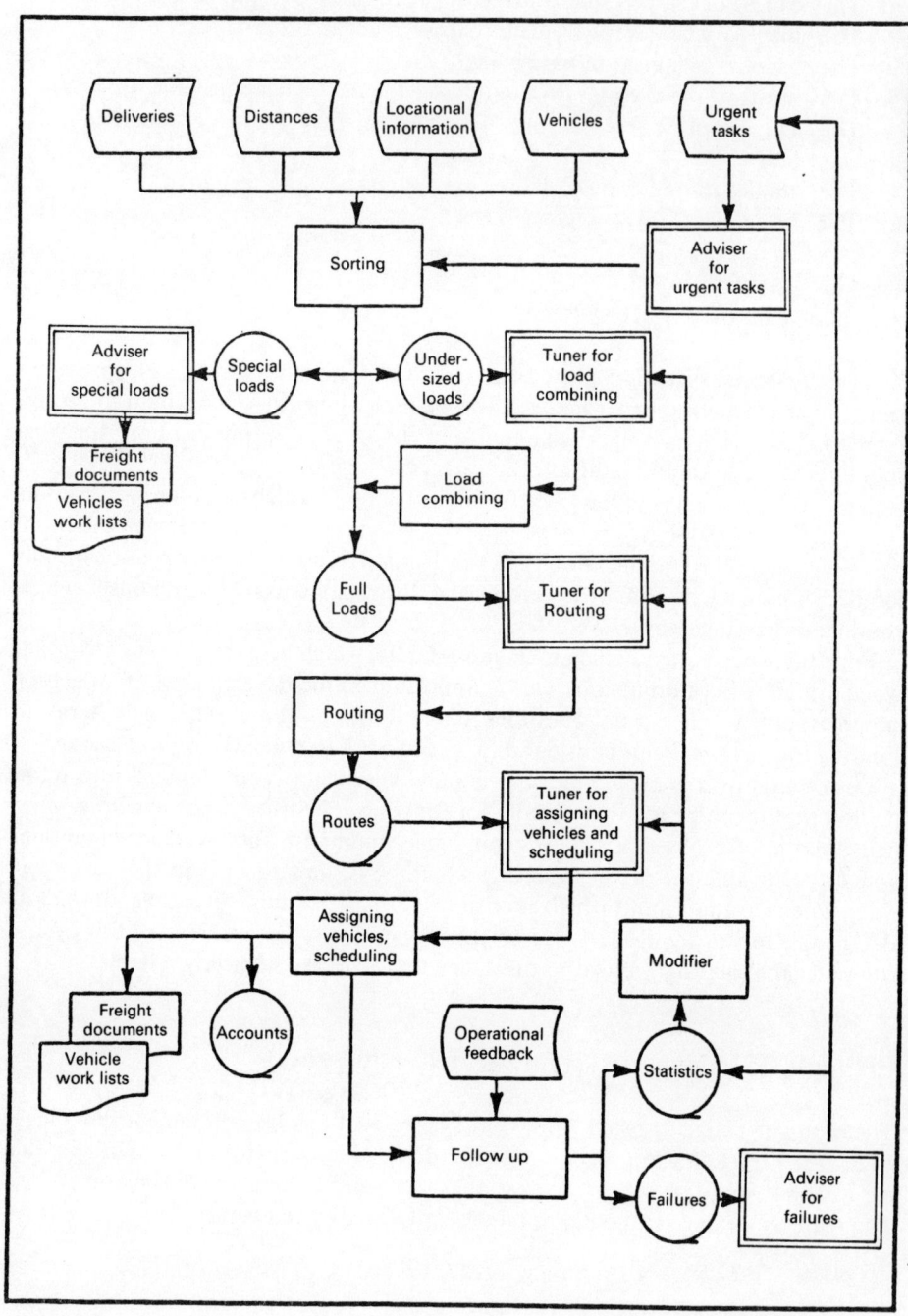

Figure 10.5   Extended system for delivery planning

routine. Then using symbolic logic, the computer can give advice on delivering these loads and display the documents that will be needed for them.

For very large deliveries, advice will be given on the choices of transportation – by road, rail, sea or air; the type of vehicles required; special handling operations; and the documentation. Details of vehicles and loads will have to be put into the module, along with costs and times and restrictions for routes, so that they can be processed according to particular rules. In this way, the field is narrowed down, and only vehicles remain that can transport the special loads in question; in all probability, only the cheapest ones!

Load-combining advisory module

Normally, methods for combining loads are heuristic or trial and error, but they will take a very long time, otherwise disasters can occur. However, if past experience is incorporated into the modules, as rules for what can or cannot be done, then logical answers can be produced. Combining loads is most likely when the number of orders are not significant for a full vehicle load; but the method chosen for combining them will be affected by the number of deliveries, the number of full loads, the number of vehicles available, and the possible routes.

This advisory module helps to reduce the amount of computing needed, but the system should be checked whenever: (1) changes occur in the deliveries – the program asks about the changes and adjusts the system accordingly, (2) a certain amount of data has been collected – the program compares it with old data in order to improve the load formations (this can be done anytime that the computer is idle), or (3) when the load combining starts – simple tests are made in order to see that the special conditions and rules are being met.

Putting a modifier module into the system enables rules to be added or removed without changing the control structure which will involve other modules. The system combines less than vehicle load deliveries and develops new routes for the full loads. Each time a full load, or a new route, has been devised, the computer asks if it is acceptable? If it is not, then, the computer asks why; finally, the procedure is checked or modified, where possible.

The reason why a new solution is not acceptable may be a lack of up-to-date information due to a recent weather forecast, or a report of local road works, or a public holiday. The modifier should include such information in the database so that alternative solutions can be presented next time. Another reason could be incorrect estimates of loading or unloading times due to broken equipment or changed working conditions.

Sometimes a solution is good in itself, but it does not comply with all the rules. Therefore, asking the operator provides an opportunity to override a particular constraint by using past personal experience.

Vehicle assigning and time-tabling advisory module

Just as loads are combined to make full vehicle loads, so routes can be combined to make full working days for the driver. When assigning a vehicle, the working hours could exceed a normal working day; so when the computer asks if the solution is acceptable, the answer will depend upon whether the driver is prepared to work overtime or not. Adding such information to the rules in the modifier will enable alternatives to be offered in future. Actually, the system can learn in this way from past modifications, since a statistical program is built into it.

In time-tabling, the opening and closing times at drop points can be questioned because they may or may not be rigid. Modifications at various points are also learnt statistically, and the computer will ask for advice whenever a time is uncertain according to its program of rules.

Urgent orders advisory module

In most cases, a delivery journey starts first thing in the morning, the load having been prepared the day before; consequently, urgent orders often arrive while the vehicle is away and special arrangements have to be made. Rush jobs, as their name suggests, have to be despatched without prior planning, although past experience is a basis for rule of thumb methods. They can be incorporated into a module for advising a computer about urgent orders; in practice, such a module is one of the most important in an expert system as far as customer service is concerned.

This module contains the rules for various degrees of urgency in order to allocate priorities to the work in hand. When an urgent job is received, the expert system considers it amongst the currently undelivered orders according to their number and characteristics in order to revise the plans most effectively. Normally, this would require too much computing time for investigating all possible combinations; however, knowledge of the best actions will provide short cuts.

The effectiveness of this module depends upon the information available to the computer for making comparisons; for instance, can vehicles be recalled and if so, where is the best place to turn back?

Since the knowledge in an urgent orders advisory module is not very well structured, the computation procedures should be independent of the control program, either as an expert system shell or prologue that includes time schedules.

Failures advisory module

This module is closely related to the previous one, because a failure to deliver a certain order on time can turn it into an urgent one. There are some differences, however, such as failures caused by accidents or breakdowns, because then extra work may be involved (like unloading a vehicle or replacing damaged goods). The most important advice from this module is the extent to which the delivery plans will be disrupted, and how they are best modified.

A delay can be the reason for not meeting a delivery schedule, due to traffic congestion or a detour; this is not a serious failure in many cases, although it means working overtime. Sometimes, part of the planned route can be allocated to another vehicle, or the sequence changed so that deliveries comply with specific opening hours. If the delay is serious, the module may include rules for re-allocating undelivered orders; however, they will usually become urgent orders that the previous module can handle.

Modifier module

This is an application of the learning system approach, the idea being to utilize idle computer time for learning how to modify programs. For example, the module allows the computer to try delivering a set of orders by a different procedure from the one actually followed. In this way, new statistics are gathered about the relative merits of comparable methods. When enough evidence has been acquired, a new priority rule may result which can be incorporated into other modules.

Another way of learning is to collect statistics of modifications made by the human operator and to associate them with particular reasons. When the frequency of a certain modification is sufficiently large it may be necessary to change the constraints already included in a module. Similarly, statistics from the effects of a constraint itself can result in a need to revise it.

Delivery plans are based upon estimated times and speeds; therefore, this modifier module is valuable for updating the estimates used. Knowledge of early or late arrivals and returns can be learnt statistically so that programs can be revised continually by this module – of course, after having asked the operator for permission. Learning from exceptions is also possible, when the reason for not accepting them is fed back; this is important if the reason is only a one-time occurrence.

Expert systems for distribution planning

As computers become cheaper and physical distribution becomes more expensive, it is worth using more computing time for distribution planning; however, this does not mean that plans will be any more accurate in practice – it means that they are made more flexible in order to cope with a wider range of eventualities. The combination of mathematical programming and artificial intelligence in the form of expert systems offers new opportunities for providing better customer service, in particular for improving delivery timeliness and reliability.

COSTS OF PROVIDING CUSTOMER SERVICE

Providing service to customers costs money; therefore, the whole of the distribution function is a cost centre, but one of the big problems when trying to reduce distribution costs is identifying them accurately. Many of the costs associated with distribution are either hidden or shared between different activities or other cost centres, thus allocating them can be difficult.

The higher the level of service offered, the more it costs. In fact, it has been shown that the cost of providing a 100% service is exorbitant. Figure 10.6 indicates that the relationship between the service level and its costs is exponential. Consequently, it is worth looking at this relationship in more detail – but first, some companies are not aware of the level of service that they are providing, let alone what is the servicing policy! The effect of offering a 97% service level instead of 99% may have little effect on product demand, yet it will cost a lot more to provide. As an indicator of the difference – a 2% service increase means an inventory increase of 14% more safety stock!

Clearly, distribution managers should recognize the implications of setting the

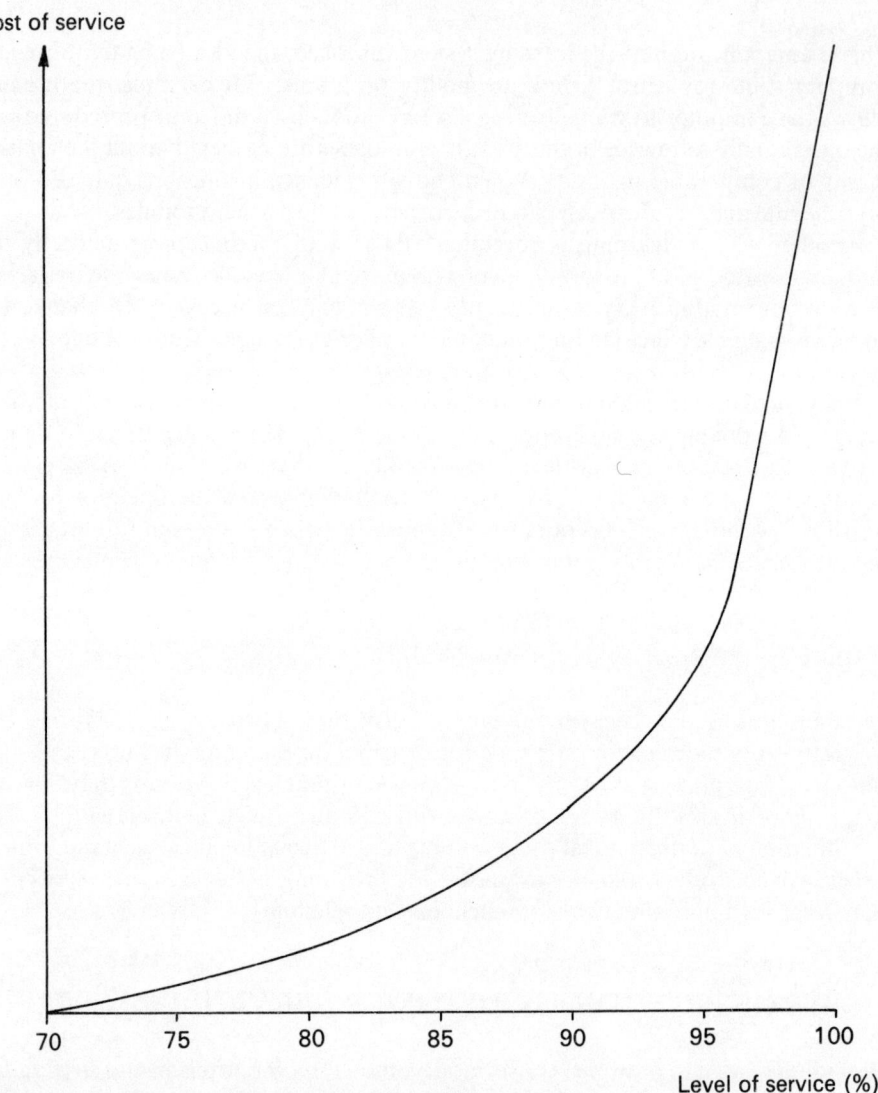

Cost of service

Level of service (%)

Figure 10.6   Relationship between service level and costs

policy for customer service. Distribution service absorbs costs that otherwise would have to be borne by the customer; for example, delivering twice a month instead of once relieves the customer of holding stock for longer than two weeks. Likewise, if the customer can rely on a high level of service, his safety stock level can also be reduced. These savings are not 'peanuts', because stock-carrying can be as much as 20% of the stock's value.

Table 10.7   Total distribution costs

	Distribution costs (%)
Transportation activity	
Material suppliers inwards	4.24
Goods operations:	
– palletization	0.11
– trunking to depots	6.67
– delivering to customer	8.09
Subtotal	19.11
Warehouse activity:	
– warehouse labour	5.38
– warehouse administration	7.48
– inventory carrying	48.97
– materials handling	3.01
– order processing	3.36
– computing	0.10
– packaging	7.51
– stock losses	0.99
Subtotal	76.80
Management activity:	
– salaries	0.80
– training	0.14
– auditing	0.13
– interest on capital	2.94
Subtotal	4.01

Total distribution on-costs = 100%

Note: Table based on information from Albert Heijn B.V., The Netherlands.

Servicing costs

All the costs of distribution should contribute to providing customer service, and not just those of transportation and warehousing. The total distribution cost, which was discussed in an earlier chapter, includes other costs such as inventory, orders processing, packaging, administration and management. Some of these costs are variable, and depend upon the distribution throughput and the type of business. A break down of the total distribution costs for a large European groceries manufacturer is given in Table 10.7; it gives an indication of the amounts involved. In this company, the distribution cost centre contributed 22.5% to the overall operating costs. Working in percentages helps management to appreciate the relative costs of different activities.

One of the benefits of being able to identify specific costs is for balancing increased costs in one area against savings in another, and being able to see the overall effect. Thus, a distribution system with five regional depots may give a slightly reduced customer service level than a system with six depots, but the warehousing costs will be much less it would appear – until the increased trunking costs are also considered. On the surface, an operational improvement in one area that looks good may not have any significant effect on the total distribution cost.

Servicing costs and benefits

The amount that should be spent on providing customer service is a question of theory because, as Figure 10.8 shows, there is in fact an optimal level of service that can be offered to customers. As the level of service increases, the number of sales lost will decrease, but the cost of providing that service will increase, and the two curves cross before the maximum service level is attained. This is the optimum.

While Figure 10.8 suggests that the point of balance is not difficult to ascertain, it is rather more difficult in practice. On one hand, there are problems of generating accurate costs data for service levels and, on the other hand, there are problems of determining the market response, namely the benefits. Therefore, what tends to happen is that managements try to find 'an acceptable balance' between costs and benefits in relation to their objectives.

Such a balance can be achieved by taking either the *cost-minimization* approach or the *service-maximization* approach. *Cost-minimization* requires specific objectives for the level of customer service and deciding how that can be met for the least cost. Alternatively, *service-maximization* is based upon a fixed distribution budget and tailoring the service to fit the amount of money available. Each has its merits; the least cost approach may be preferable in markets where customer service is very competitive; however, the best service approach may be advisable when company resources call for tight budgets.

Eventually, the costs and benefits of providing customer service have to be integrated into the whole business environment. Distribution is dependent upon marketing, production, financial and purchasing considerations, and they meet head-on when deciding the service strategy.

Service objectives

The differing needs of the various company functions mean that the customer service objec.:.es must be balanced and their constraints defined so that, overall, distribution is cost-effective. The objectives can be considered at two levels: (1) *the market standard*, which applies to the general quality of servicing groups of customers, or products; and (2) *the operational standard*, which applies to specific service levels for individual customers, products or distribution activities. An analysis of these two standards should be able to classify the different objectives in order to establish priorities.

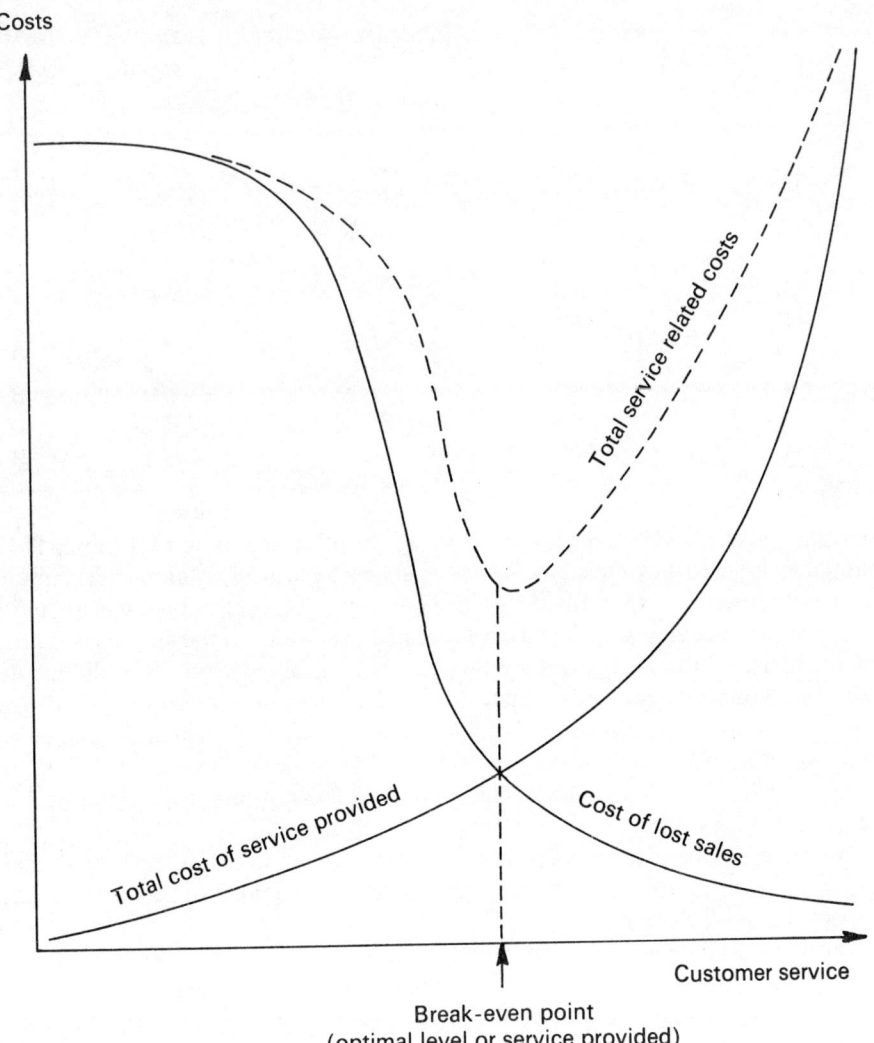

Figure 10.8 Costs and benefits of customer service

Market priorities

At the market level, either groups of customers that have similar requirements because of their size or type of business can be identified, or products are grouped according to the service that has to accompany their marketing.

Taking the customer groups first, it is important to define the objectives for each in order to reduce the number of alternatives – most markets are heterogeneous, and each customer has specific needs: that makes it very difficult to set general standards for service. It has been found that grouping customers according to needs is viable,

Table 10.9   Classification of critical service for products

Products	Ranking by returns	Critical service value			Weighted score	Revised ranking
		A	B	C		
Q	1	X			2	1
A	2		X		4	2
D	3		X		5	3
M	4			X	7	5
B	5	X			6	4
C	6		X		8	6
P	7	X			8	7
L	8		X		10	8
F	9			X	12	10
E	10	X			11	9

but they must also be *accessible* as a group. In other words so that they will have similar characteristics *and* they can be reached as a group – in a marketing and distribution sense – especially if they are members of a central buying association.

Customers needing service may be grouped according to the size and volume of their orders; or the grouping may be geographical or political. Not all customers have the same service needs, whether they are measured as lead-times, delivery-dates, flexibility, or whatever. Nor will they be equally beneficial service-wise. Almost certainly, the largest benefits will come from the smallest group of customers – the so-called *80/20 rule* applies which says that 80% of business is done with 20% of the customers.

A customer classification is possible, based upon service needs and profitability, provided that it is operationally feasible and reflects the potential profits that can be expected from the customer.

Products needing servicing can be classified in a similar way. This time, the profit contribution of products may be obtained in terms of annual turnover or unit returns. Also included should be the *critical value* of each item sold to customers; namely, the reaction to a stock-out in each case. For example, a certain product may be so vital to a customer's needs that he would have to go to another supplier in the event of a stock-out. At the other extreme, a customer may not be bothered, because an alternative product is just as good. It is useful to classify products on an ABC scale for their *critical values*, as shown in Table 10.9.

Table 10.9 is based upon the service requirements of electrical products made by a German company. The products were first ranked according to their profit margins and then assessed according to how critical they were to particular groups of customers. The critical values then added weight to the first ranking to produce a revised ranking based upon profitability and level of service.

The next step was to combine the product rankings with customer rankings, and to produce a matrix like that in Table 10.10 for a UK manufacturer of summer clothing.

The number of product and customer groups will depend upon the distribution

Table 10.10   Market service priorities matrix

Product group ranking	Customer group ranking				
	1	2	3	4	5
1	1	3	4	13	16
2	2	6	9	14	18
3	5	10	15	20	23
4	7	12	19	24	27
5	8	17	17	26	29
6	11	21	25	28	30

Table 10.11   Operational service standards

Priorities range	In-stock standard (%)	Delivery time standard (hours)
1 – 5	99	24
6 – 10	98	30
11 – 15	95	48
16 – 20	90	60
21 – 25	85	90
26 – 30	75	120

system, but the priorities will always be a combination of their weightings. In Table 10.11, the product/customer groups in the priority ranks from 1–5 can expect a product to be in-stock 99% of the time, and it will be delivered to the customer within 24 hours; whereas groups with lower priorities are less important.

Problems can occur at this stage; especially, for instance, if a customer in the second group places an order for products in groups one and five. According to Table 10.11, a product in group one has to be delivered from stock within 24 hours, but a product in group five may not be in stock because its stock availability is only 85% of the time. Another problem can arise when a full load requires the products ordered from a number of different groups. The answer is that personal experience has to have the last word in deciding the priorities for customer servicing, and the operational standards are guides for the minimum order cycle times, inventory levels or stock availabilities.

RIGHT LEVEL OF CUSTOMER SERVICE

The demand for a product is an indicator of the service provided to customers by its supplier; however, this relationship is difficult to measure directly. How does demand respond to variations in the level of customer service?

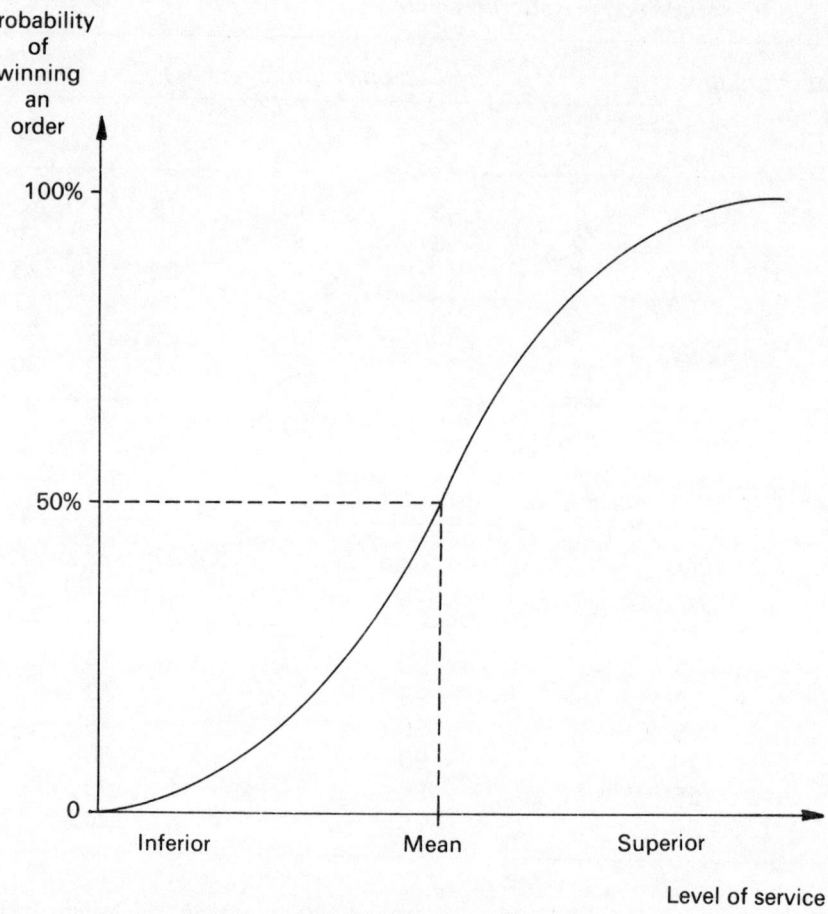

Figure 10.12   Customer service related to demand for goods

The nature of the demand responses to customer service cannot be generalized because the responses often relate to specific product or market situations. One suggestion is that customers do respond to the *differential* between the service offered by competitive suppliers, and a measure could be the relative service levels offered. The probability of successfully obtaining an order increases progressively with increasing standards of service, as shown in Figure 10.12.

The better the service offered, the better is the chance of winning an order than the competition; unfortunately, the graph does not take other factors into consideration. Those factors may be the amount of publicity, previous promotional experience, and the quality of the product itself. One way of including such factors is to carry out an *investigation* similar to a market research study. Some companies have successfully investigated the effect of service in creating demand, one being a hardware manufacturer who kept good cost records. That company compared the demand for similar products at different depots by deliberately altering the level of service offered at each location – in terms of safety stocks available at depots.

Actually, the demand differences were insignificant despite the reduced investment in stocks.

Obviously, there are dangers to this sort of investigation, but it can be useful for collecting information, and that always provides benefits in other ways. Even small-scale research can produce worthwhile results. An alternative approach is the *questionnaire*. Various factors in a distribution system that affect customers directly can be changed, and the customer asked for their comments.

Customer service policies

The extent that the level of customer service influences sales or profitability depends upon a careful analysis of the market needs, an understanding of customer reactions and an evaluation of the service costs. Companies that have such a customer service policy do report improvements in business, and in the image presented to customers. In fact, providing the right level of service is not so much a cost centre, as a source of increased income due to a value added improvement.

Example of a customer service questionnaire

1   *Order cycle*
    - What is the waiting time after placing an order?
    - How consistent are the ordering times?
    - How does it compare with other suppliers?
    - Is the minimum order size acceptable?

2   *Service level*
    - How good is the order-picking accuracy?
    - How much damage occurs?
    - What is your reaction to a stock-out?
    - Does a long lead-time affect your business?
    - Is the procedure for handling incomplete orders satisfactory?
    - Are deliveries on time?

3   *Ordering procedure*
    - Is placing an order convenient?
    - Are orders acknowledged satisfactorily?
    - Are despatch notes accurately prepared?
    - Are the invoices reliable?

4   *Communications*
    - Are enquiries handled efficiently?
    - Is the sales office competent?
    - How do deliveries compare with ordered requirements?
    - How does the supplier react to complaints?
    - Are telephone queries answered swiftly?
    - Are written communications accurate?

5   *Personnel*
    - Is the approach of sales representatives acceptable?
    - Are contacts with the staff friendly?

    – Are the delivery personnel helpful?
    – How do you rate the level of personal service provided?

6   *Packaging*
    – Do goods arrive in good condition?
    – Are the packages convenient for stock-holding?
    – Are the packages correctly labelled?
    – Are the packages easily handled?

7   *Advertising*
    – How does the service level compare with expectations?
    – Does advertising produce new business for you?
    – What is the quality of advertising in your opinion?
    – Can cooperative advertising be improved?
    – Does the distribution system enhance the supplier's image?

8   *Overall*
    – Is the level of service generally good?
    – Where can improvements be made?
    – Is sufficient information available?
    – Where do competitors do better?
    – What improvements do you suggest?

Customer service summary

The cost of providing service to customers is really synonymous with the whole cost of distribution but, in the main, it relates to the ability to satisfy orders from stock. If stock is not available at the time of ordering, it is a question of improving the inventory control; if the customer has to wait for deliveries, it is a question of revising the warehouse processing system or the delivery scheduling; and if it is a problem of damaged goods or faulty orders, the packaging and goods handling procedures need attention.

11 Computers for controlling distribution

Today, the most advanced controlling systems are based upon a computer which uses electronic data processing to compare information and decide which alternative complies best with an objective. Without the aid of computers, analysis of large amounts of data would be laborious and time-consuming. Until recently, computers were in the exclusive domain of 'systems experts', but the microcomputer has changed that. Technological advances in digitalization have put the computer in the hands of the people who know what they want it to do.

The complex nature of analogue models for distribution operations makes the analogue computer unsuitable for controlling distribution; however, digital computers can store and manipulate numbers and letters to perform calculations and similar logical operations. This makes the digital computer an ideal tool for helping distribution managers.

The basic elements of a digital computer are its central processor and the peripheral devices which supply data to the processor and record the results. Originally, the speed of a computer was limited by the input and output peripherals, which were punched cards and typewriters, respectively. However, the latest machines use magnetic discs, and the electronic processor can read, process and display data at speeds of many thousands of characters per second.

Digital computer operations are very simple – just the difference between positive and negative electrical impulses or a binary analysis – but they occur at such high speeds that complex calculations can be performed. The sequence of binary operations proceeds according to a program that is inserted into the processor so that only the relevant data is retrieved from the processor's memory and analysed.

The components and circuitry of a computer are called its hardware; while the operating instructions together in the form of programs are known as computer software.

Computer programs

The accuracy of computing depends upon the skill of the person who writes the operating program – it is the program that makes mistakes, and not the computer itself. Actually, the computer cannot innovate like a human brain, and the Israeli name for a computer is very appropriate: it is 'golam', which means 'idiot' – neither an idiot nor a computer can think for themselves!

An operating program has to be written in a language that the computer can understand, for instance, binary language for a digital computer. Programs can be written individually for specific situations, but this requires experience – it is much simpler to purchase ready-made programs from the experts. They will be standard programs, but they become specific when your own information is processed with them.

The collection of standard programs for performing a particular set of operations is called a software system.

COMPUTER SOFTWARE SYSTEMS

Computers for controlling distribution operations need not be huge or expensive today, because small ones that are quite adequate and reasonably priced are available. They are known as *microcomputers*, or *personal computers* (PC), which are compact and can be operated on a desk top. The large ones are called *mainframe* computers, and in between them are the so-called *minicomputers*.

As said earlier, all computers need software programs to tell them what to do. There are many software systems written for the distribution function which are available 'off-the-shelf', though for microcomputers none may precisely suit your needs. This leaves three options: first, choose the system that is closest to your requirements and accept the shortfall in its specifications, or adjust your operations to fit the computerized system – this is by far the cheapest option at around £1 000 for the hardware (microcomputer/PC) and £500 to £2 000 for the software; second, rewrite elements of a standard software package, or employ a systems designer to write the program for you – this is expensive, because writing software is very labour intensive (you should expect to add about £10 000 to the figure quoted above, and even then the result will take several months before all the bugs are tracked down and eliminated); third, the ideal solution is to employ a systems design team to build the whole system for you with dedicated software – naturally, the same sort of development problems will be encountered, but the final software system, at the time, will meet your specifications absolutely – the high cost will be the problem at several hundred thousand pounds, however, the copyright will be yours, and part of the outlay, if not all, could be recovered by selling copies of the package to other organizations.

Computers require considerable discipline on the part of the operators, as errors can easily creep in and pass unnoticed, since people tend to believe that computers are infallible. In truth they are, though the software may not be totally free of faults, even those written by experts; also, it is almost impossible for every permutation of the input data to be tested. It should be mentioned that Ashton Tate have resolved these problems, and its dBASE IV version 1.1 is a much improved system. Computer errors will account for as little as 2% of your problems; however, operators are people and 'to err is human'. So the first rule is be accurate at all times, and the second rule is to devise a checking system which may be done by the computer in the form of a data validation program. A set of rules can be written into the basic program so that all the data input is checked against predetermined criteria, and any data failing these tests is rejected so the operator has to correct it manually.

Computers have a limited memory bank, although it appears to be huge when the machine is purchased; but invariably, no time can be set aside to clear out the obsolete data, and in a very short time the memory becomes clogged. This may be coupled with the fact that power supplies are not entirely infallible, and data can be lost due to a power cut. Therefore, keeping back-up information is vital. So the third rule is to keep records of what is in the computer, and copies of files on floppy disks or tapes in a safe place. Good housekeeping is essential, both from the safety or security point of view, and for being able to find and gain access to files quickly. The final and golden rule for operating a computer system is to print hard copy only when needed, and then to print only the essential information. All too often, a clerk or manager is seen peering over a mound of computer paper that he does not want, but dare not throw out in case it might be useful – if only he knew what to look for!

Computers have five basic uses: for leisure, word procesing, data manipulation, communications and data storage. All business applications are variations on these purposes:

1 *Leisure* – games give an introduction to simulations, while as training packages they are essential in any organization. It is also important to keep a few games on the computer as an encouragement to the staff to use it.
2 *Word processing* is really sophisticated typing. When linked to databases that include spelling checks and grammar, thesaurus and mail merging (one letter being sent to several addresses), a word processor is very versatile.
3 *Data manipulation* changes databases and spreadsheets of source data into objective outputs. Spreadsheets are complex mathematical tools for mathematical modelling, controlling finances and scheduling vehicles. They are the basis of most distribution programs (they are discussed later).
4 *Communications* concern hard facts which computers can share and pass on, either within a company or sent outside when they act as fax machines or for accessing mainframe databases elsewhere.
5 *Data storage* is normally provided by a database, and it is merely a replacement for traditional filing cabinets. A computer memory is particularly useful for maintaining archives; however, whereas a single density floppy disk will hold all the text of this book, diagrams require a considerable amount of storage space. The new compact disk data storage can hold several million

characters of information, equivalent to a whole cabinet full of files. The space saving is huge, and may even release rooms for other purposes.

COMPUTER PACKAGES

Two main types of package for fleet managers have been developed over the last decade or so: first, one that allows fleet management to keep track of vehicle usage, maintenance and costs; and second, another type for scheduling and route finding. The latter was first on the scene with huge databases for mainframe computers; they have since been made more efficient and can fit into the smaller memory of a desktop PC. The management packages are a more recent innovation, and are often incorporated into route or scheduling programs. Their costs range from about £30 000 for a complete package to £100 for individual modules, and even they vary wildly in price. For example, AUTOROUTE costs around £150, and provides a route card and map for planning journeys between two places with an option to go via a couple of other places anywhere in the UK. In contrast, ROUTEMASTER costs 100 times as much, but includes most of the EEC as well as providing a scheduling service. PARAGON is a similar program in the same price range, and PATHFINDER, which was developed by British Road Services, is about average priced at £5 000. This oversimplifies the merits of each program, but it does illustrate the need to shop around to find what suits your needs as closely as possible and within your budget.

Databases are readily available either as blank 'do-it-yourself' program packages or as ready-made modules for transport management. The obvious use of a database is to keep a record of all the details of each vehicle, such as make, model, body type, servicing dates, test dates, capacity, dimensions, value, depreciation rate, tax and insurance costs and dates due. Those are just a few of the details in Foxgroves Choice Vehicle Management System, which has over 200 kinds of information about vehicles; it costs about £1 000. The trick with such databases is to have a questionnaire module built-in so that you can ask for statistics across the whole fleet; for example, a list of all vehicles by registration number that require servicing next week. On a more complex level, provided the data is updated daily, the program can calculate the running costs of an individual vehicle for a whole year, or of a specific group of vehicles when linked to a spreadsheet. Although designed as a fleet management tool, such programs are invaluable to planners because they can calculate answers to the *what/if* type of question. Having put the initial fleet into the program, the planner can add or subtract a vehicle and quickly get the answer to show how the fleet costs or carrying capacity will have changed.

Similarly, there are computer software packages for warehouse operations and depot siting which can be linked with the transport packages to provide a complete distribution modelling system. Freight forwarding by sea or air do not escape unnoticed by the eagle eyes of the demanding system because packages also exist for this area. The real bonus of a computer system is that it is very good at covering the tedious routine administration which, though not a direct consideration when planning a distribution system, is a valuable supplementary asset. Some of the basic rules and considerations when thinking about automating the planning and controlling of a distribution system have been outlined, and brief descriptions of the main programs available are now given, while one of the complete packages is examined in detail. The list of available packages is by no means complete, but will serve as a guide to help planners. Where possible, the name of a supplier has been included in Appendix 2 so that more specific information about individual items of software can be obtained.

COMPUTER SOFTWARE PACKAGES FOR WAREHOUSING

The *PATHFINDER* inventory system is a complete stock control and accounting system that supports trend analysis, economic order quantities, budgeting and customer records. It handles receipts, issues, returns, transfers, stock adjustments and customer histories. It uses Digital Equipment Corporation (DEC) hardware, and the source language is PowerHouse (a fourth generation computer language developed by Cosmos in Canada).

The *VAS* inventory management system controls inventory investment by tracking, analysing and reporting the stock levels for any number of items, warehouses and bin locations. The quantities in hand, on order, released, committed, available, or a back order may be interactively updated either manually or automatically. It uses DEC hardware, and the source language is PowerHouse.

WHAMS is a warehouse management system designed for controlling stocks randomly allocated within the warehouse. It uses either COBOL or PowerHouse languages on DEC or VAX hardware to recognize various types of stock movements, storage methods and information requirements. Radio data terminals can either be hand-held or mounted on operating equipment.

MAGICAL is the integrated distribution software developed by MEGA Systems. It provides for audit tracking of activities and accounting entries, multiple currency transactions with automatic conversions, flexible end-of-period processing, and it is fully integrated for running with other programs on Data General (DG) hardware.

NEGODIS software is particularly suitable for both warehousing and controlling the deliveries of perishable goods. Some of its features include transporting, ordering, invoicing, purchasing and stocks management. It uses Hewlett Packard (HP) hardware and the PowerHouse source language.

The *LARGOTIM* warehouse management system is designed to increase the productivity of warehouses and to reduce costs. It improves layouts, A-B-C activities, inventory turns, order picking and packing, stock control, and replenishments with the aid of bar-code scanning and radio frequency communication. It can be used with HP or DEC hardware.

PERSPECTIVE systems are available for entering orders and purchase order management. They automatically update accounting, inventory and sales programs, while orders may be tracked by vendor or by warehouse. They use DEC hardware and the VAX BASIC source language.

INVENTORY is a complete stock control and accounting system that uses DEC hardware and the PowerHouse source language. It handles receipts, issues, returns, transfers, stock reservations and adjustments, and maintains full online information of each.

COMPUTER SOFTWARE PACKAGES FOR TRANSPORT OPERATIONS

In the past few years, it has been realized that the logistics approach of considering distribution as a series of interdependent movements is essential for maintaining a hard won competitive position. Pressure from markets is increasing, especially concerning the reliability of services to customers, such as delivering goods on time, in the best condition and according to variable requirements. Fierce competition is also putting pressure on keeping down costs and pushing up efficiency; logistics is a most appropriate strategic weapon.

The functional attitude towards the flow of goods is being replaced by the integral approach, in which planning and control are more flexible and easier to automate. Streamlining the distribution of goods requires logical thinking, and what better training for it is there than programming operations for computer control? With increasing skills, the demand for software packages that can control distribution is also increasing. The number of packages available is confusing; fortunately, there is little to choose between them, and it is best to stick with the one that has proved successful under your own conditions, including for the model of computer that you use.

It is valuable to know what software is available if you are just moving into computerized distribution: a useful checklist was prepared in 1989 by the Dutch advice bureau Berenschot, which specializes in automation and logistics. With acknowledgement to this source, a comparison of different computer packages for distribution has been prepared, and is shown in Tables 11.1 to 11.4.

Tables 11.1 to 11.4 show how different software packages fit the different activity areas, but it depends upon the way the program functions with certain hardware, their flexibility, and the expertise of the operators. Our experience suggests that new packages are developed largely for commercial reasons rather than the know-how they contain. Due to the high cost of developing a software package, they tend to be developed for a specific purpose, and custom-built supplementary programs are added to broaden their range of functions.

Standard packages

Nowadays, it is rare for businesses to develop their own computer software, because the number of standard application programs on the market is increasing all the time. Standard programs are usually made as flexible as possible so that they can be adapted for different companies by changing the parameters. An example is the bookkeeping package that develops its own accounting program which is cheaper than self-developed programs. Less updating is necessary, because the dealer receives all the new releases, and standard packages are more quickly available.

Some caution is needed when switching to standard packages, because choosing and implementing one takes longer than expected – a package for controlling distribution might take two years before it is fully operational! One reason for this is because standard packages have a large number of options, and it takes a lot of time and effort to learn to use it efficiently for a particular situation. DRP (Distribution

Table 11.1 Software packages for distribution logistics

No.	Software package	Hardware manufacturers	Suppliers
1	AMAPS	Hewlett Packard/IBM	MSA International
2	BPCS	IBM	Consulting Associates
3	CONTROL	IBM/VAX	Cincom Systems International
4	COPICS	IBM	Cullinet Software
5	EBO	Siemens	Siemens
6	EMS	Ericsson	Hoskyns Group
7	FEROS	Quattro	Nixdorf
8	FOSS 3000	Hewlett Packard	Ordat
9	IPPS	NCR	NCR
10	MAPICS	IBM	IBM
11	MIXX	Unix	ICL
12	PIOS	IBM/VAX	McCormack & Dodge
13	PM 38	IBM	Cimpro
14	PMS	Philips	Safe Computing
15	PRISM	IBM	JJ Myers
16	PROGRES	IBM	ICS
17	PROMIS	Bull/DPS	Datashare
18	SAFE	ICL/Unix	Safe Computing
19	SAP	IBM	SAP
20	XBMS	IBM	Xerox Computer Services

Resource Planning) standard packages are available for physical distribution activities of various kinds.

When a system deviates from the standard package, it is best to divide it into modules so that a software model can be constructed from standard modules. Such an approach helps to develop the logical thinking which is needed for computer programming.

ABCAS This is a program for fleet management which was originally designed to record and monitor vehicle maintenance records and costs. Then a general vehicle history module was developed for it that could provide statistics and running costs, as a management aid. This program has continued to evolve over the years, and now consists of several modules including the inventory control of spares, tachograph analysis and scheduling. It is sold as modules which vary in price from under £1 000 to three times that amount.

AIR PACK A rather different type of program which is one of the many produced by Freight Computer Services (FCS) for the distribution function, this is primarily concerned with freight forwarding by air. The bulk of the administration involved in running an air freight agency can be handled, we believe; it is still available for the older CP/M operating equipment, as well as for modern PCs running the MS DOS operating system.

Table 11.2   Comparison of distribution software packages

Software package names and nos.

Distribution module nos.	Distribution module descriptions	AMAPS 1	BPCS 2	CONTROL 3	COPICS 4	EBO 5	EMS 6	FEROS 7	FOSS 3000 8	IPPS 9	MAPICS 10	MIXX 11	PIOS 12	PM38 13	PMS 14	PRISM 15	PROGRES 16	PROMIS 17	SAFE 18	SAP 19	XBMS 20
8.1.1	Generates transport documents (despatch note, forwarding notes, etc.)	Y	Y	Y	Y	Y	Y	Y	Y	Y	Y	Y	Y	Y	–	Y	Y	Y	Y	Y	–
8.1.2	Generates customs documents	Y	Y	Y	–	Y	–	–	Y	–	–	Y	Y	–	–	Y	Y	–	–	Y	–
8.1.3	Creates pro-forma invoices	Y	Y	Y	–	Y	–	–	Y	–	–	Y	Y	Y	–	Y	Y	Y	–	Y	–
8.1.4	Provides electronic mailing	–	Y	Y	Y	Y	–	Y	Y	Y	–	Y	Y	Y	–	Y	Y	–	–	Y	Y
8.1.5	Generates information in other languages automatically	Y	–	–	–	–	Y	Y	Y	–	–	Y	–	–	–	Y	Y	Y	–	Y	Y
8.1.6	Records the number of deliver addresses	–	–	–	–	–	–	–	Y	–	–	–	–	–	–	–	–	–	–	–	–
8.2.1	Has a route planning system	–	Y	Y	–	–	–	–	–	–	–	–	Y	–	–	–	Y	–	–	–	–
8.2.2	Checks vehicle loading	Y	Y	–	Y	–	–	–	–	–	–	–	Y	–	–	–	Y	Y	–	Y	–
8.2.3	Generates separates forwarding schedules	Y	Y	Y	Y	–	Y	–	Y	–	–	Y	Y	–	–	–	Y	Y	–	–	–
8.2.4	Simulates distribution schedules	Y	–	–	–	–	–	–	–	–	–	–	Y	Y	–	–	–	–	–	–	–
8.2.5	DRP module can actuate MRP(MPS)	Y	–	–	–	–	–	–	Y	–	–	Y	Y	Y	–	–	–	–	–	–	Y
8.2.6	MRP operates a DRP module	Y	–	–	–	–	–	Y	–	–	–	–	–	–	–	–	Y	–	–	–	–

Key: DRP = Distribution Requirements Planning; MRP = Materials Requirements Planning; MPS = Master Production Schedule; Y = yes; – = no or not applicable.

DiPS   Staying with FCS, their main program for distribution planning is the DiPS system which works on two levels. First, it models depots and warehouses as an aid to planning locations and sites that best meet the customers' requirements, including a lot of '*what/if*' options that allow planners to try out different proposals for future expansions before actually committing the company to bricks and mortar. The second level concerns similar models for forecasting vehicle utilization and running costs with trucks and routes.

DRIVE DATA, MICRODRIVE and *DRIVE 6*   These are all programs designed by FCS to handle the fleet management side of distribution operations. The main difference between the systems is the size of computer that they require: the two DRIVE programs use minicomputers in order to handle the size of database and the complex calculations; MICRODRIVE needs a larger computer, and is essentially a slightly changed version of the other programs. With the exception of DRIVE DATA, the cost of a package is a little over £1 000; DRIVE DATA is a mainframe computer program which is part of a larger package that can be accessed on a rental basis using a remote terminal in the transport office.

AUTOROUTE PLUS   This is a cheap and very good road route optimizer which, when given a starting point and a destination, will produce a sketch map and route card. It can plot routes that go via or avoid certain specified places or roads; the output gives cumulative distances travelled and times at each critical point, road junction, town and village. At a little over £300 it is extremely good value, and has been used by many of the larger transport organizations. It is produced by Next

Table 11.3   Comparison of stock control software packages

Software package names and nos.

Stock control module nos.	Stock control module descriptions	AMAPS 1	BPCS 2	CONTROL 3	COPICS 4	EBO 5	EMS 6	FEROS 7	FOSS 3000 8	IPPS 9	MAPICS 10	MIXX 11	PIOS 12	PM38 13	PMS 14	PRISM 15	PROGRES 16	PROMIS 17	SAFE 18	SAP 19	XBMS 20
5.1.1	Registers materials in and out	Y	Y	Y	Y	Y	Y	Y	Y	Y	Y	Y	Y	Y	Y	Y	Y	Y	Y	Y	Y
5.1.2	Registers independent demand (stochastic) and dependent demand (deterministic)	Y	Y	Y	Y	Y	Y	Y	Y	Y	Y	Y	Y	Y	Y	Y	Y	–	Y	–	Y
5.1.3	Makes allowance for partial orders	Y	Y	Y	Y	Y	Y	Y	Y	Y	Y	Y	Y	Y	Y	Y	Y	Y	Y	Y	Y
5.1.4	Can handle numbered order issues	Y	Y	Y	Y	Y	Y	Y	Y	Y	Y	Y	Y	Y	Y	Y	Y	Y	Y	Y	Y
5.1.5	Can handle returns	Y	Y	Y	Y	Y	Y	Y	Y	Y	Y	Y	Y	Y	Y	Y	Y	Y	Y	Y	Y
5.1.8	Can handle fixed warehouse locations	Y	–	–	–	–	–	–	–	–	–	–	Y	Y	–	–	–	–	–	Y	–
5.1.9	Can handle free warehouse locations	Y	Y	Y	Y	Y	Y	Y	Y	Y	Y	Y	Y	–	Y	–	Y	Y	Y	Y	–
5.1.10	Order numbers are related to warehouse locations	Y	–	Y	–	–	Y	Y	–	Y	Y	Y	Y	–	Y	Y	Y	–	–	–	–
5.1.11	How many stocks can be recorded?	00	1	1000	6	–	99	00	00	99	36	00	00	00	G	35	80	S	–	99	
5.1.18	Keeps history files	Y	Y	Y	Y	Y	Y	Y	Y	Y	Y	Y	Y	Y	Y	Y	Y	Y	Y	Y	Y
5.2.1	Has a demand forecasting module	Y	–	Y	–	Y	Y	Y	Y	–	–	Y	Y	Y	Y	Y	–	–	–	–	Y
5.3.1	Generates planned purchase orders	Y	Y	Y	–	Y	Y	Y	Y	Y	Y	Y	Y	Y	Y	Y	Y	Y	Y	Y	Y
5.3.2	Checks stock level against re-order point	Y	Y	Y	–	Y	Y	Y	Y	Y	Y	Y	Y	Y	Y	Y	Y	Y	Y	Y	Y
5.3.4	Stock control module is independent of MRP	Y	Y	–	–	Y	Y	Y	Y	–	Y	Y	Y	Y	Y	Y	Y	Y	Y	Y	Y
5.5.2	Re-order quantities are calculated internally	Y	–	–	–	Y	–	Y	Y	–	–	Y	–	Y	Y	Y	Y	Y	–	–	Y
5.5.5	Checks dates of perishable goods	Y	–	–	Y	–	Y	Y	Y	–	–	Y	–	–	–	Y	Y	–	–	Y	–
5.5.6	Generates maximum and minimum order quantities	Y	Y	Y	Y	Y	Y	Y	Y	Y	–	Y	–	Y	Y	Y	Y	–	–	Y	–
5.5.7	Handles packaging units	Y	–	Y	Y	Y	Y	Y	Y	Y	–	Y	–	Y	Y	Y	Y	Y	–	Y	–
5.5.8	Handles quantity discounts	Y	–	–	–	–	–	Y	Y	Y	–	Y	–	Y	Y	Y	Y	–	Y	Y	–
5.6.1	Makes stock valuations	Y	Y	Y	Y	Y	Y	Y	Y	Y	Y	Y	Y	Y	Y	Y	Y	Y	Y	Y	Y

Key: G = Gaussian; S = several; Y = yes; – = no or not applicable; MRP = Materials Requirements Planning.

Note: With stochastic models for calculating buffer stocks and deliveries, it is important to separate stochastic independent demand from deterministic dependent demand.

Base Ltd of Staines in England, who also produce a series of add-on modules, including OPTIMISATION which combines routing and scheduling. Other modules handle costing, postcodes, administrative boundaries and Isochrone planning. The latter includes:

- sales territory rationalization;
- depot location for distribution;
- catchment area analysis for retail outlets;
- response-time analysis for emergency and other services;
- office relocation.

If cost is a problem, copies of the older AUTOROUTE (not PLUS) are still available at £150, but it is better to buy the complete package for less than £1 000.

Table 11.4 Comparison of marketing software packages

Software package names and nos.

Marketing module nos.	Marketing module descriptions	AMAPS 1	BPCS 2	CONTROL 3	COPICS 4	EBO 5	EMS 6	FEROS 7	FOSS 3000 8	IPPS 9	MAPICS 10	MIXX 11	PIOS 12	PM38 13	PMS 14	PRISM 15	PROGRES 16	PROMIS 17	SAFE 18	SAP 19	XBMS 20
7	*Sales orders*																				
7.1.1		Y	Y	Y	Y	Y	Y	Y	Y	Y	Y	Y	Y	Y	Y	Y	Y	Y	Y	Y	Y
7.1.2		Y	Y	Y	Y	Y	Y	Y	Y	Y	Y	Y	Y	Y	Y	Y	Y	Y	Y	Y	Y
7.1.3		Y	Y	Y	Y	Y	Y	Y	–	Y	Y	Y	Y	Y	Y	Y	Y	Y	Y	Y	Y
7.1.4		Y	Y	Y	Y	Y	Y	Y	Y	Y	Y	Y	Y	Y	Y	Y	Y	Y	Y	Y	Y
7.15		Y	Y	Y	Y	Y	–	Y	Y	Y	Y	Y	Y	Y	Y	Y	Y	Y	Y	Y	–
7.17		Y	Y	Y	Y	Y	Y	Y	Y	Y	Y	Y	Y	Y	Y	Y	Y	Y	Y	Y	Y
7.18		Y	Y	Y	Y	Y	Y	Y	Y	Y	Y	Y	Y	Y	Y	Y	Y	Y	Y	Y	Y
7.1.12		Y	Y	Y	Y	Y	Y	Y	Y	Y	Y	Y	Y	Y	Y	Y	Y	Y	Y	Y	Y
7.1.13		Y	Y	Y	Y	Y	Y	Y	Y	Y	Y	Y	Y	Y	Y	Y	Y	Y	Y	Y	Y
7.1.15		Y	–	Y	–	Y	Y	Y	Y	Y	Y	Y	–	Y	Y	Y	Y	Y	Y	Y	–
9	*Planning*																				
9.2.1		–	–	–	–	–	–	–	–	–	–	–	–	Y	–	Y	–	Y	–	–	Y
9.2.2		–	–	–	–	–	–	–	–	–	–	–	–	Y	Y	Y	–	–	–	–	–
9.2.3		–	–	–	–	–	–	–	Y	–	–	–	–	Y	Y	Y	–	–	Y	–	–
10.2.5		Y	–	Y	Y	Y	Y	Y	Y	Y	Y	Y	Y	Y	Y	Y	Y	Y	Y	Y	Y
10.5		Y	–	Y	Y	Y	Y	Y	Y	Y	Y	Y	Y	Y	Y	Y	Y	Y	Y	Y	–
13	*Costing*																				
13.1.2		Y	Y	Y	Y	Y	Y	Y	Y	Y	Y	Y	Y	Y	Y	Y	Y	Y	Y	Y	Y
13.1.5		–	–	–	–	–	Y	–	Y	Y	Y	Y	Y	–	Y	Y	–	Y	–	Y	–

Key. MRP = Materials Requirement Planning; Y = yes; – = no or not applicable.

Like all the programs described so far, it will soon pay for itself in savings from reduced fuel bills.

FLEET MANAGEMENT A system for controlling all aspects of a vehicle fleet; it offers facilities to create and maintain disciplined control over servicing and repairs, with interfaces to accounting and reporting. DEC hardware and BASIC or COBOL software is used.

ROUTEFINDER A variation on AUTOROUTE, and again cheap, but it has the added bonus of being able to recognize postcodes of the starting and finishing points. It also includes an itinerary option for scheduling routes.

Figure 11.5a–c are sample outputs from AUTOROUTE PLUS and A to B in order to illustrate the versatility of routing programs. Each of the programs has its own particular style, and some include more functions than others. The two just mentioned are merely representative of what is available, and are not necessarily the ones best suited to the needs of your company; therefore, shop around before buying.

We asked for an optimized route from Salisbury to Salisbury via Amesbury, Ludgershall, Marlborough, Andover, Pewsey and a store in Burbage. As can be seen, Autoroute has selected a logical route to take in each of these towns and villages. For the example we asked for a 10 minute halt at each place, and a costing of £0.75p per mile for a 17 ton lorry; each of these factors can easily be changed.

This is the Calculate screen:

Routing	AUTOROUTE PLUS V2.01	17/03/91

Journey Options Speeds Rates Calculate Map Table Print Out
Calculate routes for current journey

Searching for routes from Salisbury to Salisbury
Via Andover, Ludgershall, Burbage, Marlboro, Pewsey, Amesbury

Vehicle: Lorry, Charging scheme: 17Tns cost
Routes found so far:

Route 1: 73 miles 3 hrs 19 min £54.82 Quickest
Route 2: 71 miles 3 hrs 22 min £53.43 Shortest
Duplicate route found
Finished

‹Cursor left/right to move, Return to select.›

Figure 11.5a   Computerized route planning

DATABASE APPLICATIONS

As mentioned earlier, databases control the storage and manipulation of information; therefore, they are the backbone of any distribution management software. It is appropriate that databases should be looked at in more detail in order to see what is involved when choosing or using a database. Ashton Tate's dBASE (in versions I to IV) is the accepted standard amongst micro users, but that does not necessarily mean that it is the program for you.

The first and most important factor is to check that the information can be organized and presented in such a way as to make it relevant to a particular task. This also implies to the user, who must understand the way it operates, and should not be deceived by flattering claims in sales brochures!

As with old-type filing cabinets, or even cardboard boxes under the stairs, large amounts of data are often stored as historical records – for audit purposes, to meet financial and legal obligations, to act as a basis for assessing various trends, or perhaps as useful information for future planning and decision-making. Computers allow much greater amounts of data to be retained on small floppy disks or other

The following is the Table screen produced after the journey has been calculated, a sketch map is also available:

Route 1	AUTOROUTE PLUS V2.01	17/03/91

Shortest route from Salisbury to Salisbury
Via Andover, Ludgershall, Burbage, Marlborough, Pewsey, Amesbury
Vehicle: Lorry, Charging scheme: 17Tns cost

Total time 3 hrs 22 min. Total distance 71 miles. Total cost £53.43

Time		Road	For	Dir	Towards
08:00	DEPART Salisbury	A36	1 mile	NE	Whiteparish
08:02	Turn off onto	A30	7 miles	N	Mid Wallop
08:16	Turn left onto	A343	10 miles	N	Mid Wallop
08:35	Turn right onto	A303	1 mile	E	Micheldever
08:38	Turn off onto	A3057	½ mile	N	
08:40	ARRIVE Andover				
08:50	DEPART Andover	A3057	1 mile	W	
08:52	Turn off onto	A343	2 miles	NW	
10:50	ARRIVE Amesbury				
11:00	DEPART Amesbury	A345	7 miles	S	Salisbury
11:21	Turn right onto	A36	½ mile	SW	Salisbury
11:22	ARRIVE Salisbury				Cost £53.43

Ordnance Survey Digital Mapping © Crown Copyright

Figure 11.5b   Computerized routes planning

forms of storage. Since data is an important resource, it requires managing well just like any other resource. A number of techniques and a whole technology has grown up to help you store and retrieve data that can be converted into practical information. What characterizes a useful technique is its ability to deliver the right information to the right person at the right time and, in the current climate, at the right place.

Consider the kinds of files being currently kept. Why are they kept? What data is stored in them? Would a quick selection from the files meet certain criteria, or would merging data from different files produce 'better' decision-making? Storing data is not often much of a problem. Retrieving the right sub-sets of that data is a more difficult task. In the same way that people who plan and make decisions require not more information, but more relevant or more selective information; a review of the filing objectives needs performing periodically.

Handling data is one of the prime application areas for computers (data processing), and it has been carried through to the microcomputer. That computer has

Route 3	A TO B			17/03/91

| Route Name: Demo Route
Route Info: East Midlands | Driver: Sid Synergy
Vehicle: A2B 1 | | | |

		Travel		Accumulated	
No	Location	Time	Kms	Time	Kms
1	Loughborough				
2	Leicester	0:29	19.3	0:29	19.3
3	Coventry	0:44	47.3	1:13	66.6
4	Derby	1:12	83.1	2:25	149.7
5	Nottingham	0:31	25.1	2:56	174:8
6	Loughborough	0:38	25.9	3:34	200.7

Total Calls: 6	Total Time: 3:34	Total Kms: 200.7

Move Call 4 to 5 on Route 3 to Route 1 before Call 2

Other than a difference in layout it can be seen that A to B has a dialogue box at the bottom. This allows the user to have several routes in the database and, as in this example, move calls between them. This ability makes A to B much more powerful than AUTOROUTE, but it is also more expensive. The latter is, however, rapidly catching up in both sophistication and price.

Both companies offer demonstration versions of their route planners for A to B: Synergy Ltd are based in Loughborough: Tel: 0509 232706. For AUTOROUTE contact Nextbase Ltd in Staines on 0784 460582.

Figure 11.5c   Computerized routes planning

become a sort of 'automated warehouse' for data, allowing access to records on a regular basis or on request. In large organizations with extensive computing facilities, including a large centralized mainframe computer, the usual approach is increasingly to establish a corporate database, as a central, integrated memory which can be accessed in different ways at different times by different users.

In the field of microcomputers, such an approach is generally rather limited, the aim being to replace existing manual or clerical filing systems with computer-based files. This can be done with a specific package, such as a stock record system or vehicle hire system; otherwise, a general purpose package may be obtained that requires the user to build a system by specifying its parameters. The advantage of using a computerized system, in preference to a manual one, is the ability to search the data more quickly using different selection criteria each time, and to report on findings in a variety of formats that are appropriate to the current needs.

The software packages available in this area are commonly known as Database Management Systems (DBMS) – although they are more properly called File Management or Data Handling Systems. Strictly speaking, the term 'database' should be reserved for systems in which the data is stored in one or more file(s) which are interconnected in such a way that the user (as distinct from the database administrator) does not need to know which file contains the data needed.

Data types

When first creating a file, a software package will require a title to be specified; i.e. vehicle model, date of registration, and so on; then the type of control field. Field types are generally classified as one of the following:

1 Textual (or string) fields which are purely descriptive.
2 Numeric fields, as the name suggests, hold numbers which can be used to specify these fields either as integers (whole numbers) or non-integers (decimal numbers). This is because most computer systems store numbers in a particular way which means that numeric fields specified as integers take up less storage space.
3 Data fields which are particularly awkward for computers to handle. If a package does not have the ability to handle data fields specifically, it will probably not be possible to perform searches of the type: 'list all vehicles due for a service in the next week, month, or other period'.

Data entry format

A number of packages allow users to 'draw' a form on the screen. Sometimes the screen format is similar to the one on paper; this reduces the likelihood of transcription errors. Another useful facility is the ability of assigning validation parameters to input fields so that, for example, when a distance figure is entered, a check is made to see if it is within predefined limits (this is known as a range check).

Search parameters

In order to select sub-sets of the data for certain reports, it is necessary to be able to specify the search criteria. The more sophisticated packages allow the user to specify multiple criteria which may be combined with 'logical operators', such as AND or OR; for example, 'all drivers who are over 35 *AND* speak French *OR* Italian'. If it is likely that such a search check is needed to see whether these facilities are available or not, or how easy they are to use, it is wise to check that commonly used sets of search criteria can be stored in a file for future use.

Report formats

Similar considerations apply to the format of reports as apply to search criteria. It should be fairly easy for the software to report on all or part of the data in a format designed for the purpose in mind.

Program adaptation

In any application there are bound to be some operations that occur at frequent intervals, or others that may be required on a regular weekly or monthly basis. If the procedure for setting up a particular search or report format is complex, it can be annoying to have to repeat it frequently. Some packages offer a 'macro' facility, which is the ability to store a procedure or sequence of key operations for later recall and use. In some packages such 'macros' can be extensive, being almost like small programs that can involve a number of steps or even conditional branches.

Ease of use

All suppliers inevitably claim that their packages are 'user-friendly', and demonstrations are prepared to show the packages at their best. Packages which initially appear easy to use may prove slow and cumbersome in practice. For example, menu-driven software is extremely popular, yet proceeding through a series of menus in order to reach a certain end-point often takes more time than using a direct command-driven package. Menu packages are often 'memory hungry', which mean that a larger or more expensive computer has to be bought to run them concurrently with the current database. A command-driven package, however, is likely to need greater familiarization, and thus is more suitable for an operator who will be regularly using the package.

Many packages these days have some form of 'help' facility. This means that when the user is unsure of the next action, by pressing a key on the keyboard (marked F1, or on many of the newer micros it is actually labelled 'HELP') some helpful information is displayed on the screen. Good 'help' systems are context-sensitive, that is, the information appearing on the screen is related to the task currently being undertaken, or it refers to the options currently available. A 'help' system avoids the need for frequent recourse to manuals, so it is useful for inexperienced users. However, it must only be an option, as systems that give 'helpful' advice and information *all the time* are usually slow and frustrating to an experienced user.

Security procedures

If all or part of the data in files is confidential or 'sensitive', it may be desirable to restrict access to them. Many packages require the input of a password before the files can be accessed. Others have a more flexible system, and different users can be assigned 'access levels' which govern their right to view certain data. The various fields can be given to someone with the appropriate access level; otherwise, the record may be viewed, but certain information will not be displayed.

Other features

One of the questions to consider when selecting a software package is: are the files created by this package compatible with other types of software? It is often convenient to be able to gain access to data in another package such as a word processor or a spreadsheet program. Therefore, it is vital to seek advice from independent specialists before buying a package and, if possible, to try out the system first.

When choosing a computer never skimp on the size of its memory; no matter how small your business, the hard disk memory will rapidly fill up with data. A RAM chip-based memory is also important, as most modern sophisticated business programs now demand at least one megabyte of Random Access Memory (RAM).

Finally, make sure that the system can be expanded so that it can grow with your operation; the average life of a microcomputer is eight years, while minicomputers and mainframes become obsolete after ten years. The software must last at least that long, and it may even be possible to move it over to the new machine. *Ask* your dealer to tell you about networking, linking several computers together, and expanding the system in the future.

COMPUTING SERVICES

In most cases it is recommended that advice on designing specific computer software be obtained from a reputable service bureau, such as Computing Services for Industry Ltd (CSI), which has its head office in Leeds, UK, or HCS Technology N.V. in Eindhoven, The Netherlands.

Distribution by sea

CSI won the IBM award for best computer services agent in 1990, and it has expanded to cover all the British Isles; it markets software in the area of manufacture and data collection, as well as distribution and transportation. One package for controlling export and import shipping is called EXIMSHIP, which includes provisions for customers' orders, hauliers, shipping agents, representatives, forwarding agents, customs and excise, foreign currencies, operating costs, delivery deadlines and documentation.

On-line software information

EXIMSHIP begins by organizing the information related to a shipment of goods, but not all the details need to be entered at the same time. The user may decide to enter such initial information as: consignee, shippers, route and despatch date before the rest of the details are known, like the value of the goods, type of packing, handling instructions and tariffs. The system keeps a record of previous shipments for as long as is required, which helps to organize the current shipment.

All the information entered is automatically available for producing documents and letters; therefore re-entering it is unnecessary, which saves time. Cost data from quotations will be used for working out the cost of a shipment. Using the computer's 'help' key presents an online user manual which shows what an option does and what options are available for a certain case. Also, channels are provided for collecting data automatically from another system in the computer's memory; one channel relates the online shipment information with invoicing procedures, while another gives a batch interface directly to the EXIMSHIP database.

Printing documents

After entering the online data, all or some of it can be selected in order to print out the relevant documentation. The database includes the format for the various documents, and any new information can be inserted. Everything is displayed on the video screen. The documents can be reprinted at any time, provided that the data is retained.

Controlling shipping activities

Online enquiries from the computer will show the status of each shipment against its delivery date at any time after despatch. EXIMSHIP can also be used for controlling costs. Details of each invoice related to a shipment is assigned to the party concerned, e.g. the shipper, agent, haulier or the customer. The costs can be analysed in this way according to any objective.

The system will automatically match actual costs against estimated costs and display any variances. Also, it keeps an online log of invoices entered in order to prevent double-charging for any of the services provided. Using a comprehensive set of online enquiries and the record of shipping costs allows the operator to compare figures with past or other shipments so that the costs of shipping activities are competitive.

Reporting and analysing results

The database maintained by EXIMSHIP contains all shipment details, including despatch, intermediate and arrival dates, actual costs and estimates, as well as other documented information. It allows access to both past shipments and the current online information just entered in order to prepare reports of the various activities, or to analyse their costs according to different criteria.

Directories can be set up for consignees, suppliers, routes and hauliers so that they can be searched or scanned either for reference or access. A directory contains the standard EEC codes with descriptions for different countries, ports and excises; also, they can be revised by the operator, if necessary, using the master maintenance facilities.

Benefits

This package of shipping programs reduces distribution times by providing the user with accurate and correct documentation with fewer delays; speedy completion of documents ready for despatch of the goods; reduced shipping costs through fewer delays, less paperwork and easier comparison with previous charges, as well as better control of operations. Prior preparation of reports and analysing the information improves the control of shipments, and also reduces the effort needed to satisfy customs regulations and to maintain the flow of goods. Above all, online tracking increases customers' satisfaction thanks to timely deliveries.

Computer control systems

HCS is the biggest independent distributor of automation accessories in Europe, and it specializes in control systems for industry. Its most successful software package is called PROFIT/AS which was developed originally for production control; however, it has modules for a wider range of applications. The Basic Module is used for defining the various database elements, whereas the Sales Orders module registers customers' orders according to their relevant specifications, and the Forecasting module can forecast demand based upon past deliveries.

Other modules include:

- Stock control: for the flexible control of inventory movements;
- Purchasing: for controlling the procurement of supplies;
- Costing: for estimating costs based upon standard and actual data;
- Planning: for calculating quantities and facilities required.

It is claimed that PROFIT/AS is the perfect solution for 'tailor-made' control systems. It allows great flexibility of product specifications over a wide range; the specifications are defined with MASKS, SELECTIONS and DIMENSIONS. This method is best illustrated with an example of a distributor of wines and spirits handled a confusing assortment of bottles – of different colours, covers and capacities.

Handling such an assortment was simplified with the three features mentioned above: the MASK feature indicated the colour of the bottle; the SELECTIONS feature was used for defining the covers, labels, tops and other special requirements; and the DIMENSIONS feature calculated capacities, volumes and sizes based upon defined formulae.

Batch operations

Since many distribution operations are 'one-off', it is difficult to be competitive unless everything is in control and the communications are good. Computerized control with Electronic Data Interchanges (EDI) standardize communications and allow just-in-time deliveries of goods and repeat orders. Logistics software such as PROFIT/AS ensures accurate retrievals, tracking of items throughout the storage system, inventory control, assembly of orders and costing of operations.

Computer controlled distribution systems make life easier for the operators and deliveries more reliable to customers. Nowadays, there are computer software packages available for most distribution activities, so they are performed more quickly and more accurately.

12 Logistics and successful distribution

Logistics for controlling distribution includes procedures for *reducing* the costs of investments, the times of performing operations and the waste of resources. Each person and each piece of equipment contributes to the costs and times, while each mistake is responsible for waste. Investment costs are the largest, and they should be spread over the greatest number of items as possible to improve their unit values.

CHOOSING THE METHOD OF DISTRIBUTION

The method chosen for distributing goods is specific to the goods themselves and the objectives of the distribution system. This choice is a fundamental one, and deciding it must start with a fundamental investigation of the markets for the goods in question. Surprisingly enough, the first question should be: 'Is there a market for these goods?'

The next questions will follow an affirmative answer to the first question: 'Where are the markets?', 'What size are they?', 'How should the goods be distributed there?', 'What activities and operations will be involved', 'How can they be done effectively', 'What will they cost?', and 'Can you afford them?'

In present day circumstances, markets are rarely restricted to one country, and you will have to consider exporting and importing to remain competitive. Consequently, worldwide distribution should be investigated; however, a full description would require a whole book in itself, therefore we only briefly consider distributing in European markets.

Exporting to Europe

Having decided that a market in Europe is sufficiently large enough and profitable for your company, you need to obtain information about the regulations for exporting to it. If you are based in Britain, the best place to start is the Board of Trade in London, which has connections with its counterparts in other countries. Also, it organizes export promotions and trade fairs.

The countries that interest *you* will have government representatives in your country, and it is advised that you ring and visit their embassies or consulates for further information. Britain also maintains embassies and consulates abroad. They are excellent sources of information and, from our experience, in the main they are very helpful, often going out of their way to find the information you need.

Gathering information after those initial contacts is 'part and parcel' of a logistics system, and finding information about export markets is both a useful training exercise for logistics, and an opportunity for logistics experts to provide a practical service. Our advice to anyone wishing to learn more about distribution overseas is to speak to your bank manager – Westminster Bank publish an informative series of booklets that describe the most important export markets for British goods. These booklets are valuable reading for distributors everywhere, because we can all learn from others when we put our minds to it. A similar service is provided by the NMB bank, in the Netherlands, and other leading banks.

Communications in Europe

If data is the life-blood of distribution logistics, then language is the blood vessels that form the network through the body of a market! English is the primary language for international communications, but the proficiency of using it will vary from country to country. In Europe, the chances of making yourself understood in English differs widely, as the following summaries indicate for different parts of the continent:

An excellent understanding of the English language obviously applies to the British Isles and former colonies such as Malta, Cyprus and Gibraltar.

A good understanding of English will be found in the countries that traditionally have been trading partners with Britain, particularly where the languages spoken originated from German. Few problems with the English language will be found in the Netherlands, Scandinavia, Iceland and Switzerland.

A reasonable understanding of English for business purposes exists in Belgium, Luxembourg, Finland, Greece, Turkey and in the western part of Germany.

A fair understanding of English applies to parts of some other countries in the EEC, and to those countries like Austria, Yugoslavia, Hungary and Poland which cater for an increasing tourist trade from abroad.

Some understanding of English will be found in all other countries, but it will be poorest in the Eastern European countries, although it is on the increase due to improving communications and the news media.

The more you can learn about your markets, the easier it becomes to distribute your goods, and firsthand experience cannot be bettered. The closer you get to

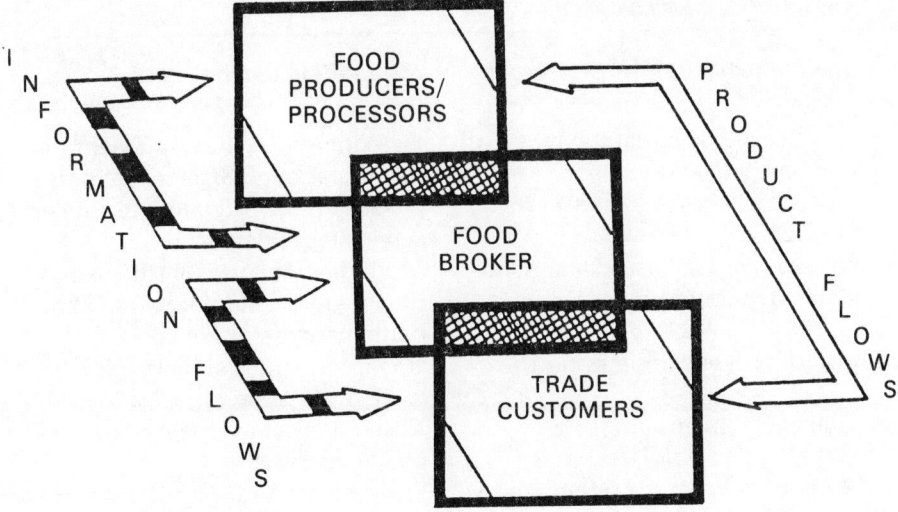

Figure 12.1   Key informant in distributing processed foods

the market, the more you will learn about it and discover the benefits of cooperating with your agents, partners and other participators. Setting up a distribution office abroad is an added expense, and an agency may be a better bet. Somebody 'on the spot' can overcome difficulties in countries like Japan, where an intimate knowledge of the indigenous market and powerful backing are essential for distributing there.

Collecting logistics information

Effective logistics differs from efficient logistics because it recognizes that controlling costs is only half of the equation for successful distribution management. Effectiveness also requires development of the customer service that brings repeat purchases. Understanding the nature of customer service can be a real logistics exercise because it will help to measure satisfaction. Formerly, the reaction of customers was determined with questionnaires and market research in direct contact with the customers, but that takes a long time and costs a lot of money. However, an alternative investigation methodology is appropriate for enquiring about customer service levels. It is called the *key informant method*, and was developed in the USA.

Applied to distribution, the key informant method depends upon the existence of key individuals who know all about storing and moving goods for markets; they are often intermediaries in the distribution network. For example, in a study of distributing processed foods, the key informants were found to be the food brokers who negotiated transactions between the manufacturing industry and the retail outlets (see Figure 12.1). Even when food products were delivered directly from a factory to the trade customers, the related information was

Table 12.2   Key informant method: measures and criteria

Information measures	Information criteria
1. Number of years that the broking firm has been in business.	Five or more years is sufficient for gaining enough experience for the purpose of investigating customer service requirements.
2. Number of years associated with a certain supplier/manufacturers.	More than one year is sufficient to provide relevant information about a particular type of transport.
3. Size of broker's organization.	One informant is sufficient for small to medium-sized organizations.
4. Title of informant.	A single informant needs to be a key policy maker.
5. Number of years the informant has worked for the firm.	Five or more years is sufficient to gain enough experience for the subject of investigation.
6. Number of days per week engaged with the supplier/ manufacturer.	At least one whole day per week is sufficient to acquire the requisite knowledge of the supplier of goods distributed.
7. Number of days per week engaged with the trade customers.	At least one whole day per week is sufficient to understand the service requirements at the retail outlets.

processed by firms of brokers. Consequently, the broker was in a position to be knowledgeable of the customers' experiences with the suppliers.

The method began by questioning the broker's policy maker in such a way that complex social judgements were excluded; this was accomplished by asking for information on observed distribution activities concerning the actual order cycle time or product availability. Finally, specific reports were prepared on the distribution service offered by individual suppliers in order to prevent generalizations.

In this way, the key informant method obtains a wide range of relevant information from a single informant. Some of the measures and criteria for the kind of informant to look for in the food industry are shown in Table 12.2.

The critical issues of implementing the key informant method are the selection and qualification of the informants. A preliminary visit to the firm of food brokers provided a valuable insight into the suitability of staff as key informants. However, the main advantages of the method are: reduced complexity of the investigation; better quality of data collected due to the careful selection of informants and questions; increased understanding of the nature of problems and working conditions, due to the objectivity of being a 'third party'; and more effective data collected for logistics models.

COMPARING THE COSTS OF DISTRIBUTION

Individual distribution systems and methods of operating differ in many respects, and no single measurement can characterize these differences; some of the differences that can be compared include:

1 *Availability of customer service*: the number of depots, the range of stocks, inventory levels and delivery times.
2 *Reliability of service*: the safety stock levels, order picking and packing, age and types of delivery vehicles and their maintenance.
3 *Capital investment*: the size and number of warehouses, the vehicle fleet, materials handling equipment and the inventory investment.
4 *Operational costs*: the warehouse operations, delivering operations, mode of transportation, logistics operations and order processing.

Distribution investments and operational costs can be compared using a capital charge or return on capital investments in order to convert them into annual running costs. One approach to making a cost comparison is:

1 Set up alternative systems, and vary the transportation modes and the service reliability levels in each of them.
2 Determine the availability of customer service and the reliability of service for each alternative system.
3 Total the costs of the activities for transportation, warehousing, data processing, inventory-carrying and investing in resources.

The choice of comparison will depend upon the cost-effectiveness of the alternatives, based upon the improvements that can be made in excess of the least cost system. The actual evaluations have to be made within the framework of each case, although customer investigations, competitor effectiveness and market penetration will provide guidelines for these evaluations. Table 12.3 summarizes the investment costs in a series of similar distribution systems, in which the number of depots in the distribution system differ for a network throughout the USA.

From Table 12.3 it can be seen how the activity costs of distribution interplay so that a change in one produces one or more changes in the others. For instance, increasing the number of depots from 5 to 17 increases the one day order availability at the 80% reliability level by 34%, but the three days availability by only 2%. Similarly, increasing the service reliability requires different increases of investment. Although these figures came from a study in America, they show the trends that can apply anywhere in the world; it is only the monetary values of the distribution resources that are different.

SYSTEMATIC RESOURCES PLANNING

The interplay between the different distribution activities are important when planning the resources, or facilities, that each needs. A systematic method requires 12 steps in order to decide the plans for a functional organization like that shown in Figure 12.4:

Table 12.3 Comparison of distribution system costs ($000 000)

Comparisons	SYSTEM A			SYSTEM B			SYSTEM C			SYSTEM D		
Number of depots	5			17			25			50		
Service reliability levels (%)	80	90	95	80	90	95	80	90	95	80	90	95
Stock availability for orders (%)												
– after one day	24	27	29	58	66	69	65	73	77	70	78	83
– after three days	70	79	84	72	81	86	72	81	86	72	81	86
Investment costs (p.a.) =	174	239	296	315	437	542	336	466	580	520	730	920
– inventory	1275	1275	1275	1335	1335	1335	1350	1350	1350	1405	1405	1405
– facilities	1450	1515	1575	1875	1770	1875	1685	1820	1930	1925	2135	2320
– total	90	90	90	110	110	110	125	125	125	160	160	160
Depot operating costs (p.a.)	265	265	265	225	225	225	210	210	210	195	195	195
Transportation costs (p.a.)	395	415	435	455	490	520	465	540	540	535	595	650
Capital investment costs (p.a.)	750	770	785	780	820	850	800	835	370	885	950	1000

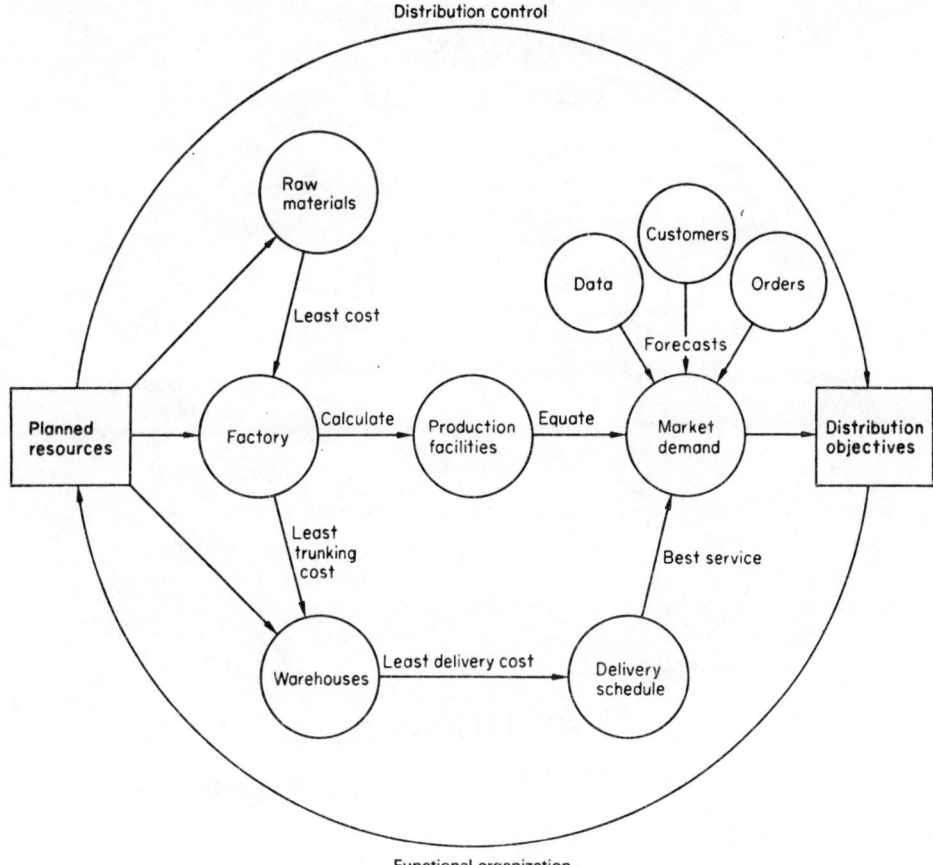

Figure 12.4 Schematic distribution resources planning

1 Forecast *market demands* for the planning period under consideration, and set the *distribution objectives*.
2 Calculate the *production capacities* available at *factories*.
3 Decide the *production facilities* required to meet the *total market demand*.
4 Site the *factories* near to the sources of raw materials or locations of demand so that *overall delivery costs* will be minimal.
5 Develop the *demand data* in terms of number and locations of *customers*, sizes, frequencies of *orders* and delivery lead times.
6 Decide the *warehousing* requirements and site the *warehouses*.
7 Determine the need for *trunking* and decide the *vehicles and routes* required if it is necessary.
8 Determine the *vehicles and routes* needed for *local deliveries* to customers.
9 Prepare *delivery schedules* for the vehicles.
10 Analyse the *functional distribution* requirements and structure a *management organization* for the distribution system.

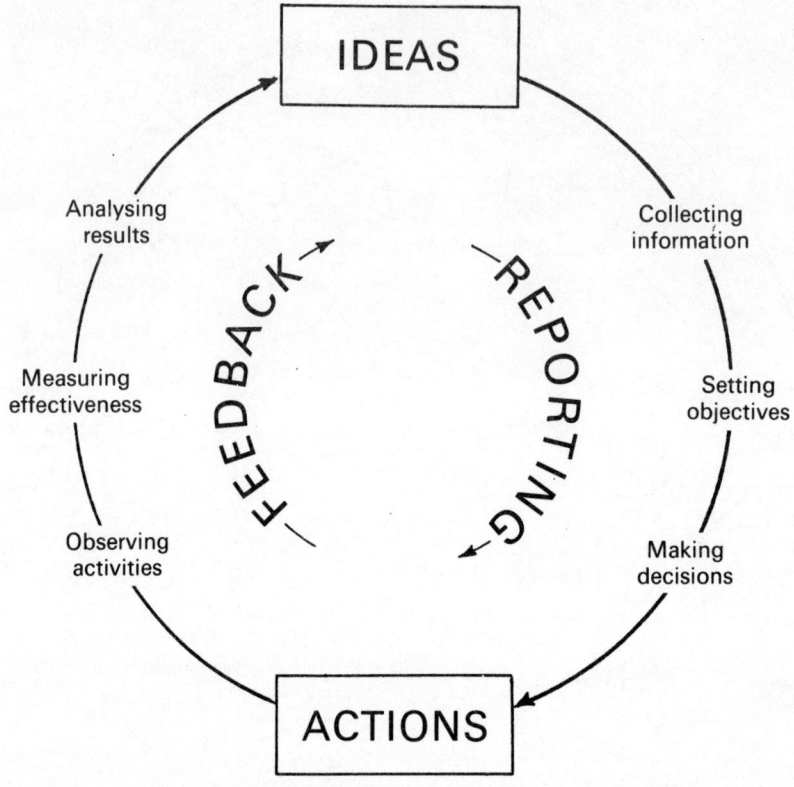

Figure 12.5   The communication wheel

11. Decide the *control* procedures needed in the system for satisfying the customers.
12. Implement the *planned resources* and operate the system according to the *strategic plans* for achieving the *distribution objectives*.

Good distribution management begins with planning followed by comparing the results with the plans to see if the objectives have been achieved satisfactorily. This comparison represents *control*, and it is easier to control a system that is well-planned. Understanding this is a logical process, and it is necessary for constructive thinking to fill in the details of plans in action. Those details provide the information that helps a manager to plan for uncertainty, because the more facts available the more realistic are the plans.

A distribution system is like a gearbox – it has a power supply input and an objective output, but in between are gearwheels and interlocking teeth, each of which influences the output. Power efficiency is lost at every contact point in a transmission system, but losses can be reduced with lubricating communication; therefore, the more appropriate the information, the smoother the system will run. Figure 12.5 is a diagrammatic expression of how information keeps the *communication wheel* turning.

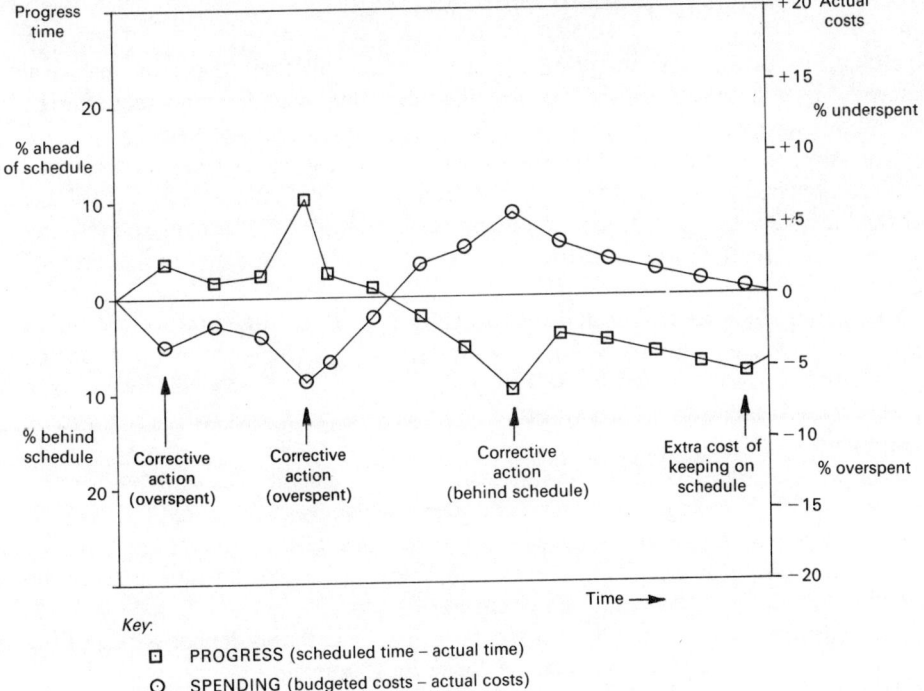

Figure 12.6 Heuristic control chart

Heuristic control

Management is a heuristic process because it is based upon discovery through personal experiences, and heuristic control involves the use of inductive reasoning. A manager who is able to forecast what will happen under unusual operating conditions will be able to take corrective action before serious damage occurs. Some managers rely on computer programs and others rely on hunches, but heuristic control combines the two. There is a place for electronic accuracy *and* personal intuition in modern management, provided that the manager is able correctly to analyse information and communicate rational decisions. Good communication is necessary for heuristic control, since speaking to people and asking the right questions is the best way of obtaining the right information and putting decisions into practice effectively.

A heuristic control chart is shown in Figure 12.6, which represents the time span for processing a customer's order. Whenever progress falls behind schedule it is accompanied by cost-cutting, while over-spending is associated with rush jobs when trying to keep on time.

The datum line represents the planned schedule for an order, and plotting the deviations from it in terms of time and cost will show where corrective actions need to be taken; particularly when the process is significantly behind schedule or over-spent.

Network analysis on a microcomputer

The elements of any system interact and interplay, but their relationships when described by a network need to be simplified in order to understand them better. Although preparing a network takes time, it is the best way of learning about a system's operations; fortunately, network analysis can be performed quickly with a microcomputer. In the past, a number of complex software programs were available for the lucky few who had access to a mainframe computer, but the microcomputer makes simpler versions available to everyone, giving more confidence in the results if they are under personal control.

Microcomputer packages usually have well-designed, friendly input routines that are suitable for casual users. Someone with computing experience can pick up the manual and produce a network model in a short time. This allows the office staff to run the models themselves rather than relying on *remote* experts with a mainframe computer.

Manipulation of a model by the staff who have to deal with the problem is more relevant, and the manager gets results sooner after suggesting changes. This promotes better participation in decision-making, and testing the alternatives to observe their effects gives an opportunity to appreciate the relationships between the different activities in a distribution system.

The objectives of a system have implications for the design of its network and the requirements of a computer software package; they are:

1 *Flow of information*: people can be very good at their own jobs, but unaware of how their actions affect the whole system. A well-designed analysis network provides a structure for the flow of information throughout a distribution system. The model must be simple and comprehensible to the participants to aid their understanding rather than add to their bewilderment. It is better to work in 'penny packets' by collecting small amounts of essential information regularly than amassing large amounts of dubious data, even at the risk of losing some realism by omitting less important steps.

   Too much data can clog up the memory of a PC anyway. Actually, the restrictions of a PC – such as limited size of the network, slower data retrieval from a diskette (hard disks fill up too quickly with back-ups and models for alternative scenarios) and more laborious analyses – do have an advantage: the models are kept simple!

   Good reporting leads to more effective information transfers, so that everyone who is involved can find out just what affects them without wading through a morass of printouts! It is important that the software allows plenty of flexibility in the design of reports so that information can be selected and sorted according to needs. Typically, the report should be a summary of progress in key areas with specific details for each individual, giving them an outline of what is expected of them and what information is required for updating the model.

2 *Modelling*: the aim of network models should be to provide a means for predicting the results of changes without a long wait or the risk of damage. The information should be presented in sensible reports that suggest the likely results of decisions. Mainframe computers do not encourage experimentation, but the easier and quicker output of data with a PC enables planners to examine

several alternatives at one time, or to explore different ways of reducing activity times.

Some software packages allow all the information related to certain tasks to be stored as a single module. That module can be loaded into the network model, and all the interconnections are made automatically. This facility speeds up the construction of models when considering the answers to 'what-if' questions.

Resource planning models for use with a PC may not be sufficiently broad-based for making overall plans; of necessity, microcomputer models are narrower and more specific. However, cumulating the results from a number of small models can offer a useful guide to general outcomes. Some PC resource analysis packages are quite sophisticated, but they are not really needed for most distribution planning strategies.

3 *Operation control*: the essence of control is comparing expected and actual results to discover discrepancies and similarities. That is only possible with microcomputer models when they are realistic and properly maintained. One of the most common faults is people forgetting to report their intentions, which can affect the progress results. If somebody thinks that a task is not likely to start on time, that must be included in the overall plan. A PC's reporting facility should be flexible enough to include feedback that can modify the objectives regularly.

4 *Ease of use*: in many cases, running distribution programs on a computer is only *part* of somebody's work; therefore, the package chosen should be easy to use occasionally. The requirements are:

- good documentation;
- well-designed display layout for easy manipulation;
- conveniently arranged menus;
- logic checks on networks and highlighting of critical paths;
- choice of notation to match previous experience;
- flexible updating that automatically revises all modules;
- overriding of automatic revisions as required;
- provision of intermediary information before an activity is completed.

5 *Good reporting*: many objectives for the activities in a distribution system require reports that can be interpreted in different ways by different people; therefore, the software package should have a flexible reporting facility. Some of the features required are:

- a choice of event times – start/finish/early/late -- and activity durations;
- a responsibility code for detailed reports of relevant aspects for individuals;
- selection of information by period of time;
- information on progress indicators for individual or grouped tasks;
- different specifications retrieved or saved according to circumstances;
- combination of information into a single report;
- quick reference summaries for a number of similar activities;
- bar chart outputs as required;
- linkage to a database package in order to increase the scope of a report.

6   *Resource analysis*: sometimes an overview of the effects of a specific activity can be useful. This requires a software package to be able to:

- attach resource codes to activities;
- describe varying resource availabilities;
- describe resource demands during an activity's duration;
- combining requirements for resources over a period of time.

7   *Connections with other systems*: some network packages are modules of larger systems, and this allows connections with other databases, or a new database can be created for storing information on past results, costs or times.

In concluding this section of software packages for network analysis, it should be realized that programs for running with a PC are easy to use, suitable for different networks including heuristic, critical path or PERT analyses, and reasonably priced. However, no system is successful unless somebody assumes overall responsibility for it. That person must have sufficient authority to make sure that the necessary information is collected and processed; while a general appreciation of the potential benefits from networking with a microcomputer can be used for planning a more effective distribution system.

COMPUTERS AND LOGISTICS

Throughout this book, references have been made to different computers for performing the operations of controlling a distribution system, and it may be confusing to decide which is the best for distribution logistics. A study was undertaken into the computing needs for operations research work in the British Gas Corporation, and the costs for alternative computers were calculated to compare mainframe, mini and PCs. The results of this study have been interpreted in the light of logistics for distribution, and it is hoped that the following synopsis will provide guidelines for distribution managers.

Nature of logistics work

The nature of the work to be done will have a great influence in the choice of computer for logistics; in the main, three kinds of work have to be considered:

1   *Data analysis and modelling*: data is required for producing models that help managers to make decisions; these models are generally small, and can be run on any computer. On occasion, however, simulations for resource planning in large organizations need access to corporate-planning data, and such a database will be too much for the smaller computers to handle.

2   *Information systems development*: operations of a system are mainly concerned with simple choices; as a rule, they can be performed satisfactorily with a PC. The data for a distribution system comes from outlying places where a large computer would be too cumbersome and immobile anyway. A large computer would be needed for originally developing the system, but not for operating it; nevertheless, software packages are readily available.

3   *Decisions support*: personal computing facilities allow managers to obtain

spreadsheet information from the field, for which just small programs using BASIC are quite adequate. Reporting packages ensure that the information is supplied in the appropriate form for making particular kinds of decisions.

Costing computer operations

The British Gas study was carried out in 1983, and the actual cost figures are now out-of-date; however, they are useful for comparing trends in the cost-effectiveness of different computers. The software requirements had to be met by a computer, otherwise it was deemed unsuitable for the study and excluded from the comparisons. The size of the logistics group did not exceed ten staff members, and the facilities were one computer, four video screens and one printer.

In practice, the cost differences were small; a large computer would cost more to run, but this was counterbalanced by the salaries of the extra staff needed to operate an equivalent number of small machines. Provided that a computer was available, the logistics staff were capable of adapting the data to their needs regardless of computer type. Consequently, it was concluded that the cheaper types were quite adequate, and that small personal computers also had other advantages (for example, they gave more personal freedom and less dependence on a central authority). Against this was the need for maintaining compatible data sets, and having access to more powerful data sources, on occasion.

A case appears to have been made for microcomputers – in particular personal computers – for logistics operations; not so much from any cost advantage, as from the factor of independence afforded to operators.

Microcomputer characteristics

The characteristics of microcomputers are helping them to overcome the former barrier to automation in a distribution system and, technically, they are more appropriate to the nature of distributed operations. As a consequence, they show a great promise in the field of logistics for distribution.

The biggest attribute of a microcomputer is its low cost without loss of computing speed or memory capacity. Its price is within the budget of even quite small distribution operations, and its size prevents the fear of staff of 'domination by computer'.

More significant than the cost aspect is the accessibility of microcomputer systems. The small decentralized scale and relative ease of operating modern software programs by non-specialists has improved the image of computers in businesses. This message is important to managers because it destroys the 'black box' image, and puts the function of a computer within their control.

A microcomputer provides the opportunity for more flexibility, and it can identify the capabilities and limitations of a system; especially for implementing a process step-by-step so that automation can be adopted in manageable bits. In many cases, little formal preparation goes into the acquisition of a microcomputer, and its applications will just grow with time as more and more experience is gained. This is not a bad thing, because applications will develop in response to the motivation of the staff, and this increases personal involvement.

The true effectiveness of distribution logistics depends upon the ability of a distribution manager to take advantage of all the benefits offered – including reduced costs, improved services, more appropriate control and, above all, more successful performance of duties.

Appendix 1   Case studies

AUTOMATED RESUPPLY IN RETAIL BUSINESSES

This case study is based on work done by British Home Stores (BHS) in the UK when they automated their distribution data processing from store level to the computer control centre in Luton. The process is then reversed out to their suppliers. We shall digress from the real world situation to simplify some areas and generally improve the readers' ability to learn from the case study.

For the technical aficionados, the BHS system is based on the Viewdata principle, and runs on a McDonnell Douglas Sequoia mainframe based in Luton. The suppliers use IBM compatible PCs fitted with a modem link, which connects them to Luton utilizing standard telephone links. A stores' link is much more specialized, and uses an IBM data network to connect the Electronic Point of Sale (EPOS) minicomputers in the high street stores to an IBM mainframe. It should be pointed out that each mini is capable of handling more than one store, so to reduce costs some shops were linked together using leased telephone lines. The simplified method of operation is as follows:

1   The customers choose goods from shelves and rails in the stores and take them to the EPOS terminal, where a sales assistant will key in the item code number, quantity and price. This information is stored in the controller minicomputer along with the shop code, which it generates automatically.
2   At the end of the day the financial information is tallied for management purposes, and the item codes are used to quantify the total sales on each item. This latter information is essential as part of the management information system, but it is also the start of the distribution planning chain. An algorithm is used to decide whether an item should be restocked or not. Clearly, it is pointless ordering one blouse when the shop still has a dozen of the same type in stock. Any items that fail to meet the ordering criteria of the algorithm are

noted in a separate area of the computer's memory, and added to the next day's figures.

3   During the night the Luton mainframe computer receives the management information and the restocking requirements. The latter data is consolidated by area and item and passed to the buying department, who are linked to the MD Sequoia. First, the restocking requirements are compared with management policy; for example, is the line being run down and replaced by a new fashion? Assuming the item is still required, the supplier database is interrogated to find out if the stock is available. BHS deals with some 500 suppliers, 60% of whom provide 90% of volume of the stock required. It is this group who are linked by PC to the mainframe through a bulletin board system where orders, invoices, packing lists, delivery instructions and messages are left. Due to the amount of traffic over the telephone lines and a desire to make use of cheap rate line time, a direct one-to-one link is impractical. The PCs contact Luton automatically (and vice versa), and once the terminal has passed the security checks the information is transmitted.

4   During the following day the supplier prepares and packages the goods in accordance with the BHS instructions, which includes labelling and bar coding. These items are sent electronically from Luton with the instructions and printed out at the supplier's office. While this is happening, the main computer is generating tasking details for the transport contractor. The instructions tell transport operators what has to be collected from each supplier, and the vehicles are allocated according to size and route. All goods are brought in from the supplier to a central distribution centre at Atherstone in Warwickshire. Here, goods arrive grouped by supplier and are regrouped by store. The vehicles bringing goods in from a supplier are unloaded and immediately reloaded with stock to be delivered to shops on particular routes. The warehouse is almost totally automated, which is why goods are packed by store and bar coded by the suppliers.

The BHS distribution system is managed by the mainframe computer, and utilizes the ROUTEMASTER system. On a daily basis, all the orders due for collection from suppliers and goods due for delivery to stores are fed into the system. ROUTEMASTER is basically a scheduling system which has been preloaded with store locations, weekly schedules and vehicle details. From the fixed data and the daily variable information, ROUTEMASTER generates vehicle routes, delivery cycles and loading tables for each vehicle. The software provides not only route cards for the drivers, but all the paperwork that they need. Finally, because the routes are known, an estimate of the time at each point can be sent out so that store managers can make staff available to handle goods when they arrive.

The expense of the system has been more than covered in terms of service efficiency and reduced costs. Overall, it minimizes road distances and therefore fuel and running costs for the vehicles, as well as reducing journey time. It also acts as a human resource scheduler, assisting store managers and suppliers as well as the distribution staff.

This brief case study highlights what can be achieved in a large company which is able to spend large amounts of money in the short term in order to get a longer term return on the investment. The key lessons are that communication costs are a major factor in such a system, security of data can be a problem with so many people linked into the system, and above all else, that efficient systems management is vital for success.

ROWNTREE MACKINTOSH AUTOMATED WAREHOUSE

In 1985, when it was opened by the Lord Mayor of York, the finished goods store at York was the largest computer controlled warehouse in the UK. The warehouse holds stock from most of the British factories within the company, and is the hub for their national distribution. Naturally, as a confectionary store it is environmentally controlled; the main warehouse is a *people free* area, other than the occasional maintenance crew.

At the time the complete system cost £7 million, which is a major investment, particularly as at the time the company was production-dominated and distribution was a poor relation. It must be remembered, however, that the 1980s saw a very rapid growth in major retail outlets such as superstores, and demand for confectionery in bulk consignments increased. RM operate a centralized system based on York which handles bulk goods, and a series of smaller area depots which receive and break bulk into small consignments for delivery to shops. As the group has factories in Norwich, Manchester, Hull, Glasgow and North London it was decided that the central warehouse should be located in the Midlands. This would achieve the best balance between trunking products in from the factories while serving the bulk of their customers in the South. Having investigated the costs of buying ground planning permissions, and so forth, it was decided to compromise by utilizing a cricket pitch belonging to the company at York, The facility is located close to the transport depot and the main factory site, making the choice very convenient, if a little north of the Keefer optimum position.

This case study will not consider further the distribution network, but concentrates instead on the scale and operation of the warehouse facility. The building is of standard modern construction, a metal lattice frame with cladding; the floor, however, is a particularly strong reinforced concrete slab. This is because not only does it carry the weight of the building and machinery, but also 30 000 pallets of produce stacked 11 high. The building is a little over 150 metres long by 50 metres wide and 25 metres high, with 16 loading bays for road vehicles and a ten wagon rail siding.

The main warehouse is a sealed unit with all doors normally locked, the only openings being two windows through which the pallet conveyors pass, and even these have polythene flaps. This measure is necessary both to preserve the environmental controls and for safety. The automatic pallet movement system cannot detect the presence of people, so excluding them avoids anyone being run over or hurt. Heat and fire is, however, detectable by 908 smoke detectors, plus other sensors for the air-conditioning plant. Fire is dealt with by 12 500 sprinklers linked to two 100 000 gallon water tanks; when devising the system disposal of the water became a major problem.

The racking is arranged into 24 pallet rows, the outer ones being double and the inner ones quadruple arrangements. This allows six pallet cranes to work the system, with each crane having a reach of two pallets to either side. Figure A1 displays the

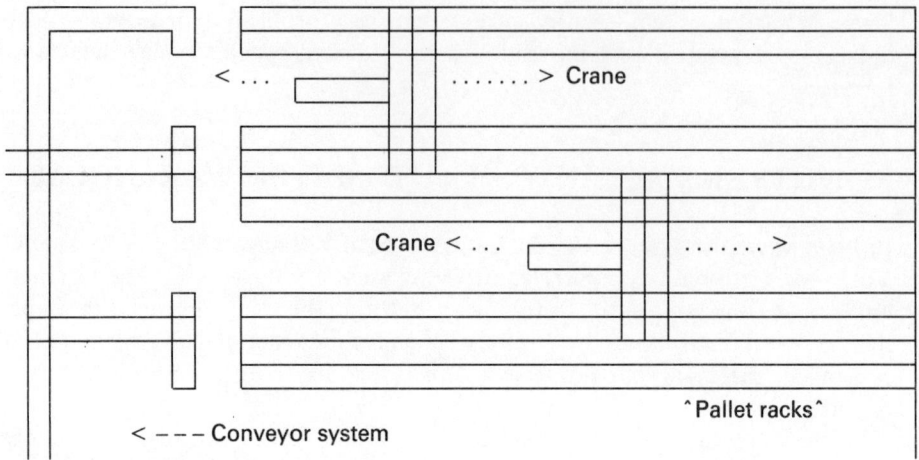

Figure A.1   RM racking arrangement

arrangement at one end, two crane bays of the warehouse, with the conveyor pallet mover on the right.

The pallet cranes move on rails up and down a single aisle dropping pallets onto a roller conveyor at the left hand side of Figure A1. This has a series of turntables to move pallets in different directions, and detectors register the location of the pallet so that each section knows when to power up and transport the pallet. Each aisle is 112 pallets long by 11 high and two deep on either side, which gives each crane access to 4 928 locations.

The pallets are all bar code marked: when they arrive at the inbound bay the code is read into the main computer using a hand wand and details about the contents added by keyboard. The pallet is then moved onto a short section of track where it waits for the computer to decide on a location for it. There is no apparent logical order for the location other than that new pallets are placed on the inner location of any cell. During slack periods the computer reshuffles the locations so that the oldest pallets are in the outer more easily reached locations. Several other factors, however, are taken into account, and what appears to be illogical is in fact a very complex computational problem. Another factor considered when placing the pallet is that it is located close to the next outbound pallet that the crane is to collect. This is to save on travelling time for the cranes, which is conducted at a gentle 7 mph (30m per minute).

Floor loading was mentioned earlier. The computer takes this into account, and the software algorithm ensures that weight is evenly distributed throughout the warehouse. It is essential that the racks remain absolutely level for the cranes accurately to place their forks under the pallets. The other key factor is ensuring that each product line is evenly represented on each aisle. This means that during maintenance periods when a crane is switched off, the remaining five cranes can still work normally and orders can be picked correctly.

The outbound area is much larger than the inbound one, and the floor is marked out with a representation of the load space of 16 articulated trucks. The computer plans the load for each truck and assigns a loading dock for it; it then prints out a

Table A.2   RM warehousing statistics

Total floor area		:	12 600 sq m (136 000 sq ft)
Volume		:	191 800 cu m (6 777 000 cu ft)
Cost 1983–85		:	£7 000 000
Dimensions	length	:	159 m (522 ft)
	width	:	47 m (154 ft)
	height	:	23 m (75 ft)
Pallets	max weight	:	1 tne
	capacity	:	24 lanes 112 long by 11 high
	total	:	29 568
Controls		:	2 mini computers in parallel controlling 6 pallet cranes each with its own microprocessor and 250 metres of logic controlled conveyors. A direct link to the company mainframe provides stock control and management information.
Environment	light	:	nil normally
	humidity	:	65%
	temperature	:	13 C (55 F)
Transport	Roadliner bays	:	16
	Rail siding	:	10 PAL vans.

loading list in the outbound area. The computer delivers the necessary pallets to the convey siding in the area where the staff using conventional electric forklift trucks make up each vehicle load on the floor adjacent to the loading dock. Rowntree Mackintosh make their own trailers, each of which takes 56 pallets due to the light weight of chocolate products. When the truck arrives, its load is waiting and all the paperwork has been prepared, so turn round time is kept to a minimum.

Appendix 2 Computer software packages

The following list of software companies and their services illustrates the range of computer packages that are available. It is not exhaustive, nor will it be up to date when you read it. Should a current list of products be required, the reader is urged to contact the Chartered Institute of Transport in London, or one of the specialist bodies listed at the end of this appendix.

ABCAS	Dillon Computing Services, Bristol, UK Tel: 0454–413928
AIRPACK DIPS DRIVE DATA DRIVE 6 MICRODRIVE	Freight Computer Services, Enfield, UK Tel: 081–367–4200
AUTOROUTE AUTOROUTE PLUS	Next Base Ltd, Staines, UK Tel: 0784–460077
dBASE	Borland International, UK Tel: 0734–320100
DRP	Caldicus Systems Ltd, London, UK

EXIMSHIP   Computing Service for Industry, Leeds, UK
                                Tel: 0532–342211

FLEET MANAGEMENT   Fraser Williams Ltd, Liverpool, UK
                                Tel: 051–227–5995

FOXGROVES CHOICE VEHICLE MANAGEMENT SYSTEM UK

INVENTORY   Pathfinder Software Inc, Vancouver, Canada
                                Tel: 604–682–6633

LARGOTIM   Largotim Warehouse Management Systems Ltd,
                                Milton Keynes, UK
                                Tel: 0908–79423

LOCATE   Cleveland Computing Associates, USA

MAGICAL   Mega Systems Ltd, Surbiton, UK
                                Tel: 081–390–8500

NEGODIS   Temsys, Cheval Blanc, France
                                Tel: 090–716107

PARAGON
PATHFINDER   British Road Services, UK

PERSPECTIVE   LIOCS Corp, Lombard, USA
                                Tel: 0312–953–2220

PRISM   J J Meyers BV, Best, Netherlands
                                Tel: 04998–99925

PROFIT AS   HCS Technology, Eindhoven, Netherlands
                                Tel: 040–444545

ROUTEFINDER   SIA, London, UK
ROUTEMASTER   Tel: 081–730–4544

VAS Order Management   Snow, Stewart & Strickland, Birmingham, USA
                                Tel: 0205–933–7484

VAX   Utility Software Systems Inc. Kaufman, USA
UNIX   Tel: 0214–932–2690

WHAMS   Computer Systems Devt Ltd, London, UK
                                Tel: 081–837–3676

XDG   Data General Ltd, Hounslow, UK
                                Tel: 081–572–7455

SPECIALIST BODIES

Cranfield Institute of Technology,
Cranfield,
Bedford MK43 0AL, UK
Tel: 0234–750111
Fax: 0234–750875

Royal Institute of Navigation,
1 Kensington Gore,
London SW7 2AT, UK
Tel: 071–589 5021
Fax: 071–823 8671

Polytechnic of Central London,
Transport Studies Group,
35 Marylebone Road,
London NW1 5LS, UK
Tel: 071–911 5000, ext 3103
Fax: 071–911 5057

Cambridge Academy of Transport,
11 Hinton Way,
Great Shelford,
Cambridge CB2 5AX, UK
Tel: 0223–845242
Fax: 0223–845582

Chartered Institute of Transport,
80 Portland Place,
London W1N 4DP, UK
Tel: 071–636 9952
Fax: 071–637 0511

Institute of Logistics and Distribution Management,
Easton House,
Easton on the Hill,
Stamford,
Lincolnshire PE9 3NZ, UK
Tel: 0780–56777
Fax: 0780–57610

Management Systems Committee,
America Trucking Associations Inc.,
2200 Mill Road,
Alexandria VA 22314, USA
Tel: 803–838–1721

The Logistics and Transportation Review,
University of British Columbia,
1924 West Mall,
Vancouver V6T 1W5, Canada

Index